Small Wars and Their Influence on Nation States

1500 to the Present Day

Small Wars
and Their Influence on
Nation States

1500 to the Present Day

William Urban

Frontline Books

Small Wars and Their Influence on Nation States
1500 to the Present Day

This edition published in 2016 by Frontline Books,
an imprint of Pen & Sword Books Ltd,
47 Church Street, Barnsley, S. Yorkshire, S70 2AS.

ISBN: 978-1-47383-792-8

CIP data records for this title are available from the British Library

Printed and bound by CPI Group (UK) Ltd, Croydon, CR0 4YY
Typeset in 10/13 point Palatino

For more information on our books, please email: info@frontline-books.com,
write to us at the above address, or visit:
www.frontline-books.com

Contents

To the faculty of the
United States Military Academy at West Point, Summer 1985.

You taught me much that appears here.

Foreword

This interesting study exemplifies the extent to which history is not only what happened in the past but also how we, today, provide accounts of the past. Our concerns play a key role in this shaping, and William Urban is alive to the particular concerns of the present. A modern age in which jihadists and terrorism play a major part provides the context within which Urban examines others on the periphery and considers the challenges they posed to more settled peoples. As he argues, the success of Western globalisation and technological progress from the sixteenth century led to a marked tendency to treat tribal peoples as peripheral and redundant, and he successfully presents several key instances of this process. Both imperial systems and academic anthropologists categorised these peoples as redundant and bound to fail.

However, this modern approach appears less pertinent today because of the resilience of these peoples. This, then, is a book about centres and peripheries, one that ranges with confidence across time, offering a distinctive, often opinionated, frequently controversial and problematic, but always arresting, account. Much of the book addresses the imperial experiences of Britain and America, but other empires are also discussed. The energy of the writing is accompanied by a range of example and allusion that requires continual effort on the part of the reader. This effort is further to the fore because the approach is thematic rather than chronological, but that helps provide a welcome coherence.

There is also an instructive geographical range. For example, there is a good use of Morocco in order to throw light on the military balance both with Christian Europe and with sub-Saharan Africa. Morocco provides a useful perspective from which to consider military history because it problematizes the usual pattern of Western expansion. Thanks to Portuguese efforts, such an account appears relevant for the fifteenth and early sixteenth centuries, but in 1578, in a dramatic and total defeat, the Portuguese army was destroyed and King Sebastian killed. Portuguese Morocco was rapidly rolled up by the victorious Moroccans, and Western pressure on Morocco did not become a major theme anew until the mid-1840s. This is a good example of how military history frequently looks most instructive if considered in contexts other than that of the leading power. Indeed, works such as that of Urban remind us of the folly of adopting the conventional approach of focusing on the supposed paradigm power.

In such cases, Urban valuably sketches the extent of a 'deep history' that affects the present day. When, in Mali in 2012, Tuaregs seeking independence allied to jihadists advanced south within the state toward the Niger Valley, they did so with great success until French troops helped drive them back into the Sahara Desert. As Urban notes, this did not exactly parallel earlier Muslim penetration into Black Africa, such as that of Morocco from the 1590s, but the comparison is not irrelevant. The extent and impact of 'deep history' are made clear, while the range and variety of the non-West and the peripheral peoples emerges clearly.

Attention subsequently profitably switches to the Americas. Urban explains the limitations of British regulars in the American War of Independence. While not an original topic, this is a useful one, not least because of the extent to which the American Patriots can be seen as peripheral in so far as Western power is concerned. Given the Patriot approach to the Native Americans, the majority of whom were allied to the British, this then becomes a matter of many peripheries, which helps greatly to complicate the situation. From a different angle, rivalry between the peripheral peoples frequently provided their settled rivals with many advantages. Thus, the European Americans benefited from the divisions between Native Americans and the major weaknesses of pan-Nativist movement. Conversely, divisions between the European Americans were significant. This point helps explain the significance of repeated American attempts from 1776 to conquer or intimidate the British in Canada.

In an instructive juxtaposition, the focus then moves to Inner-Asia, and notably to the Chinese advance in the eighteenth century and to its Russian counterpart, both aspects of longstanding processes. The strengths and limitations of the native opponents are ably illustrated. A key limitation again was the divisions among the opponents to both Russia and China. For example, conflict between Kazakhs and Dzunghars helped the Chinese advance into Xinking.

The periphery in literature and military history follow as topics that enable Urban to make a range of points about the wide-ranging impact of frontier warfare. The multiple nature of the frontier emerges clearly, and its consequences for military history. This then is a vigorous work that reflects a fertile mind capable of a broad range of reference. Both the important topic and William Urban's study deserve much attention.

Jeremy Black
April 2015

Introduction

Frontier wars are often associated with terrorism. Irregular warfare—the weak against the strong—has always included tactics that run counter to the moral codes of regular armies, and it often provokes a counter-terrorism more terrible than the provocations. Therefore, the subject of terrorism has to be faced immediately and put into context. It is both a strategy and a tactic, and it reflects the values and traditions of people who have no other way to make war.

Any concentration on terrorism alone would inevitably distract from the fact that centres have problems with peripheries that involve the survival of tribal and clan identities opposed to everything the modern secular and industrial world represents. This was true even in industrialising nations in the nineteenth century, where alienation produced by urbanisation led recent arrivals in the cities to search for new individual and group identities, or to seek utopian solutions such as anarchism and communism that promised a simpler and more just society. Often the nation-state simply took the place of older local and family traditions. As long as this seemed to promise prosperity and pride, it was sufficient to satisfy citizens who did not want to emigrate or return to rural poverty. The Great War of 1914-18, however, gave a great blow to hopes that nationality could provide a centre for disordered identities, much less cope with unemployment, crime and poverty. Fascism and Communism quickly arose to take the place of national identity and nationalism. Then, after the failure of those ideological systems, there seemed to be nothing authentic, nothing to be proud of or fight for. For many there was prosperity and pop culture, and, when it came to unpleasant jobs, there were immigrants from the Islamic world, or Africa, or Mexico to do them. But there was a spiritual emptiness, a lack of vision and purpose.

Similarly, in the Islamic world and elsewhere in Asia and Africa secular national states failed to satisfy rapidly growing populations. Religion—cleansed of complicated regional accommodations with ancient practices and Western scepticism—arose to declare that fundamentalist beliefs were more valuable than material wealth, especially material wealth that was just out of reach; these beliefs were sufficiently simple to be understood by everyone, and violence was used on those who were too stubborn to submit. This development is most obvious in Islam, but it can also be seen in African Christianity, Hinduism, and even Buddhism.

These are themes this book will touch on. It will also look at the ways that Westerners have written history, not just their own history, but those of non-Western civilisations that now insist on writing their own, 'authentic', histories. This includes peoples who have failed to make themselves into well-organised states and who show no interest in becoming a part of one—the peoples living on the periphery or beyond; the tribes in frontier regions. These people are often alienated by interference with their traditions and practices, and with the displacement of tribal leaders and local religious figures by outsiders. This has been true the past 200 years, and especially for the post-colonial epoch, but the roots of this phenomenon can be easily traced farther back. Consequently, much of this book will be about frontier warfare from 1500 to 1800.

This book has only a few general themes. First, that small wars will continue to break out despite all efforts to eliminate them; this is partly because the major powers will concentrate on domestic issues first, then on one another.[1] This allows small problems to grow into large ones. Second, that most of the wars of our era, like those of the centuries described in this book, will be in tribal regions where honour is valued and material possessions disdained. Third, that these wars will draw in governments that, in order to reduce casualties among inappropriately trained recruits, use professional armies and elite forces; then, to reduce further the political costs, first replace draftees with volunteers, then employ non-citizens (British Gurkhas, the French Foreign Legion), and lastly true mercenaries, often men drawn from the frontier regions themselves—sturdy, proud, and accustomed to handling weapons. These men occasionally bring old feuds with them, so that when they are employed against tribal enemies, they do not care all that much about rules and guidelines, and whatever brutality they commit is rarely reported. Fourth, that the wars are caused partly by central governments failing to understand the dynamics of tribal life described above.

Whatever peace is achieved in local conflicts does last forever, or even long. That said, no government can ignore the conflicts, and the situations are not hopeless—the centre often wins. However, these wars can draw in competing outside powers which the tribes can manipulate against each other and against local rivals. The Great Game can be played out in many places other than Central Asia.

The history of the Basques offers some insights into how difficult it can be to suppress a people's desire to be independent. Basques have long fought to maintain their language and culture, and they have a formidable military history—after Charlemagne lost his rearguard to an ambush in their mountains, he never bothered them again; later they honed their skills by serving as mercenary soldiers. Intensely religious, zealous in defending their ancient customs and independence, for centuries they have frustrated Spanish efforts to create a unified nation. Infiltrating the ranks of their armed resistance can't be done because of group loyalty; also, since their language is reputed to be impossible to learn and, because everyone seems to know everyone else, outsiders are quickly identified. Persuading individuals to become informers hasn't been successful, either. Yet Basques have shown great creativeness in fitting into the modern world, and Spanish politicians from differing parties have managed to keep the nation together.

It is easy for outsiders to ignore problems presented by Basques and similar peoples, since normally they do not involve others directly. That is not true when insurgent activities have the potential to lead us into another great war, or when they acquire weapons of mass destruction. Our politicians assure us, as European statesmen did in 1914, that a general war is not likely. But some damn-fool event in the Balkans can always throw our calculations out of whack.

Wars just over the horizon of our awareness are nothing new, as the examples in this book will illustrate.

Wars Do Not Vanish

Matthew 24:6: *And you will hear of wars and rumours of wars.*
See that you are not alarmed, for this must take place, but the end is not yet.
(Modern Standard Version)

The modern world's potential to destroy itself has made this Biblical passage and the horrible descriptions of the Last Days match the fears of the early Christian church. Two great wars in the twentieth century, separated by a world economic crisis and followed by a long Cold War that could have resulted in an exchange of thermonuclear weapons, make us aware of the fragility of modern cultures. The conclusion of this passage from the book of Matthew promises salvation to those who remain faithful through the wars, famines and earthquakes, but the envisioned utopian future of that era is much different from that imagined by today's increasingly materialist secular culture. The austere authoritarianism in the East is evolving into a revived Sino-centrism based on economic and military power, and the chaos in the Middle East has conflicting religious fundamentalisms which only agree that the modern world is a mistake. Some Christians and many secularists see this as a sign that the Last Days are upon us. The many contradictions and exceptions to today's complex religious and political realities have confused a Western public increasingly reluctant to read or think deeply, leading some to ignore the danger of war, some to take refuge in work, drugs or alcohol, and others to concentrate on the social fads of the moment.

Even well-educated elites believe that the end of the world is nigh, coming via thermonuclear war, or the starvation and epidemics that would follow a clash of civilisations, or, increasingly, long-term climate change. These groups are often not well equipped to deal with potential catastrophes because they seem to believe that reading about war or talking about it will cause the deadly conflicts to come about. Hence, they prefer to ignore conflicts that arise on the periphery of their settled societies.

Climate change is a much safer topic. No government will draft its young people to fight in that war, and if we lose, it will not be our generation that suffers.

Frontier Wars

Ours is not the first era to believe itself safe from barbarian onslaught. Most Romans thought that their world would last forever (*Quando cadet Roma cadet et mundo*), the Chinese believed that they were safe behind their Great Wall, and the citizens of Baghdad in 1258 expected that Allah would protect them from the Mongols. These were all true clashes of civilisation, or, as they thought of them, civilisation versus barbarians. The barbarians won. However, civilisation's defeat was not followed by total anarchy and mayhem, at least not forever; and we no longer think of barbarians as devoid of culture or civilisation. Germanic tribes, Vikings, and Mongols each brought new vigour and new ideas into the lands they conquered, and the empires they overran were not as lamented as we might think—as the Chinese say, these empires had lost the mandate of heaven. More accurately, the rulers of those empires could not get their subjects to fight the barbarians. The Greek historian Herodotus noted in the fifth century BC that wealth makes men soft, and the masses of servile peoples in the armies of despots have no reason to fight well. Only free men, men who are poor but proud, they said, make good warriors. This gives frontiersmen a significant edge over individual soldiers in the armies of advanced nations, an edge that is often sufficient to offset the latter's superior weaponry. This advantage, however, does not usually last long.

The great Arab historian Ibn Khaldun (1332-1406) noted that tribal groups have more social cohesion than larger societies, so that when motivated by religious fervour, inspired leaders, or opportunity, tribal warriors can defeat declining states. If they take the state over, inevitably urban habits and civilized vices will weaken them; within a few generations the victors will adopt the culture of the conquered and become soft, after which they will fall to the next group of motivated barbarians.

We are often told that we need to understand our enemies, but for Ibn Khaldun's contemporaries, whether Arabs, Chinese, Turks, Indians and Europeans, the problem was not that they did not understand what the barbarians wanted, but what to do about them. The memory of Genghis Khan was a reminder of what could happen.

This book is not so much about the clash of civilisations as Samuel P. Huntington thought of them—Communism versus Open Societies, then Islam versus the West—as another idea that grew out of the failures of the War Against Terror. *This is that the jihadists' anger comes less from radical Islam than from tribal societies that feel themselves threatened by modernization. Islam is more a justification of violence than an incitement to war.* It is a classic case of those on the periphery feeling themselves alternately insulted and ignored by the sophisticates of the centre.

This book was well along by 2013, when Akbar Ahmed's book, *The Thistle and the Drone*, appeared not long after Jeffrey Kaplan's *Terrorist Groups and the New Tribalism* explained how terrorism often appeared in waves. It also came to me that today's honour-based tribal societies were actually fighting against another honour-based institution, the armies of the West. Sophisticated academics might sneer at the West Point Motto— Duty, Honour, Country—but that would only demonstrate how little they understand 'the other' (jargon for anyone not like yourself, who is different and usually inferior). Soldiers, and especially officers, are different from the rest of us, but, being as proud as jihadists, they don't like being treated as inferiors. While professional soldiers may hate guerrillas for using unconventional tactics, they do not despise them; academics, by contrast, they respect too little to hate.[2]

Space limitations will not allow me dwell on this subject, but I urge readers to keep it in mind.

Mercenaries

As readers of my earlier books will know, I have long been concerned with two problems—first, how to create an armed force able to protect a nation, second, how to prevent the masters of these armies from abusing their power. Modern armies arose in the era of absolute monarchs. These rulers were not, as it happened, as absolute as we once imagined, but it was many years before parliamentary bodies learned how to wrest power from them. When they did, they found themselves facing some of the same problems that their late rulers did—conflicts with other states, conflicts on unsettled frontiers, and uprisings inside their borders. The need to have a strong army made it difficult at first to instill in generals the importance of beings servants of the state, not the masters, a task that has been accomplished by the national military academies, which train future officers for a profession—fighting wars—under the direction of elected presidents. A draft army can limit the ability of a government with free elections to behave arbitrarily, because families of draftees are seldom happy to see their sons fighting a long war on a distant frontier.

It is not easy for governments to turn their backs on frontier conflicts. As the title to Walter Laqueur's well-known book on terrorism indicated, there is *No End to War*. Much as we might wish otherwise, for the foreseeable future there will be wars in corners of the world where modern secular society has not taken root and technology makes extremist movements dangerous. Bringing order to chaotic regions was one of several reasons for colonialism, but few states today are willing to act as colonial powers (and none is willing to admit it). Instead, there is a widespread belief that such efforts are nothing but a cover for making the rich richer and disempowering everyone else; there are occasional remarks that there was no good reason to fight Hitler or the Japanese militarists.

Universal peace is not going to arrive soon. Wars will occur, but none will mean the end of the world, no matter how that is defined, unless it is closely tied to superpower rivalries. Individuals, groups, even nations will suffer, but life will still continue; it will often be even better. Getting to the future will not be easy or pleasant, at least not if historical experience means anything.

Europeans in the early modern era lived and died without experiencing Armageddon. Yet many experienced wars, and even when general wars slackened off temporarily, there were rumours of war. In many cases these were wars on the periphery of their known world, their frontiers. One characteristic of the colonial era—the use of mercenaries—has become important again. In recent decades white mercenaries have fought in African revolutions—South Africans, Brits, even Cubans and Swedes, supporting one African tribal group against others. More recently African soldiers have hired themselves out to the UN or the United States to replace combat troops in dangerous situations—Iraqi insurgents would happily have killed an American soldier standing guard, but saw no propaganda value in assassinating a Kenyan.

Misunderstanding the Past

Modern Europeans and Americans know little about long-ago wars on the periphery, but African and Asians (and certainly everyone in the Middle East) are very aware of them.[3] To understand these regions today, we need to look into the ways that European wars affected them centuries earlier. Yes, we all know about the colonial era, but some of the most important examples predated colonialism. That does not make them any less important...or less interesting.

Local politics are complex. While we are accustomed to our own politicians changing their positions, even their alliances, we assume that distant lands, especially 'backward' ones, will be today and even tomorrow much as we imagine they were in the past. This may be historical arrogance, but it is common to many who think of themselves as culturally enlightened, good hearted and well-intentioned.

Anyone expecting a clear narrative on conflicts in modern peripheries that everyone agrees with, might as well not read at all—there are too many conflicting viewpoints. While historians are now better able to say what happened in Asia and Africa centuries ago than could any previous generation, they cannot agree on a common story.[4] The reader who does not want to throw in with whatever version of history is current at the moment can be left at a loss. If he agrees that foreign intrusions beginning in the sixteenth century destroyed a golden age, say, of African culture, he must ignore evidence that not all was well in those years—as one chapter in this book indicates, this was a period of Islamist expansion across the Sahara that coincided with the arrival of European merchants on the coasts; meanwhile, Muslims were sailing along the shores of the Indian Ocean to purchase slaves just as Europeans were arriving. Thus, while this story places the blame for African problems on outsiders, most importantly Europeans, it seems that it was more complicated than that.

Some post-colonial historians say that foreigners had little effect on African states—proud Africans were in charge of their own destinies, as they are today. If that is so, all earlier accounts of African history are worthless, or so biased as to be worse than worthless. Also, if colonialism is responsible for all of today's evils, why is there violence and starvation now that the African states are independent? The most common explanation is that neo-colonialism—the product of foreign interference, the Cold War, capitalism, and do-gooder idealism—is to blame, corrupting native rulers, especially military elites, to allow the continuation of colonial exploitation under the cover of national independence. In the end a reader might just conclude that, with ideology trumping dispassionate analysis, there is no way he can figure it out.

It is much the same with the Indian subcontinent. In the era when British and French companies began establishing trading posts along the eastern coast of India, the distant Mughal Empire was weak—attacked by Persians from the north and the Maratha Confederacy from the south—and ineptly led. Yet the Empire survived, partly because everyone was accustomed to its providing a stable centre to political life; the shah had become a living fiction by the time the Europeans arrived, but he was a convenient fiction. The Europeans took advantage of a chaotic situation, but they can hardly be accused of causing it.

Anti-colonialist arguments try to absolve native rulers of all guilt (except those who invited Europeans to help them against domestic enemies) and blame the outsiders who took power from them, while those who see the advantages of colonialism (the end of domestic violence, improved transport, a modern system of justice, better medical services, new international languages) are often less persuasive than nationalists whose very idea of a nation-state was inspired by the Westerners.

The poor reader who relies on European accounts of the colonial era can be considered an apologist for foreign rule or a racist; if he cites the wrong authorities, he is guilty of being a traitor to the future.

Fortunately, this intellectual dead-end is no longer universal. Ideological winds blow this way and that, and eventually some historians grow weary of propaganda masquerading as history. Authors like Douglas E. Streusand, *Islamic Gunpowder Empires: Ottomans, Safavids, and Mughals,* illustrate how much progress historians have made in cutting through the mythology and ideology of the past. Streusand calls these three states gunpowder empires only because he cannot imagine a better way to describe their common characteristics—they were not created by firearms, but such weapons were new when they rose to greatness. Military successes had been followed by sophisticated innovations in governance, great economic activity and more tolerance for ethnic and religious minorities. The decline came because religious fundamentalism and incompetence at the top provoked revolts that were exploited by colonial powers.

This failure was not confined to Muslim states. China had seen the collapse of the Ming dynasty, the Holy Roman Empire lost its preeminence in Europe, and the Polish-Lithuanian Commonwealth disappeared completely.

The collapse of the great Polish-Lithuanian state between 1772 and 1795 offers a similar temptation to condemn outsiders for manipulating a constitutional system that contemporary Poles seem to have liked. Alas, Polish freedom applied only to a small percentage of the population, and while nowhere in Europe did all citizens get to vote, Western nations had at least abolished serfdom, whereas Poland had not.

All these examples are like the one that troubled Edward Gibbon (1737-94), whose *History of the Decline and Fall of the Roman Empire* presented us with a narrative that may be the only one worth serious consideration— why states fail. Why, moreover, among all the potential successor states of Rome, did some have an influence on everything that came afterward and others did not? Gibbon assumed that Rome was the centre of Western civilisation and that somehow Romans failed to maintain it. Decline is hard to detect, but few states vanish at their height.[5]

While inspired individuals can see the problems of contemporary societies, they cannot always correct them. Therefore, it falls to historians to describe the weaknesses in the foundations of each destroyed civilisation and suggest that a similar fate awaits all of us if we are not careful.

The Continuity of History

Not so long ago the crusades were almost forgotten, and, in the minds of those who counted, deservedly so. Americans thought of crusades as any movement designed to correct a problem—say, to cure cancer, or the War on Poverty; and almost no one in recent years, not even the most sturdy defenders of Israel, advocated recovering the churches and religious sites in the Holy Land. The Muslim world, in contrast, saw their struggle against colonialism as a continuation of the crusades; the most radical Muslims believed that a Christian/Zionist conspiracy was not only trying to take

Palestine from its proper owners, but seeking to prevent the establishment of an Islamic state that would first unify all believers, then bring the entire world into the religion of peace. Thus, Westerners who innocently use the term 'Moslem' rather than 'Muslim' are showing a lack of respect, and any who deny that imperialism is a secular form of crusading is insulting Muslims everywhere; those who say that the foundation of Islam is not peace, but submission, are regarded as Islamophobic.

Medieval Europeans were fixated on crusading, so much so that any history that forgets this is sure to be misleading. Nobles were honour-bound to defend their Church, and many commoners shared that sentiment. In that era the concept of honour helped maintain a stable society. Men advanced their careers by military prowess and women by defending their virtue. Rules regarding class were strict, but they allowed everyone a certain level of dignity. Awkwardly, this emphasis on tradition and social stability made it difficult for Christians to deal with people who did not fit into the easily recognized system of values—Muslims and frontier people. Nevertheless, the traditional society could not be maintained forever. Not even firmly established classes (which sometimes recognized how recently they had come to power themselves), could stop the process of change.

The Mongol hordes of those centuries remind us that peoples on the periphery could be very powerful. When Mongol armies overthrew great empires in Europe, China, and India, they were perceived as enemies of agriculture-based civilisations; today we see that they were also intermediaries for transmitting ideas and technology from one distant civilisation to another. From the sixteenth century onwards firearms began to nullify the horsemen's greatest advantages—numbers, speed and archery. That made it easy to look at the peoples of the periphery as interesting but irrelevant ethnographical specimens.

This is not possible today. Under the right conditions, tribal peoples have always been able to hold their own against modern armies. Offended dignity makes them fight, and honour will not allow them to surrender; properly equipped, they can inflict sufficient casualties on foreign armies to undermine their enemies' political will, and once the cost of a war reaches an unacceptable level, the invader will pull back. Little has changed over the last centuries except the weaponry and means of communication.

We tend to worry about weapons of mass destruction, but the jihadists of 9/11 used only box cutters to take over the aircraft that they flew into the Twin Towers of New York City and into the Pentagon; and all had lived in the West, some apparently happily, and were educated in Western universities. Modern jihadists do not reject the West entirely—they are very happy to watch porn on computers or use social media—but they reject its acceptance of alcoholic drinks, gay rights and women's liberation. Atheism they cannot understand at all. Their enthusiasm is kept vibrant by imagining a return to a utopian tribal past.

This book will show that such combinations of pride and anger were widely shared by those who lived on the periphery in earlier centuries.

1. The story of Archias in Plutarch's *Pelopidas* might remind us how this works: Archias was the hated despot imposed on Thebes by the Spartans about 383 BC. When Theban exiles slipped into the city to assassinate him, he was at a party, drinking heavily. A messenger arrived with a letter warning him that he was in danger. Archias took the letter from the messenger's hand, set it aside, and, when the messenger said that it had to be read immediately, he replied, 'Business tomorrow'.

2. It was very different in the 1960s, when Clifford James Geertz (1926-2006) was explaining the Viet Cong insurgency as a reaction of traditionalist peasants against modernity imposed by the central government. Perhaps this was because his emphasis on semiotics made his 'thick descriptions' difficult to understand. More importantly, to pursue the slow, non-coercive policies he recommended required time, and the North Vietnamese with their modern weapons and the modern concept of nationalism were already invading the South. Also, the predictions he made in *Islam Observed* (1968), to wit, that secularism would ultimately triumph, seemed sufficiently off the mark that political and military figures saw no point in listening to his prediction that Islamic fundamentalism was on the rise.

3. Mike Martin's *An Intimate War: An Oral History of the Helmand Conflict 1978-2012* shows that while British politicians and generals thought they were in Afghanistan to support the American war against al-Qaeda and the Taliban, the Afghans saw it as a third British invasion. John Fairweather, in *The Good War*, said that any other nation's troops should have been sent there, as long as they weren't British.

4. One is reminded of Walter Raleigh having observed a quarrel below his prison cell in the Tower of London. After hearing various accounts of the incident, none of which agreed with each other or his own observation, he wondered if he could trust any of the accounts he was using for his History of the World.

5. The Assyrians conducted campaigns of terror to prevent a massive uprising of their subjects, but the prophet Jonah was ordered to warn them of the disaster that awaited if the people did not repent and change their ways; they were spared momentarily, but were ultimately destroyed so thoroughly by angry neighbours that only a few centuries later strangers could not get local people to tell them who had lived in the huge, empty cities they saw lying in ruins. The Aztecs similarly alienated the subject peoples at their periphery, and the Incas were fighting a civil war as well when a handful of Spaniards arrived.

Chapter 1

Centres and Frontiers

It is useful in any book to have an early look at some of its central concepts, then an overview of the places that will be studied. The areas covered here range across the globe, but have much in common. Sometimes the narrative involves states in crisis, but more often states with problems across the frontier. It is a complicated story because history does not run along the ordered lines of fiction.

A frontier is a region where an ordered society gives way to disorder. This disorder may have complex and fixed rules of its own, but those rules are traditional rather than written and practical rather than theoretical. In any case, a frontier is not a border, which is a line marking where one organised entity meets another.

Organised states have capitals, usually cities, where art, literature, science and politics are concentrated. Borderlands have villages, sometimes towns, but rarely cities. Frontier regions are usually populated by nomadic or semi-nomadic peoples. Their culture is what they can carry with them.

The centres of great civilisations are always exciting. Any reasonably educated person hearing a name—Rome, London, Paris—will recognize it. It is not the architecture, avenues or parks alone that spark this response, but the self-confidence and wealth that exude from cities which are centres of great empires. The peripheries—borderlands and frontiers—are different. Poorer and less populated, they are easy to ignore. However, by their very nature peripheral regions can be perceived by neighbouring states as 'their' peripheries, too—even their natural prey.

Peripheries are not vacuums, but regions that do not have one dominant tribe or coalition of tribes. Historically, when peripheral areas are organised by a charismatic chief and the central power is temporarily weakened or in decline, this inspired leader can overrun powerful empires, even ones with

1

proud military traditions. Thrace, Herodotus noted, was the most populous and richest region of his time (c 500 BC), but it was only later, when Philip of Macedonia conquered the region and added its warriors to his army, that it became a danger to the Greek city-states. Mongolia was usually weak, but when Genghis Khan unified the tribes he was able to begin the conquest of China and wide areas to the west right into Europe and the Middle East.

Borderlands and Frontiers

In practice most people use the terms border and frontier interchangeably because they do not see a distinction. But we talk about border crossings and frontier forts. The first implies peaceful movement from one nation to another, the other a potentially hostile encounter with people very different to ourselves.

Two examples: The Ukraine lay between the Tatars, Russians and Poles; that is, between Muslims, Orthodox Christians and Roman Catholics. Poland later lay between Orthodox Russia, Protestant Prussia and Roman Catholic Austria. Both Ukrainians and Poles found it difficult to defend themselves, much less to develop the institutions and habits of governance that Western Europeans thought were normal and just. The Ukraine was on a sparsely settled steppe, while Poland-Lithuania was surrounded by powerful and greedy neighbours. The first was periodically depopulated by invaders; the second was carved up and exploited. Together they are models for situations historians see elsewhere throughout the centuries.

Western Europeans who had trouble finding a political equilibrium themselves in this era considered the eastern European borderlands chaotic and ungovernable. Yet, many of the problems were the same. There were powerful nobles who dominated ancestral lands and demanded freedom from taxation and service to the crown; there were state churches that wanted a monopoly on matters of belief and the money of the believers; commerce grew only slowly, partly because the rulers wanted to tax it, and that could be done best if the state regulated everything. The temptation to raise taxes ever higher undermined commercial growth.

While borderlands did not have the same system of tribes and clans typical of frontier regions, the difference was sometimes only a matter of nomenclature. Still, borderlands did tend to have more and closer contact with urban elites and royal courts, and as far as possible copied them faithfully; the more distant from the centres of commercial life and education, of course, the less people in the borderlands felt their influence. Rural people knew that they were backward in material wealth and the social graces, but their goal was to become rich and sophisticated, while the people in frontier regions wanted to retain their independence and their traditional simplicity and morality. Thus, while the two regions had much in common, they had fundamentally different aspirations.

Walls can be Borders, but the Frontier lies Beyond

Every British schoolchild is familiar with Roman efforts to control the Picts, but few learn much about the Picts other than that they dyed their skin blue and fought naked in the northern cold. Indeed, even experts know relatively little about them. Archaeology gives some insights into their society, Romans wrote a bit about their customs, and Christian monks described their conversion. They were replaced or absorbed by Scots from Ireland. Other than this, theirs was a dark era indeed.

Our experience with the Picts is, alas, fairly typical of how little we know about the peoples who lived beyond the frontiers of literate societies. Since many of the Celtic peoples were divided into tribes and clans, and since Scotland was so divided later, we assume this was true of the Picts; we also assume that what was true of regions closest to organised states was true of those more distant. But assumptions can be in error. Thus, we can speculate about the range and power of tribes, but we know that new information can change that understanding significantly.

Our lack of firm knowledge of this region is strikingly similar to our ignorance of other frontier regions today or in the more recent past. There are the physical barriers of geography and distance, the intellectual barriers of language and culture, and the ideological barriers of religion, superstition and tradition.

Nationalist scholars increase our uncertainty more by projecting modern tribal practices back into a semi-mythical past as if they had existed without change forever. This is then confirmed by post-colonialist scholars who accuse their predecessors of bias, racism and dishonesty; other Western scholars, some gravely sorry for the abuses of Western imperialism, are reluctant to criticize the governments of former colonies. Western states, leery of offending dictators, offer apologies. The poor reader who does not have multiple lives to spend investigating these claims can be left in confusion.

What is clear is that frontier societies often display violence, brutality, sexism, and outbreaks of religious fanaticism (pagan, Christian, Islamic). But it seems that the elites of the western world are reluctant to see anything which does not fit into the concept of the Noble Savage, a belief that primitive peoples were more authentic, more moral. This idea was widespread in the eighteenth century, attributing great virtues to peoples who lived far from the attractions and vices of Paris. It is a popular view today.

Ordinary people have no difficulty in choosing between the attractions of big city life and those of rural poverty. Urban Arabs do not want to be Bedouin again, and retired bandits in every society surround themselves with technology and luxuries. It is their children who have the romantic dreams of the simple life.

Nothing is new about this. The *Wanderjahr* of German romantics, the Continental Grand Tour of British nobles and gentry, Americans going to California to join a commune, demonstrating against the government, or joining the navy, are representative of a tradition of discovering oneself. The Clash of Civilisations, a theory popularized by Samuel Huntington in the 1990s, may have less to do with a stagnant Islamic world confronting a dynamic West than with young people who are disenchanted with the failure of their leaders—kings, dictators, clerics, and despots who may have been mentally unbalanced. All failed to deliver the prosperity of modern Americans, Europeans and Asians.

The more isolated young people are, and the less educated, the more they see their own worth reflected in their ancient concepts of honour, group solidarity, and suspicion of outsiders. A warrior society is tightly bound together even when the motto is 'Me against my brother, My brothers and me against my cousins, then my cousins and me against strangers'.

Is this the way to understand the Middle East and similar tribal societies around the world? That is the contention of Philip Salzman in *Culture and Conflict in the Middle East*, a book quietly published by a new press in 2007; his thesis—that tribalism, not Islam, drives political extremism—has become more widely discussed as prevailing theories of how to deal with terrorism fail. Salzman argues that the seventeenth century political theorist Thomas Hobbes, in his 1651 work *Leviathan*, comes closest to describing the realities of the modern Arab world. Hobbes stated that mankind's original state of nature was not the Garden of Eden, but a war of all against all, with the only hope for change being to have a king strong enough to enforce law and order. In short, the way to a peaceable kingdom was through a despot.

Whether the aftermath of the Arab Spring confirms or invalidates this concept remains to be seen, but it is interesting that scholars are looking back to yesterday's philosophers to understand today's world.

Romanticism versus Realism

Scholars, once each gets past their common tradecraft and their efforts to be fair and honest, are often either romantics or realists. This can be seen to reflect the influence of Jean-Jacques Rousseau (1712-78) and Voltaire (1694-1778), the two greatest thinkers of the French Enlightenment. Neither was religious, neither was conventional, but both brought the power of intellect to the problems of their age, changing forever the way we see the world. Rousseau squeezed his readers' hearts, while Voltaire poked at their ribs. These methods were vast improvements over royal hands grasping at pocketbooks and courtiers quarreling over which of them was permitted to carry the royal chamber pot to the window, but their ideas about what made for a good society did not always lead to a better one.

Rousseau had the better of the contest over what made a nation, and why—despite his views that the best rulers might, for a time, be despots. The creation of national units, his courtship of kings and empresses suggested, required some temporary compromises. Voltaire cared less about nationhood than freedom, but he was willing to sacrifice either for a *bon mot*. Society women who ran the fashionable salons of that era much preferred the witty Voltaire to the dour Rousseau, but around the campfires of distant tribesmen the words of Rousseau would have resonated more.

Discussion over the existence of a centre, or its non-existence, summarizes one aspect of post-modern scholarship derived from Rousseau—whether any people, region, civilisation or race are to be 'privileged' over any other. Obviously, those peoples who form a traditional centre are usually, more numerous, wealthier, and more literate; they are militarily dominant, so that they have the potential of taking whatever they need from lands on their periphery. However, the cost of taking this rather modest wealth being fairly high, it was wiser to make a client of an ambitious chief who would look aside at economic exploitation as long as the outsiders kept their thoughts to themselves and their hands off the women.

Whether these urban centres were culturally superior to those on the periphery has been a part of Western intellectual dialogue since Rousseau published his essay *Discours sur les sciences et les arts* in 1750. When Rousseau sent Voltaire a copy of *Du contrat social ou Principes du droit politique* (*The Social Contract*, 1762), which began, 'Man is born free, and everywhere he is in chains,' he received a famous rebuke that began, 'I have received your new book against the human race, and thank you for it. Never was such a cleverness used in the design of making us all stupid.'

If anything, the tenor of the debate has only worsened since post-colonial and post-modern scholarship became popular. According to this viewpoint, we should not be proud of belonging to cultures that are temporarily popular, especially not the American variety. This concept of cultural equality (or the superiority of more authentic natural practices) extends to music, food and sexual habits. Of course, ordinary scholars, like ordinary citizens, ignore much of this. Social change occurs slowly—often no faster than the death rate—so that fast food and fast-paced history remains popular even in academic institutions. The centre remains secure in the belief that its music, food, and sexual practices are obviously superior. And often the peoples of the periphery come to believe this, too; at least the Western educated, urban elite does.

Is this not proof of Rousseau's thesis that civilisation corrupts? Vice attracts, as does entertainment, leisure, and over-eating. This makes it easy even for Westerners who are only moderately self-indulgent to idealize those uneducated, rural folk who denounce self-indulgence as destructive of their purer, more authentic culture. If the tribesmen use simpler words, that makes them only more authentic.

We humans can marvelously contradict ourselves in so many ways. But we are usually wise enough to see that cultural differences are a matter of degree. In a complex world a virtue in one situation might be a vice in another. Our prejudices can also be humorous. Nothing is funnier, perhaps, than a person claiming to be unbiased, then expressing an opinion you know to be prejudiced.

Everything being relative, even backwater centres can claim an ancient culture that allows them to look down on neighbours who are not equally fortunate. There are levels of centres, some larger, some more technologically advanced, but all share the experience of having to deal with peripheries. Cities, towns, villages, countryside, frontier—the line between one and the next is not always clear, but each sees itself as superior to those above and especially to those below it.

This is part of what makes frontier zones so interesting—the interaction of differing cultures, religions, systems of thought. For generations Western historians have written about the 'Holy Land' of three millennia ago being influenced by Egypt and Mesopotamia, but striving to remain independent of both; or the Romans fighting to keep barbarians invaders out of their empire. Indian and Chinese historians may have little interest in these Western matters, but they understand their ancestors' fears of barbarians on their northern peripheries.

However, even this commonplace observation can be contentious.

William McNeill, in *The Rise of the West* (1963), argued that Muslim traditionalists triumphed over reformers in the sixteenth century, dooming their lands to a blind conservatism until the middle of the nineteenth century, when military despots using Western methods rose to oppose both native traditionalists and European colonial powers. Niall Ferguson, widely considered the twenty-first century's best-known contrarian, writing at a time when Muslim zealots were making headlines almost daily, argued that the Islamic world had adopted the superficial technologies of the West without accepting the underlying values that had produced the technology—competition, science, the rule of law, medicine, consumerism and the work ethic. Whatever one thinks of Ferguson, he is never dull. Nor, to the philosophically inclined, is this whole debate. Not even the most hard-headed realist can dismiss the academic back-and-forth shouting as pointless.

These themes connect to one that intellectuals used to agree on: how civilisation softens its people, making the state vulnerable to attack by 'barbarian' outsiders with more vigour and self-confidence. Often rulers attempted to strike before the danger was acute, expanding their frontiers outward to conquer, then 'civilize' those regions. But sending unwilling subjects to war in distant and challenging conditions risked popular anger that might lead to their overthrow. Inaction, therefore, had much to recommend it; inaction was further justified if the frontier peoples presented no immediate threat.

Indeed, conquering frontier regions was usually difficult, especially before 1700, before military technology improved. The rulers of great states and their advisors knew that barbarian tribes and nomadic peoples often lived in dense woods, difficult mountains or wide deserts, but not having observed those places first-hand, they did not fully appreciate the difficulties their generals would face. Well-organised armies that were too small were ineffective; armies that were too large could not feed themselves. Weapons and tactics appropriate to fighting civilized enemies were less effective in the small scale operations on frontiers. Worst of all, these attacks would cause the barbarians to join together, becoming thereby much more dangerous.

Military historians seldom deal with these conflicts—the sources are scattered and less detailed, the outcomes of the wars were often ambiguous, and the significance questionable. Also, potential readers seem to be more interested in clashes of large armies than in obscure conflicts. The debate was limited, therefore, to a conversation between experts on geopolitics. This debate became heated in the nineteenth century. First,

7

there were those who believed in the thesis of Halford MacKinder (1861-1947) that whoever controlled eastern Europe would dominate the Heartland (Central Asia), and thus dominated the 'world island' (Europe, Asia and Africa). Opposed were those who believed in Sea Power, most importantly, Alfred Thayer Mahan (1840-1914); this group was focused on commerce and overseas trade. For much of the nineteenth century and some of the twentieth, the two views appeared in public debates whenever Russia appeared likely to acquire a warm water port. This led those who feared the tsar or the Communists to argue that no Russian ruler could be allowed to consolidate his hold on the heartland. This contest became known as The Great Game.

There are exceptions to the public ignoring backward places, of course. Whenever the leader of irregular forces possessed enough charisma to make himself exotic or romantic—or useful later to nationalist historians—tales or books soon appeared to exploit popular interest. The range of such leaders is extraordinary—well-read Westerners will recognize Vercingetorix, Hermann, Robin Hood, Rob Roy, Geronimo, Pancho Villa, Lawrence of Arabia, Mao, Che Guevara, Ho Chi Minh, Osama bin Laden. Well-read Asians, Africans and Latin Americans have their own lists. In all cases, the outlaw leaders we remember raised guerilla armies, fought lengthy campaigns and were often victorious; all fit some contemporary need for a mythic leader, and some made up their own mythology, suppressing all other versions of what had actually happened.

The ones we forget are characterized by having allowed their poorly organised guerrilla forces to exploit the common people, who failed to develop a 'narrative' that justified their actions, or who were defeated by better-led and more effective military forces. Their bandit armies, often mere collections of criminals, committed terrible atrocities in order to enrich themselves, or simply to get enough food to survive, or to retaliate for crimes committed decades or centuries ago. Occasionally, they tried to impose a political or religious ideology, but more often they only wanted to terrorize potential enemies into submission, or to take revenge on tribal enemies, or personal ones. Often enough this so angered the local population that potential recruits turned into committed enemies. Examples coming to mind are al-Qaeda provoking the 2007 Sunni Awakening in Iraq, or Sioux Indians seizing buffalo-hunting grounds from other Plains Indians, causing them to assist the US army.

Faraway central governments can misunderstand the dynamics of local politics. A financial crisis in 1765 led British politicians to believe that they could levy taxes on their American colonies, then they believed that a little show of force would bring about compliance, and finally, they were astounded to find a supposedly unmilitary people fighting an amazingly effective war against the best troops Europe had. When the campaigns in the northern colonies failed to yield victory, they turned their attention to the southern colonies. Every expert thought that these were the most loyal to the crown—the dominant class there was composed of two aristocracies, plantation owners and merchants; and the fear of a slave revolt was even greater than Britons had of another rebellion in Ireland or riots in lower-class districts of London. This opinion held sway until the British army led by Lord Cornwallis (1738-1805) arrived. His most dashing officer was Banastre Tarleton (1754-1833), whose 'British Legion' (a mixed cavalry and light infantry unit composed largely of loyalist Americans) defeated larger patriot forces time and again. However, it was not long before the Legion became infamous for 'Tarleton's Quarter'—the murder of prisoners and suspected rebels. Even Tarleton's natural allies were appalled by his massacres and confiscations, and patriots were energized to fight harder and even to commit atrocities of their own. However, Anthony Scotti, Jr, in *Brutal Justice*, denies that Tarleton was especially cruel. This was a vicious civil war, he said, and Tarleton was a convenient villain for patriotic narratives. The British Legion was a model anti-guerrilla force—swift, deadly, and seemingly everywhere. Terror was not, however, the way, in Sir Henry Clinton's words, 'to gain the hearts & subdue the minds of America'. This phrase will come to mind for every American who can remember the war in Vietnam.

After surrendering at Yorktown in 1781, Tarleton had reason to expect trial and execution. However, George Washington (commander of the Continental Army and later president) observed the laws of war by releasing him on parole; but he gave him none of the honours and hospitality he extended to the other British and German officers.

The American colonies stretched along the coast, a large, lightly settled region of swamps, woods and low mountains. Local military habits had been developed over a long period of desperate warfare with the Native Americans, some of whom had long sided with the Britons and Americans against traditional enemies. The Spanish and the French had also made alliances with native tribes hostile to the British and their Indian allies. These conflicts were as close to total war as the era saw anywhere. The American War for Independence was a civil war, with the British making alliances with Indians and promising freedom to slaves who ran away from the rebel owners, but they were reluctant to offer loyalists constitutional concessions that could have prevented the war in the first place. Each side confiscated food and fodder, each confiscated the property of enemy landowners, and anyone trying to remain neutral was crushed in between.

What is interesting in the context of these wars is how little the British government understood what it was doing. The practice of sneering at Americans was almost universal; no American could purchase an officer's commission, and even the American loyalists who enlisted to fight for the crown were given a green uniform instead of the more prestigious red one. Tarleton himself found it difficult to advance his career by demonstrated competence and valour in regular cavalry units—that is why he accepted command of the British Legion rather than await the slow process of gradual promotion that might well forget the son of a Liverpool merchant. Tarleton had the favour of Sir Henry Clinton, who commanded the His Majesty's army in America from 1778 to 1782, but appointments were made in London. Tarleton's future, therefore, depended on the impression he made in the capital.

Tarleton returned home to a hero's welcome and, wearing his green uniform, had Joshua Reynolds paint the portrait that is now in the National Gallery in London. He entered into a long career in Parliament, where he became a strong voice for continuing the slave trade, and eventually enjoyed a military command in Ireland.

Cornwallis returned home on the same ship as the American turncoat, Benedict Arnold (1740-1801), and was greeted by cheering crowds. Soon he went to India as governor-general, where he instituted sweeping reforms that on one hand limited the abuses of the East India Company and on the other guaranteed British supremacy throughout the sub-continent. He strengthened the hold of Indian landowners over the peasantry, believing that a landed aristocracy made for the best and most stable government, but he did not allow any Indian nobles to think themselves equal to Britons. Transferred to Ireland, he suppressed the uprising of 1798 and defeated the French army that had come to the rebels' aid. He is remembered in India for his reforms, in Ireland for his execution of prisoners; and in America as the talented general who underestimated George Washington.

American Wars on the Periphery

Americans are no more immune to misunderstanding what they are facing on the frontier than other peoples, but their historical frontier was populated by weak and fragmented tribes. The frontier wars were, they believed, steps on the way to empire.

In most successful frontier wars there was overwhelming power on one side, on the other only genius, enthusiasm and justice. Victories were celebrated by poets and historians who saw expansion over neighbours as preparation for the nation's future greatness. The Roman historian Livy tied the skirmishes of the early Republic to the later acquisition of empire, with an emphasis on the development of civic characteristics that turned a band of exiles, runaways and unwilling subjects into dedicated soldiers and politicians. Livy was a model for nationalist historians across Europe.

Recently Max Boot, in *The Savage Wars of Peace*, made a less ambitious contribution to understanding how an American nation with little interest in empire acquired one, then eventually became the only surviving superpower. Boot's thesis is provoking. He argued—cogently, critics think—that the traditional view of historians was misleading. Historians had long seen the origin of American imperialism in the nineteenth century Indian wars; he saw it in twentieth century interventions in Latin America. Indeed, the westward movement of American miners, ranchers and farmers did not result in a foreign elite ruling over large numbers of natives, whereas America's twentieth century involvement in troubled regions such as Cuba, the Philippines, Panama, China, Nicaragua, and Mexico did. Also, in Boot's view, American intrusions overseas were often based as much on idealistic motives—to suppress tyrants, to oppose European colonialism— as to protect capitalist investments.

This is not an argument likely to impress Marxists of any persuasion except his suggesting that, while commercial interests were important, the potential of future markets was more important than immediate profits; this suggests that strategic goals had priority over capitalism. Similarly, he pointed out that American churches and other 'do-good' organizations were exhorting both Republican and Democratic administrations to protect their efforts to Christianize and uplift the 'backward' peoples of these regions, or to feed them. In short, mixed motives abounded, all brought together in the belief that nothing could be done in these nations (or done by the local populations) unless political stability was restored.[1]

Boot argues that the American military learned the lessons of modern war in these interventions. Small unit actions trained a generation of military leaders who had primarily understood that the American Civil War provided only one important lesson for the American Way of War—to use overwhelming force, to employ technology and transport, and to seek total victory.

It might be noted that infantry tactics changed little between 1865 and 1917 because a mass army can only be raised and employed quickly by training regiments to attack in mass formations. This reduces the human tendency to ask 'what the hell are we doing?' Officers do not want soldiers to look around to see if someone else will take the lead in what seems to be a suicidal gesture. Human beings in crowds will do stupid things. The distribution of alcohol helps. In fact, the system worked right until the widespread employment of machine guns and artillery. Afterward, experienced officers argued successfully that training men to fight as a small platoon was time well spent.

Boot's small wars saw little of this debate—since generals would not send large armies to fight guerrillas, local commanders had to develop small unit tactics appropriate to countering raids, ambushes and terrorism. The strategy of temporary military occupations required a concentration on state-building rather than developing colonial policies. This meant an emphasis on training local military forces and having American administrators demonstrate how to run an honest and efficient government (lessons that were usually quickly forgotten). Whatever the strategy's shortcomings, it allowed the president to withdraw the American forces before the domestic opposition to colonialism became too loud. This seemed to work even in countries suffering through post-colonial chaos and domination by a series of military strongmen. Unfortunately, Boot suggests, much of the experience gained in these wars was contained within the Marine Corps without affecting the Army or Navy. One might easily imagine that American generals and admirals were more interested in the annual Army-Navy football game than in Central American or Asian affairs.

This attitude changed somewhat later, though Boot was unsure whether this was cause-and-effect or the result of battlefield experience. By 2006 a new U.S. Army/Marine Corps Counterinsurgency Field Manual appeared, with an emphasis on flexibility, knowledge of local conditions and people, and small unit tactics. Combined with reinforcements that politicians and generals said would make no difference, it turned a lost war in Iraq into what was thought to be a victory. Since the strategy was revised again following the election of Barack Obama—pulling out of Iraq while announcing a similar plan for Afghanistan—Boot said that it was too early to judge the results. At the time of writing, with the situation in the Middle East uncertain, one is tempted to think that the long-term American policy is to vacillate between doing too much, doing too little, and doing nothing.

One lesson Boot's book should have imparted was that it did not matter whether Americans had any interest in places they could not find on a map or not, because they would learn that a political vacuum draws outsiders in. In the early twentieth century this meant that if Americans did not act in the Philippines or China, or elsewhere, then Germans would.[2] Also, that politicians could be motivated by political idealism even more quickly than by money or office; this was especially true if it involved the connected virtues of Democracy and Protestantism that were part and parcel of the Progressive movement in both major political parties. It was Theodore Roosevelt (president 1901-1909) for the Republicans, Woodrow Wilson (president 1913-21) for the Democrats; and, almost surprisingly, William Jennings Bryan (1860-1925), long a strong voice denouncing the excesses of capitalism and war, for the Populists.

Some of the American presidents who advocated intervention, from Wilson (in Mexico 1914-19) to George W. Bush (in Iraq 2003-08), expected that the people they freed from tyrannical governments would be grateful and even eager to embrace the American form of democracy. Realists like Theodore Roosevelt (and perhaps Ronald Reagan) were disliked for their emphasis on having a military capable of enforcing their will and their seeming willingness to use it. As Roosevelt predicted, those who feared America power usually became sufficiently quiet that it was unnecessary to use it, but no rule is without an exception—even mentioning this truism will likely provoke dissent from those who dislike any form of Western imperialism and militarism. Wilson, alas, disliked preparations for a major war as much as he hated German militarism. Therefore, he entered the Great War with so few well-equipped troops that it was a full year before American ground forces did anything beyond boosting British and French morale. His good intentions in the Fourteen Points and the Versailles Treaty are not often praised by modern historians, who see them either as ineffective or as producing nationalism, ethnic cleansing, and then Lenin, Stalin and Hitler. Wilson's interventions in Mexico also gave him results opposite to what he wanted.

The larger lesson is to recognize that while Rome, Great Britain, France, Russia, China, and the United States of America were either the centres of empires or desired spheres of influence, they cannot be fully understood without some acquaintance with the ways they met challenges on their peripheries. And, as often happens, the efforts to control the periphery took on a lives of their own, drawing sustenance from the centre even as they ignored policies intended to control it.

To take one step backward—to look at why the centre even cared about what happened on the periphery—gives us three reasons why these wars occur. First, someone or some group in the centre thought that occupying peripheral lands would be advantageous. This advantage could be strategic

(Rome trying to shorten its long fortified frontier against the Germans), economic (to acquire resources), prestige (postage-stamp imperialism in the nineteenth century), or political and patriotic (particularly in the mass newspaper era). Second, the centre was protecting itself from attack. The Romans built the Antonine Wall and Hadrian's Wall to protect Britain from the Picts, but had to abandon both when manpower was not available to defend them. The Chinese built the Great Wall, but were still overrun by the Mongols and the Manchus. Last, the centre gets sucked in, often without intending to. Gladstone (1809-98, four times Prime Minister of Great Britain) was against invading the Sudan, but events (and General Charles 'Chinese' Gordon) forced his hand.

Sudan could be considered the pivot point of northern East Africa, making it more valuable in linking east and west (the French plan) or north and south (the British hope) than for its wealth. Geography and climate had limited Sudanese influence over neighbouring peoples who were different in race, culture and religion, but there as in India Islamic fundamentalism made conquest by British armies difficult. Thus, while once the Sudan was important only for trade in slaves and ivory, it became the centre of a regional Great Game played by distant politicians poring over maps that provided less information than flights of fancy.

Practical Experience

In early modern times, three great 'gunpowder empires' occupied the area from southeastern Europe to the farthest extent of the Indian subcontinent. The Ottoman Empire, the Safavid Empire, and the Mughal Empire bestrode the Islamic world for two centuries after 1500. All three empires developed similar responses to problems that had proved fatal to preceding dynasties. Traditionally, warrior kings had parcelled out authority to tribal leaders who in return contributed warriors and a portion of whatever taxes were collected. Given that animals were more important than money, and that grazing lands were limited, tribal leaders found it difficult to share their wealth with both their ruler and their people. As a result, rulers could not always support their armies on such contributions; at such times they were forced to squeeze the subjects at the centre of their realm for additional taxes, and when wars came, they had to rely on hastily raised mounted troops. Trade would be curtailed by war, after which revenues from commerce would collapse, and they could not pay their armies. This had to change.

Since cannon, muskets and other military supplies could not be acquired and maintained in such an ad-hoc manner, the rulers established bureaucracies to raise incomes, dispense justice, and appease the needs of minority populations so that they did not perceive themselves as abused subjects or belonging to an inferior culture. Whether it was the 'millet' system of Turkish government, the somewhat more complex Persian administration, or the multi-layered Indian state, each was a pragmatic adjustment to local needs. The result was wealth beyond previous memory, a bloom of artistic and literary creation, and exceptional freedom for individuals and groups.

The wealth and prestige did not last, of course, but the memory of that long era of greatness still causes a blush across the faces of modern youth in these lands when they realise that the world thinks of them as poor and backward, and a look around them shows that the world was right. At these moments the religions that had once been vibrant and creative turn into vehicles of violence and revenge on those believed responsible for their loss of power and pride.

For these reasons it will be useful to look at these great empires of the past, then compare their experiences with other, more modern states and the ways that they interact with the peoples in the lands and nearby.

Suraiya Faroqhi's 2004 book, *The Ottoman Empire and the World Around It*, is aptly named. Indeed, it looks squarely at the problems any centre has when trying to control or govern a periphery. One area of concern was the vast region south of Egypt. The Sudan may have been the centre, even the heartland of northern Africa, but from the viewpoint of urbanised Egypt, it was a wild and dangerous frontier.

It had always been that way. The Greek historian Herodotus reported that nobody had ever explored the upper reaches of the Nile, and when a millennium later, Arab armies poured into the region, they could do so because they had come from a similar dry and desolate region and had enough horsemen to persuade the tribes to convert to Islam—which they did, though incorporating many tribal traditions into the daily practice of the new religion. The Egyptian domination did not last. The Sudan may not have produced many scholars, but its warriors were valiant beyond reason; quickly the zealous horsemen drove out the garrisons of the Egyptian sultans and Mamelukes and of the Ottomans who succeeded them. The Ottoman sultan, desperate for a means of defending this frontier, restored the Mamelukes to power there. Ultimately, the Mamelukes replaced the Ottoman governors in all but name, much as they had done with the sultans.

In nearby Arabia, the sultans chose to pay the Sherifs and Bedouin who protected the holy places in Mecca and Medina. Stationing garrisons was impractical—too little food, too much isolation, and too expensive. However, the pilgrimage to Mecca being a religious duty of all Muslims, the sultans could not ignore their responsibility to protect the pilgrims.

Christian pilgrimages to Jerusalem were less important, but the Ottomans tolerated a limited number of worshippers as long as they were discreet and did not offend Muslim sensibilities; the money they paid went to the maintenance of mosques and other civic buildings.

Here, as elsewhere, the Ottoman policy was a sophisticated pragmatism. This usually took the form of an unsophisticated 'muddling through'. The ideal of a centralised bureaucratic state—and the desire to expand the faith— ran contrary to actual policy in which direct imperial control was rarely imposed on frontier regions. Rule was usually indirect, through local elites, or, as in the case of Egypt, through what amounted to a buffer state. This allowed the sultan and his high officials to concentrate on more important matters—rivals in Europe and Asia, poetry, tulips, and their harems.

Africa was, in fact, only of marginal importance to the Ottomans. The sultans had other frontier regions that they considered more significant— the Caucasus Mountains, the Crimea and the steppe, and the Balkans. They found it impossible to govern any of those areas effectively from Constantinople (the name Istanbul came into common use only slowly). Yet, if they gave those regions autonomy, they would eventually have to put down efforts by governors and tribal leaders to make themselves independent. Governance was a matter of balance, not too much, not too little—and inevitably the administrators in the capital occasionally guessed wrong.

The border with Persia was no problem. That was a real border, a dividing line between two civilisations with different ethnic majorities, different languages, and differing versions of Islam. It was not a frontier, but only an imaginary line drawn where the nearly level plain of Mesopotamia ran up against the foothills of the Zagros Mountains, more or less along the border of the modern states of Iraq and Iran.

In general, the Ottoman wars against the Persians resembled the Roman and Byzantine conflicts with the Persians' predecessors. Whoever controlled Armenia (now southeastern Turkey) controlled the region. If the Ottomans held the mountains, they could protect Syria and invade Mesopotamia; if the Persians dominated, the Ottomans were in trouble. North of Armenia were mountain peoples that were alternately Christian and Muslim, leading one to suspect that religion was more a means of asserting ethnic identity than convictions about a moral life that led to paradise.

The Caucasus Mountains to the north of Armenia provided a different challenge because the diverse peoples there could withdraw into difficult terrain and call for help from neighbouring powers—the Persians and Russians were always willing to support any uprising that provided complications for the Ottoman sultans, and Ottomans, too, on those occasions when enemy influence was strong in the region. But this rarely mattered because armies moved through the less rugged lands along the Caspian Sea, not through the mountains.

As a result, Georgians, Azeris, and Chechens survived. However, few Circassians did. This people along the Black Sea, once so numerous that it provided many slave soldiers to the Mamelukes, was almost eradicated by Russian armies, with the few survivors fleeing into Turkey.

North of the mountains lay a giant steppe inhabited almost only by nomads. To the east were the Kazakhs, to the west Tatars. Tatar raids into Russia and Poland-Lithuania carried away huge numbers of blond prisoners for sale in the Muslim world; the fierce horsemen also provided a cavalry screen for Turkish armies in the Balkans. Awkwardly, Tatars usually disappeared when there was a likelihood of heavy causalities; the very lack of discipline that made them so formidable as marauders and foragers rendered them unsuitable for pitched combat. The best that the sultans and grand viziers could do was to hope that the khans who led the Tatar hordes would be more help than trouble, and that when Turkish armies found themselves in trouble, that the Tatars would remain around long enough to extricate the men and their weapons.

It seemed that the Tatars were forgotten by modern history, but when the Russian annexation of the Crimea took place in 2014, we were reminded that they existed, and that they did not want to be ruled by Russians. Cossacks were there, too, and for them anything that Russia did was perfectly fine.

The Balkans were generally ruled through vassals, usually Christian monarchs or governors. The mutually jealous peoples kept one another in check, with imperial policy encouraging an ever greater complexity of ethnic identifications. By and large Catholics, Orthodox Christians, Jews and Muslims governed themselves from the village level upward, most paying reasonable taxes, providing supplies and labour for campaigns, and, when appropriate, adding their forces to the sultan's armies. Service at a distance from home was rare, but some Christian communities were subject to a tax in young boys.

The young men thus recruited by Ottoman officials were technically slaves, which meant that in their future roles as warriors and administrators, they could be rewarded or punished without offending any important Turkish families; in time they came to dominate the Ottoman state, even removing incompetent or incompliant sultans. The slave soldiers known as Janissaries were the best musket-wielding infantry in the world.

Some Janissaries remembered their origins sufficiently to see that money was spent on civil projects in their homelands, or that younger Janissaries were promoted to the extent their talents permitted. In time, of course, as their enthusiasm deteriorated into a love of the good life, sultans decided that they were no longer necessary.

The way was open for a debate on how Turkish the Ottoman state should be. That is a question that still remains open, one that has great significance for the non-Turks inside the borders of that modern nation-state.

This, in a wider context, is one problem this book will investigate.

1. This argument parallels recent criticisms of foreign aid and what leftists call neo-imperialism, in that large corporations, NGOs, the United Nations, American anti-Communism, and local elites combine to establish and defend stability in the newly independent third world nations. Even aid to starving peoples goes astray—first to the compromises of the legislative process that require the purchase of American aid, then the inability to prevent its theft and resale at the point of delivery—with the unintended result of causing local prices to crash, ruining local farmers. Reactions to any failed programme can be so severe as to cause a 'yo-yo' effect that undermines the governments the policies were intended to support. The degree to which this leads to corruption, local unrest, and eventual military intervention deserves more attention than it gets.
2. German imperialists, who arrived late into the colonial game, did not disguise their interest in Africa, Samoa or even in Mexico. In 1914 the Japanese gleefully seized their colonies in the Pacific and China.

Chapter 2

Gunpowder Regimes
The Spread of Firearms

This chapter looks at the rise of European armies, their wars against each other, and then their successful employment in Asia, Africa, and the Americas.

Firearms gave Europeans superiority over peoples who relied on spears, swords and bows, and over those whose social values continued to emphasise cavalry. Since the origins of gunpowder weapons lay in the East, it has often puzzled historians why it was the West that developed those first primitive firearms into deadly weapons, then spread the technology back to India, where it had long been believed to have originated.

We are now certain that gunpowder was invented in China; but we still wonder why its various uses as an explosive, in rockets, and in firecrackers did not change warfare there significantly, or why firearms did not supplant traditional weapons. Only after gunpowder appeared in Europe during the thirteen century and became important in the fifteenth, did everything change, eventually everywhere. The military innovations introduced in Europe between 1500 and 1650 have been called the Gunpowder Revolution. This is not quite the same as the subsequent Military Revolution or more recent Modernisation, but it was essential to both.

This is an important matter because, as Marshall Hodgson notes in *The Venture of Islam*, there were already sweeping political changes underway around 1500—in addition to the rise of France, Spain and Austria in Europe, Persian and Ottoman states were becoming more powerful, the descendants of Timur (Tamerlane, 1336-1405) were conquering northern India, Portuguese captains were sailing onto the southern seas, and Russian tsars were looking to occupy the steppe.

Rulers of these new empires all employed cannon to capture hitherto impregnable fortresses and to strike at troops beyond the range of spears and arrows. Still, as Hodgson notes, gunpowder was often not the most decisive factor, only the most easily identified.

The Gunpowder Revolution was a slow moving event. Although firearms eventually had a permanent impact on warfare, it is easy to imagine, incorrectly, that they were quickly accepted. We tend to see spectacular and memorable moments—pitched battles—that condense our sense of time into easily remembered 'world-historical' events. However, what we see as sweeping changes were not always so understood by contemporaries. This was especially true in Eastern Europe and much of East Central Europe, where geography lent itself more to raids by nomads than to defence by knights and local militias. Because matchlocks were awkward to use on horseback and too slow for infantry to employ effectively against charging horsemen, firearms were rare there until the development of the wheel-lock pistol and the flintlock musket. Moreover, so great were the distances between fortified cities and castles that cannon could scarcely be dragged there for sieges. Undermining walls was an ancient technique, but only in the gunpowder era could a besieger set off a 'mine' and follow it up with an infantry assault. This was much more effective than digging out a large chamber under a wall and then setting the timbers afire.

It is often said that cannon outmoded the old curtain wall of traditional castles, but it would be more accurate to say that the combination of cannonballs and mining did so. Cannon could hit a tall wall more often and more effectively at a single point, weakening it until it collapsed, but the noise from the bombardment also disguised the sounds made by sappers as they dug their way to the wall, then stacked the barrels of explosives.[1]

With the more common use of gunpowder weapons, much changed. Not everything, of course, and not everywhere, and certainly not at once. Some changes—such as the metallurgy necessary to cast cannons, and clockwork mechanisms adapted to firearms—had been long underway. Traditional weapons continued to dominate for various reasons—sometimes out of class pride, sometimes because of expense, and sometimes because the tried-and-tested was actually better. But when it became obvious that walls around castles and cities could not withstand artillery or exploding mines, Europeans came around. At least, those with the money to buy the new weapons and hire dependable soldiers came around. The political chaos of the late Middle Ages sorted itself out so that only a handful of Western states remained important—Spain, Portugal (as a naval power), Austria and France.

There was a second tier of significant states—England, Holland, Saxony, Bavaria, Poland, Denmark, Sweden, Naples. There was a numerous third tier which was slow to recognize that the rulers were significant only when allied to larger powers, and that political independence was more theoretical than practical.

The Great Armada and the Spanish Netherlands

The most critical moment in the history of the English-speaking peoples might have been in 1588. Had Spain gained control of the Channel, their 130 ships could have carried troops from the Spanish Netherlands (modern Belgium) across the short passage to overwhelm Queen Elizabeth's small and outmoded land army. However, by keeping her wits, Good Queen Bess kept her head. Although it was afterwards possible for the Spaniards to keep commercial lanes open, so that individual ships from Spain could slip past the loose English blockade, it was impossible to transport large numbers of men and equipment to the army in the Low Countries—the region around the mouth of the Rhine and other great rivers. North of the Spanish Netherlands were Dutch speakers who had become Protestants, then joined together to create the United Provinces (better known by the largest province, Holland) in order to defend their religion and their political autonomy from Spanish governors. Now their daring sailors joined English and French Protestants in attacking Spanish shipping. Confident of their ability to take on lumbering troop carriers, and eager to take booty that included chests of coins, they made it impossible for the Spanish crown to send reinforcements north by sea. Consequently, Spanish military units had to march from Italy to the Upper Rhine, and thence north, recruiting young men and refining their soldierly skills along the way. This 'Spanish Road' was the imperial life-line: if it was cut, the emperor might lose his most valuable provinces, the industrial lands that make up modern Belgium.

This war had unusual aspects. The effort to subdue the Dutch was partly religious, partly economic (for taxes and to control competition); the conflict with Catholic France was largely dynastic. But a study of the two long conflicts tells us not to expect politics to follow the cold predictability of logic. Hot blood, luck, and bending to practical necessities made that impossible.

The Spanish army was not composed entirely (or even largely) of Spaniards, but they were its vital core. Its complicated tactics were quickly learned by recruits from all the Spanish domains or wherever Spanish armies passed—drill, drill, drill, and more drill. Young men, then as now, yearned to be part of something great; joining the finest army in the world

21

was the fastest way to do that. They were also paid well and they were fighting for their Church and their king.

Money was important for mercenaries, but it wasn't the only consideration in choosing an employer. In the case of the Spanish army, pride predominated, after which came religious identification, hatred of national enemies, the absence of other opportunities for employment, boredom with village life, and a desire to travel. Dependable pay outweighed the promise of higher wages, and thanks to the bullion from the New World, Spain had full-weight coins to disperse to its troops. The uniforms were attractive, too, and there is nothing as good for attracting girls as a combination of uniforms, ready cash and swagger. Stories of travel and battle, and a reputation for being passionate lovers also helped. While Spaniards were not known for having bushy beards, their moustaches were cute.

Lastly, the people in the Spanish Netherlands were fervent Catholics with a tradition of resisting French aggression. But even this and the Spanish army might not have been enough to preserve their independence if the French kings had not periodically diverted their resources to invasions of Italy or Germany. However, frivolity was a royal prerogative, and the kings exercised it. To the north, the Dutch were striking out in a new direction, too—commerce and overseas possessions—that provided them the money to maintain their armies and navy and their fortified cities. The Dutch were Protestant, to be sure, but their religious beliefs were not well defined until the Spanish hammered them into shape.

The Spanish army stationed in the Low Countries was a first rate fighting force, one that at first had beaten the French to the South and the Dutch to the North. However, once those enemies had built huge fortresses on the borders, this army could make little headway against them. These fortresses were not yet the scientific defensive works of Vauban (1633-1707), the French designer who made engineers indispensable to kings and commanders, but Michelangelo (1475-1564), who had designed some of the fortifications of Florence, would have admired them. The new principle for fortifications was indirect fire—luring attackers into a killing zone, then slaughtering them with cannon protected from suppressive fire. These characteristically had lower walls that could not be bombarded easily, a glacis that allowed attackers into the killing zone (but made it difficult to get out), ravelins (detached outer works that sheltered the main wall from direct fire and broke up attacking forces), and cannon buried deep in the fortification, reached only through protected galleries and firing through ports that were too small for infantry to enter.

Sixteenth century field commanders experimented with new formations that allowed better employment of muskets and cannons, but they still relied on masses of infantry bearing pikes (at which Swiss and Germans were most skilled) or nimble swordsmen who could slip under spears or climb over the rubble of collapsed walls. Cavalry was still dominated by the nobility, but even well-born horsemen were smart enough not to charge into massed pikemen; pistols still needed more development to be effective when fired from horseback and so were less often employed than sabres or lances. Field artillery was still cumbersome. Training was often minimal, which meant that commanders emphasized hiring veteran warriors who understood both the use of their weapons and the drills that brought the unit to the most effective place to confront the foe.

The Spanish army, thanks to its units serving longer than most of its opponents, was simply a better fighting force; and its morale was unsurpassed. The English, in contrast, had relatively few men and officers with battlefield experience, and the forces that could be raised for local defence were not even well-prepared to fight the last war that had taken place on English soil—the War of the Roses, almost a century earlier. Queen Elizabeth's Tudor dynasty began at the decisive battle of Bosworth Field (1485), but Shakespeare did not write about it—*Richard III*, made famous by the line, 'A horse, a horse, my kingdom for a horse!'—until 1592, four years after the Great and Invincible Armada was defeated and dispersed.

England, safe from further attack, could now send out its Sea Dogs to attack the Spanish Main. Piracy enriched the queen and made her subjects proud. Protestants could wipe their brow, certain that their heads would not be detached from their bodies, or that they would be subject to the notorious Spanish Inquisition.

It is no surprise that contemporary philosophers, like Erasmus, might say that any unjust peace is better than any just war. But if men are sheep to be led by dogs, there are also wolves in the world. Erasmus could enjoy his well-stocked library, his circle of friends and his glass of red wine because princes provided law and order. He could, nevertheless, see that the storms of religious controversy, dynastic ambition and commercial competition were building up to blow down the walls of his comfortable existence.

Colonialism

Wars were expensive, and kings relied on hard cash to fight them. This came largely from taxes, especially those on commerce, then on loans, currency manipulation, and the sale of offices.

Since the most easily collected commercial taxes came on colonial products, this meant that the king with the most colonies had the most money; and, in lands with large native populations, their contributions were important, too.

Spain and Portugal created the first great European colonial empires. In an important sense this determined the ways that the nations along the Atlantic coast behaved. Portugal, Spain, then France, Holland and England became wealthy from overseas commerce in ways that Poland and Austria-Hungary or even Germany could not—the Hanseatic League declined because regional trade in grain and fish and salt, fur and beeswax and amber, iron and cloth and beer, were insufficient to make a handful of city-states into a great empire. Holland and Denmark, then Sweden took its place.

Colonial expansion was not a simple process, nor a well-planned one. After some floundering about, the Spanish crown developed a system based on the cooperation of state and church that encouraged economic exploitation of the native peoples and resources without provoking rebellions or outraging its own religious sentiments.

Those nations which acquired colonies later were unable to duplicate this achievement. Most importantly, there were no more great empires to overthrow. In North America tribes could just withdraw into the wilderness. The islands in the Caribbean were too well defended by great fortifications and navies. Africa was filled with strong native peoples, too much disease and too much heat; it was very much the same in Asia until the eighteenth century—a time when the British East India Company eliminated its French rival and worked with native princes.

John Darwin, in *Unfinished Empire*, listed five different ways that the British established colonies: the most important was a war of conquest, with Ireland as a model. This was also intended to deprive England's enemies of a base for attacks on the western coasts of the British Isles.

Darwin's analysis of the origins of the American War for Independence is especially worth reading. First, there was the policy of 'salutary neglect' that reflected the British parliament's preoccupation with trade and war elsewhere that lasted so long that Americans had become accustomed to self-government. This ended when a British government struggling to repay the debts from the Seven Years War (1756-63) without taxing its nobles and merchants concluded that the people and products of America could produce the needed revenues; Americans were, after all, not paying their fair share of the cost of the common defence, and they were better off than the average Briton. The ministers believed that these incomes would help pay for future wars against France and further commercial expansion into the Spanish empire and India. Lastly, American taxes would help preserve the system of corruption that was a part of politics in this era.

Time was short, however. The Americans were become numerous and self-assured. If they crossed the mountains into the interior—a development that Native Americans were unable to stop—their numbers would soon equal those of the mother country, and they would demand to be treated as equals. To forestall this, Parliament moved to forbid westward expansion, then imposed taxes, and when it met resistance, it threatened to use force to collect them.

It was too late. Events showed that Parliament lacked sufficient troops to intimidate the population across such a vast area, was reluctant to build a royalist party by rewarding loyalists, and did not understand how to play the diverse interests of the colonists against one another. The conflict of British self-interests against colonial self-interests became an 'accelerating slide into violence and war.' Unable to allow the colonists to continue their self-government, and unable to persuade them that the taxes were legal, necessary, and quite small, Parliament resorted to emergency rule by appointed governors backed by too few troops.

Misperceptions were joined to all-too-clear perceptions of what the opposing parties wanted. Most importantly, Americans had come to see themselves as separate from Britons. America had too many well-educated and eloquent leaders with a vision that clashed with the long-term plans of British leaders.

Parliamentary leaders, unwilling to sacrifice short term gains for long term advantages, misjudged the situation in 1775. By 1781, when they gave up the effort to suppress the insurrection, their debts were much greater, their empire smaller, and their reputation damaged. Britons began to rethink their empire, making changes that would have warded off the great catastrophe if they had been applied sooner. Peace with France came just in time. Soon they would have to meet the challenge of the French Revolution, then Napoleon, without American resources that would have contributed significantly to the war effort.

Spanish colonial policies were much more effective. Only Napoleon occupying Spain, then putting a brother on the throne, began the complicated process of unravelling that empire.

The Cost of Firearms

Muskets and cannon could not be produced by the economically backward states or frontier regions. The necessary infrastructure was not there. Also, though blacksmiths repair firearms, and members of the lower class could do the dirty and dangerous work of making gunpowder, no traditional society has ever produced an upper class willing to get its hands dirty.

Aristocrats, clan leaders, whatever their rank and status, preferred to fight from horseback. Partly this was to get a better overview of the battlefield, but it was more often simply a matter of status or comfort. Since commanders tended to be middle-aged or older, even the lowliest warrior could usually walk faster and longer than they could. To not be outdone, commanders avoided allowing anyone to see their weaknesses; and when they were tired, they were liable to make bad decisions.

When flintlocks first appeared on European battlefields about 1700, their superiority to matchlocks was obvious—the soldiers did not need to light a fuse and keep it burning, there were fewer accidents with gunpowder, the rate of fire was somewhat faster, and it was easier to attach bayonets to the barrels. Even so, the cost of replacing many muskets at once was beyond the resources of many European princes, thereby eliminating them from the game of power politics.

The European states with the resources—generally the large kingdoms—became more powerful as the weapons became more expensive. This was not due to the cost of the weapons alone, but also to their ability to hire mercenaries to use them. Not all military units were composed of the kind of mercenary the popular imagination conjures up—moving from army to army in search of higher pay—though there were plenty of bounty jumpers. Most soldiers were recruited locally, with pay as the incentive. But if pay fell too far in arrears, soldiers deserted. And once the bullion from the New World ceased to enrich Spain, every ruler struggled to square the circle of inflation and stagnant incomes, and payments on the debt.

One exception to limited employment opportunities were exiles from the British Isles, who could join fellow Irishmen and Scots in continental armies. Another was the officer corps. Low-ranking officers generally came from minor gentry or families involved with commerce, and since there was little money in the profession—they even had to buy their commissions—their careers were usually short. Like their continental peers, they loved the uniforms and may have had occasional hope for a heroic moment that would give them local fame, but their long-term plans were marriage, society life, and an enjoyable retirement in the country; few had opportunities to demonstrate their talent for command—that required a patron, perhaps a good marriage, and sufficient money to shine at court. In contrast, high-ranking officers with experience in continental wars were in high demand, sought by kings and princes from every land and clime. Such men could demand high pay and rewards in the form of lands and offices. These were the true mercenaries of the 1700s. However, after 1789 royal employers were less interested in hiring foreigners who might slip off for better pay elsewhere. The new military academies were developing a new class of talented commanders, and the French Revolution had demonstrated that those men could be better generals than those whose training and experience consisted largely of genealogy and hearing relatives boast of great exploits.

Meanwhile, the intricate drills that had allowed generals to take advantage of terrain and opponents' errors had become less important. Armies trained to manoeuvre for slight advantages found themselves overwhelmed by masses of enthusiastic French revolutionaries, who, not dependent on supply lines, seemed to be everywhere, attacking with surprising discipline in heavy columns and breaking their line formations. French generals could do this partly because the opposing commanders were cautious about exposing their expensive, highly trained troops to pitched battle; they could not replace losses easily, while the French could.

As it turned out eventually, the French enthusiasm did not last. It never quite died away, but though cries of *Vive le Roi* were replaced by *Vive la France*, these were eventually met by similar nationalistic shouts from their opponents. French nationalism gave birth to national feelings in Italy, Germany, Poland and even Russia. Greater equality of opportunity meant more chances for men of talent to make careers in the new national armies.

The early Industrial Revolution made it possible to arm these new armies, then to clothe and feed them. Moreover, the willingness of common men to volunteer meant that enlistment bonuses did not have to be as generous as before. Armies were at last relatively cheap.

One might be excused for thinking that such armies could easily deal with poorly-armed rabble in frontier regions. But that was not so. Napoleon learned that he could not simply put his brother on the Spanish throne or send an army to Haiti to return the rebellious slaves to servitude. Moreover, armies that rely on enthusiasm are prone to easy discouragement, and disease can cut down more men than weapons.

Impact on the Periphery

Peoples living in the mountains and deserts never fought in mass formations. Perhaps their cavalry charges gave the impression of huge numbers, but that was what infantry was supposed to perceive. The speed of the assaults, the surprise of the ambush, did not lend themselves to counting.

Frontier warriors had little use for the standard infantry musket, which was cheap and sturdy, but lacked accuracy. The knife, the sword, and an expensive long rifle were their standard weapons. A small number of warriors with long rifles could pick off their enemies at a distance, and when they caught pursuing regular soldiers in an ambush, there was little danger of being harmed in return. They knew that cannons were too cumbersome to carry along, and if the enemy somehow managed to get some in position, they could shoot the exposed crews down. Consequently, generations of warriors carried the long rifles, elaborately decorated weapons that were passed down from father to son and displayed to friend and foe as proof they were men who could defend themselves and their families from any threat. They could similarly decorate their women with gold and silver, a gesture that the women probably assumed was a reflection of their own value, when the real purpose was to demonstrate to other men how powerful the husband was.

These are the people described by Ahmed in *the Thistle and the Drone*. He sees local society in the tribal areas of his native Pakistan as reflecting three institutions: 1) the tribal chiefs, 2) the local mullahs, 3) the distant government as represented by local experts. Tribal societies, he says, are like thistles—they are hard to uproot, their narrow sharp thorns are painful, and they survive every hardship; they may be poor in possessions, but they are rich in pride and traditions.

This repeats a point that Walter Laqueur made in *No End To War* (2003), that 'tribal loyalties, language (or dialect), and the place where a person was born were often more important than religious solidarity'. Laqueur being one of the most important Western authorities on terrorism, his book was widely read and cited. This point, however, seemed to have been overlooked. Instead, generals and politicians alike found it easier to believe the jihadists' claims that their motivation was religious.[2] It was a missed opportunity—the jihadists knew that tribes and clans were natural rivals of each other, and that a call for Islamic unity would bring support from far and near. Had the West emphasized the tribal nature of the jihadists, they would have at a minimum raised doubts in the minds of Muslims who were wavering as to what they should do. If you believe that only war for Allah is noble, dying for anything less makes no sense.

This stands in strong contrast to modern Western materialism. Christians were once doughty warriors for their faith, the jihadists say, but now the West is composed of secular states that worship nationalism and practise orgies of sexual promiscuity, drugs, alcohol and sodomy—all financed by colonial exploitation and racial oppression. It is, they say, the crusades all over again, and explains why the crusaders lost.

Ahmed's second point is tribal customs are very puritanical, especially in matters of sex.

There is nothing, he says, in the Koran to justify female genital mutilation or honour killings; these grew out of internal Muslim disputes when leaders claimed leadership of Islam by being, as we say in the West, 'More Catholic than the Pope'. One way of discrediting opponents is to accuse them of being secular or corrupt or un-Islamic. Thus, both the jihadists and those who look to the Koran to understand the jihadists have misunderstood what is going on. Muslims who kill innocents or put on suicide vests may be reflecting ancient tribal customs, not the sophisticated theology of Islam.

Some tribal leaders today are content to maintain their petty tyrannies in the hills, but until 2014 few wanted to reestablish the Caliphate that was abolished by the secular Turkish state of Ataturk in 1924; awkwardly, the Caliphate never functioned as modern jihadists imagine, but such a misunderstanding is not unusual for true believers in any cause. Dreams can be more real than reality. On such dreams the jihadists build sand castles in the sky, each housing seventy-two virgins, each houri decorated with gold and silver jewellery.

Many jihadists believe that once they make themselves supreme over all Muslims, then over the entire globe, world peace, justice, and morality will follow. Awkwardly, the West remains strong, so there is a war to be won, a war in which virtue and cleverness face technologically superior weapons. Their strategy is to use terrorism to paralyse their effete and unmotivated foes, pitting not only the true faith against the infidels' unbelief, but also the demands of oppressed tribes for justice and revenge against the corruption and cowardliness of the West and its Middle Eastern imitators. It is a matter of honour—the jihadists show little respect for hypocritical Wahhabi princes of Saudi Arabia who combine American vices with lavish gifts to those want to destroy America.

In practice, Westernizing Muslims kill many more tribesmen than Americans do, but it is easy for angry tribesmen to believe that without American money and weapons, the puppets of a foreign culture would quickly be overthrown. In short, the leaders of modernising states can be as clueless about the origins of their problems as American presidents. Or so Ahmed suggests. First the Near Enemy (Israel and Muslim states that emphasize secularism), then the Far Enemy (the West, especially America).

If Ahmed is right, the Israeli-Palestinian dispute is of little importance. If that were settled by some means we cannot imagine, he says that the contest of city and country would still be with us—and that is what drives jihadi terrorism.

Ahmed's thesis runs up against establishment views that cannot be changed quickly, because nobody likes to admit that decades of theory were wrong and that trillions of dollars were wasted. Also one may question the practicality of his advice to restore stolen lands to the tribes and leave them alone. Modern states have expanded too much into the periphery to pull back, and even in Developing Nations people demand some hope for enjoying the good life they see in the West. In short, city people do not like to starve any more than country folk, and they have a sense of pride, too.

Oriental Gunpowder Regimes

While it would be an exaggeration to say that firearms revolutionized warfare from Ottoman Turkey to India, traditional arms became ever less important in that vast region. Thus was it ever: dynamic societies are forever undergoing change, and the idea that the Middle East was changeless is now hopelessly out of date. Our awareness of the contribution of gunpowder weapons to the process of change is not absolutely new, either. Richard Hellie (1937-2009) opened historians' eyes in 1971 with *Enserfment and Military Change in Muscovy,* arguing that modernisation was paid for by making Russian peasants into serfs. Marshal Hodgson had expressed similar views twenty years before his *Venture of Islam* appeared post-mortem in 1974, providing persuasive reasons why Ivan the Terrible and his successors came to mistrust the boyars who had previously dominated the military forces. Defeats in the Livonian War of 1558-83 and the ensuing Time of Troubles seemed to come from relying on an old-fashioned cavalry force; to create a modern army similar to those of the Swedes and Poles, the tsars hired foreign mercenaries and vastly increased the use of muskets and cannon. Hellie tied this together with an explanation for the survival of serfdom, which (in the absence of commerce that could be easily taxed) was the only way to pay for the new army.

In 2011 Douglas E. Streusand's *Islamic Gunpowder Empires: Ottomans, Safavids, and Mughals* played an equally important role in revising stereotypical thinking about the armies of the three great Muslim states of the early modern era. These states extended from the Atlantic to modern Singapore and included local cultures which were more easily governed by moderating Islam than in imposing practices more suitable for desert nomads and isolated villages.

Traditional arms remained important, but the tribesmen increasingly served as auxiliaries to specialists trained in the use of firearms. The goat herder who once could defy armies from the crest of a ridge by throwing rocks at them now had to learn to duck cannonballs, and horsemen had to expect to dodge or jump over the fallen mounts of those who had led the charge against the foe.

More importantly, Streusand explains how and why modern nationalist historians interpret the past of these gunpowder empires. Because Turkey and Persia were never colonised, the study of history in those nations is less contentious than in India and Pakistan. Thanks to the imperial archives having been opened, western-style research is possible in Turkey, and historians do not have to fear accusations of being colonial stooges and apologists; consequently, while it once took a lifetime to master the history of the Ottoman Empire, today any scholar can understand its basic outline.

While Indian and Pakistani historians agree that colonialism was bad, they hold very strongly contrasting views about why Britons were able to dominate so many peoples who were culturally and intellectually superior to them. Hindus and Indian secularists emphasize the destructive religious zeal of Muslim rulers who antagonised Hindu 'infidels' beyond endurance, so that they were willing to serve foreign rulers in order to fight them. Akbar's policy of universal toleration had brought peace and prosperity, but his reign (1556–1605) had seen a diminished purity of Islamic practices, the rise of Sufi orders, even the mixing of Muslim and Hindu rituals; the tax on non-Muslims had been abolished and inter-faith marriages had been approved; Muslim religious leaders lost some of their favoured status, and non-Muslim political and military leaders had been promoted. Reversing all this provoked rebellions and civil war. In Indian eyes Auranzeb (shah 1658–1707) was the villain who began the destruction of the Mughal Empire.

Muslims, in contrast, say that the reforming shahs were insufficiently zealous in crushing unbelievers, so the country remained divided. Auranzeb brought about a return to central authority. This made him the richest man in the world, but his empire was so large that he had to employ governors fearful of exhibiting too much competence and ambition; they were unable to put down the rebellions that cost him so much in manpower and treasure. He died exhausted, without a competent heir to complete his tasks.

Each side makes good points. Moreover, the ranks of the combatants did not always correspond to modern efforts to simplify the story to racial and religious stereotypes. Hindus and other religious minorities fought on both sides, and the *Taj Mahal* was built right in the middle of the period of transition. Mughals relied on heavy cavalry, which, when combined with some gunpowder weapons and a wagon fort, was sufficient to defeat armies that relied on elephants and infantry; their muskets and cannon were inferior to Ottoman or European weapons, but they were better than those of their Hindu opponents and rebellious officials; offering generous terms of surrender could bring a quick end to some wars, but hardly intimidated determined rebels. The Mughal Empire was based on seeking to accommodate every important group in a vast region. It was easy to do too little or too much.

Any government based on compromises needs a ruler who is flexible and nimble. This was not easy to do in a territory as large as India, where the shah was continually travelling and fighting; and whenever the shah had to spend years in distant provinces, he was represented elsewhere by cautious officials who were reluctant to act without his approval. Also, shahs inevitably became aged and infirm. Harem politics came into play, and the influence of favourites and courtiers. Compromises can be maintained when policies are predictable, but the hallmark of the all-powerful ruler is to make unconsidered anger and whims into laws.

Contemporaries did not realise the extent of Mughal decline, if they sensed it at all, any more than we do in prosperous nations today—the world is sufficiently contradictory that positive changes are often more apparent than negative ones. Streusand argues strongly that the historians' judgments reflect their national bias. Indians, like English writers before them, blame Aurangzeb's religious bigotry; Pakistanis blame the artificial balance of religious communities, when a strong central government and adherence to Sunni Muslim practices would have provided a secure ruling class that could have quelled rebellions and warded off foreign intrusion.

The impact of Marxism on the study of this era becomes significant when historians shove the Indian subcontinent's mosaic of politics into a framework of capitalist economic exploitation. There was, of course, economic exploitation, but that came after the decline of Mughal authority, after the peasant revolts, the famines, the rise of Hindu and Sikh states, and the governors (nawabs and rajahs) becoming what we could call princes.

All this happened before the arrival of capitalism, which was nevertheless blamed for the problems. There were food shortages, as should be expected after military conflicts disrupted agricultural production and commerce. Was there a general cultural decline? Or faulty government policies? Or incompetence at the top? What happened was that once the princes could not collect enough revenues for both themselves and the central government, they kept the money for themselves; the shah might complain, but he no longer had the resources to force his princes to obey. As the shah became a distant symbol of authority, the princes quarrelled among themselves, disrupting commerce and agriculture. Some were total incompetents in everything except holding onto power; and to achieve this, they welcomed French and British merchants who provided what had once been produced locally; soon they were buying weapons from those merchants, then hiring military instructors, and finally they were begging for military alliances. Inevitably, the weaker princes sought more and more outside help, until finally the foreigners and their armies and navies were indispensable. The British eventually beat the French, then took over, leaving the princes in place as figureheads but in fact managing everything from tax collecting to dispersing money, from passing laws to supervising the judicial system, and ultimately introducing a British educational system to make their subjects into slightly darker imitations of themselves.

Streusand's sophisticated analysis is not likely to please nationalists who want their history presented in short, one-sided sound bites. He refused to blame the simultaneous decline of the three great Islamic states (Ottoman Turkey, Safavid Persia, and Mughal India) on pressure from rising European states. 'It would be tidier and trendier that way,' he admits, and more politically satisfying, too, but the stories are too complicated for a simple explanation. Persia collapsed having allowed its military to deteriorate, so that what would once have been a minor crisis led to the collapse of the central state, and the provinces were unable to come to the rescue. The Mughal state fell because the centre did not provide provincial officers the security and advancement that they felt were due to them; consequently, the governors competed among themselves without rebuke from the top. Very soon 'the idea of Mughal sovereignty remained intact and unquestioned; Mughal government had disappeared.'

The political breakdown opened the way for foreign intervention. The traditional way of describing this is 'divide and rule'. However, the Mughal governors had already divided the state. All the British had to do was to support the weakest side, then make themselves indispensable. They did so with local troops—the sepoys—who were at first mostly Brahman Hindus commanded by Hindi-speaking British officers. Considering how the Mughals had alienated their Muslim and Sikh subjects, it was no surprise that these groups, too, preferred British rule, especially through those years when the British interfered relatively little with local affairs; British tolerance in religious matters was especially appreciated.

The Ottomans, in contrast to Mughal and Persian practice, adapted themselves and their institutions to meet the new challenges. It was not an easy matter, and only the minimum number of necessary changes were adopted—as elsewhere, religious beliefs and national pride stood in the way—but they were sufficient. There was a loss of territory and prestige, and self-confidence, but the state did not collapse for another two centuries.

Because Streusand published in 2011, he was able to analyse the early years of the War on Terror in its various manifestations. This was, he said, not a Clash of Cultures in the sense of Huntington's thesis. The origins of jihadist beliefs do not reflect their oft-stated aspirations to resurrect fallen empires as much as complaints about the rulers of those empires, nationalist views from the nineteenth century, and more modern totalitarian ideologies.

From the viewpoint of today, however, the rise of the Islamic Caliphate in Syria and Iraq suggests that he should have included the Arabs in his study.

Lessons?

Military technologies so far seem to indicate that might makes right. Except perhaps on the frontiers, where governments (especially popularly elected governments) find the costs of conquering and occupying too hard—and especially hard if restrained by moral considerations that a Genghis Khan, or Timur, or Auranzeb would have laughed at. Hitler or Stalin cannot be brought into this dialogue except by those lacking any sense of proportion.

Only gunpowder regimes can create great empires. But they cannot perpetuate themselves without the money to pay soldiers, buy weapons, and support all the governmental functions necessary to a great state. Whether in Europe or Asia or elsewhere, the basis of the state must be the citizenry. People work best and are most productive and creative when they are secure, when they feel respected, and when they share in the benefits of being a great power.

France had the most potential to dominate Europe militarily—as it did briefly under Napoleon—and long did so culturally. But Great Britain had more successfully released the talents of its citizens.

Similarly, today Israel has made itself a military power, and its citizens have made their unpromising land prosperous. Its neighbours have done neither, and, worse, are mired in internal strife so terrible that it is difficult to imagine their taking the steps necessary to escape their troubles.

Israel would be hopelessly divided, too, if the very real prospect of suffering another Holocaust did not require the parties to work together.

This is something that all democracies share—they will raise a large army only for emergencies or to face long-term threats (the Cold War comes to mind). When the crisis is past, they want to spend that money in other ways.

Whether this is a good idea or a bad one can only be seen in retrospect.

1. The Guy Fawkes plot ('Don't you Remember, The Fifth of November') of 1605 involved putting gunpowder in the parliament basement, then waiting for the king and the members of parliament to assemble. That is why fireworks are still the proper way to celebrate the holiday, even though the only explosion was in the movie *V for Vendetta*.
2. After the 9/11 attack on the Twin Towers, Western scholars hurried to assure everyone that jihad was a quest for personal improvement. They were correct in so defining the Greater Jihad, but forgot that there was a Lesser Jihad that every Muslim warrior since Muhammad has understood to mean war on behalf of the Faith. Protecting the faith from defilement and women from unclear hands and eyes is central to this.

Chapter 3

The Frontiers of Christendom

Europe's most famous response to a challenge to its political and religious institutions was the crusades. This was a series of international military campaigns that were more dramatic and far-reaching than any local struggle against pagan or Muslim attacks had ever been; it began as a response to Turkish tribes overrunning much of the Byzantine Empire and the Arab states which had made it difficult for pilgrims to visit Jerusalem. It would be a stretch to think that medieval crusades are a model for the United Nations' efforts to deal with threats to international order, but the principal problem may be nomenclature; Dwight Eisenhower was never criticized for entitling his book about the Allied effort to overthrow Nazism *Crusade in Europe*, but times have changed. There is an international effort today to stop Somali pirates from attacking shipping; and recent Islamist attacks on Christian communities in the Near East, on insufficiently fundamentalist Sunni Muslims and on Shiites, on Israel, and on semi-secular Arab states, have reached Western states that once considered themselves a part of Christendom. So, while the word cannot be uttered in public, perhaps there is something in the concept worth thinking about.

Crusading was not a static institution. It evolved from an effort to recover the Holy Land to an international Christian response to the advance of Ottoman Turks into Europe. Threats from the Muslim world were nothing new, but earlier generations of Christians had found it nearly impossible to station troops on threatened frontiers. European borders could be defended by fortresses and vassals who took turns serving as the garrisons; but for the castles of the Holy Land, where local resources were insufficient, only a force of volunteer knights without families and ambitions could hold fortresses until help arrived from far away. These warrior monks (actually friars) represented a development that the early Christian church could never have imagined.

The early Christian church had responded to the desires of its members by developing three distinct traditions—the secular church (led by bishops—the Bishop of Rome developing into the head of the Western church—who oversaw the priests and parishioners), hermits (who practised solitary penance, prayed, and meditated); and monks (who lived, usually in monasteries, by a set of rules requiring prayer, study, work and rest) and friars (whose spiritual work led them into secular society). The hermit tradition eventually waned, but the monasteries thrived, with new monastic orders taking on ever more specific roles. The number of new foundations increased after AD 1000, with military orders becoming popular after 1100. In the military orders the usual vows of friars—poverty, chastity, and obedience—were joined by one to fight for the Church. The knights of these Orders came as fully trained adults, and they soon made themselves important on the frontiers of Western Christendom, most notably in the two centuries of the crusade in the Holy Land, but also in Eastern Europe, the Baltic, the Balkans and the Iberian peninsula.

Medieval Military Orders

The military orders were founded to conduct wars on the periphery of the Roman Catholic world. Volunteers had captured Jerusalem during the First Crusade, and volunteers were always ready to march to the rescue when Muslim armies threatened the Holy Land, but the distance from Europe to Jerusalem was so great that the armies always arrived too late. Also, problems in Europe often made it difficult to recruit a force sufficient to have any effect.

The new military orders—most importantly the Templars and Hospitallers—became feared and hated by their Muslim foes because they were skilled and relentless and as determined in their religious views as any jihadist a sultan or emir could recruit. They were professionals who spent their days in prayer, fasting, and training for combat. They had no family to worry about, no incomes to put at risk, and no concerns for either their earthly or heavenly futures.

The fact that all officers were elected rather than inheriting their posts was a great advantage in resisting the threats of the Old Man of the Mountain, the semi-mythical leader of the Nizari branch of the Ismaili sect of Shiite Muslims whose power over his hashish-drugged followers was described by Marco Polo. The cult's assassins terrorized Muslim and Christian leaders through the twelfth century and into the second half of the thirteenth, collecting great sums of tribute and intimidating political rivals. Opponents besieged its central fortress in what is today northwestern Iran, but without success; only the Mongols, who had learned their siegecraft in China, persuaded the defenders to surrender. After that the assassin cult disappeared, its fanaticism reviving only in the twenty-first century when Sunni suicide bombers appeared.

The military orders suffered a hard blow in 1307 when the Templars were arrested by the King of France, tried on questionable grounds, and then either imprisoned or executed; monarchs and clerics quickly confiscated the Order's wealth and looked around for more victims. The grandmaster of the Teutonic Knights quickly moved his residence from Venice to Marienburg in Prussia, where he was safe. The Order flourished there, as did the associated Livonian Order that ruled along the Baltic coast to the north. Other orders hurried to demonstrate their usefulness to important monarchs and to the Church; some aided the Portuguese and Spanish crowns in conquering the last Moorish states on the Iberian Peninsula, then in suppressing pirate raids from North Africa and in exploring the African coast.

The Protestant Reformation undermined the effectiveness of all military orders in Central Europe, but the Hospitallers and newer orders provided men and officers for the naval forces that resisted the Ottoman expansion by sea. The sieges of Rhodes, Cyprus, and Malta, the Christian victory at Lepanto, cannot be read without marvelling at the courage of all of the combatants, but especially that of the warrior-monks of the military orders, some of whom were Protestants, and some who only served for a short period.

The Teutonic Knights in the 1700s

The Teutonic Knights had been founded during the Third Crusade to provide hospital services, then, because so many knights had joined its ranks as orderlies—a job for which they had little talent and no training—the pope gave it a military function similar to the Knights Templar and Knights Hospitaller. The only significant difference was that the two older military orders were largely French and English (which, in an era when the King of England ruled much of France, was an overlapping category). The Teutonic Knights were German, as their name in German made clear: *Der Deutsche Orden*.

Another difference was it possessed a territorial base in Prussia, with an associated, less centralised base in Livonia (modern Latvia and Estonia). It fought against Lithuanian pagans, Orthodox Russians, and Roman Catholic Poles who raised claims against its possessions of Prussian lands.

Unlike the other military orders, the Teutonic Knights had a special responsibility to the Holy Roman Emperor; a relationship that sometimes clashed with its obligations to the pope. The knights were not mercenaries, but as early as the thirteenth century they hired knights and men-at-arms for garrison duties and their field armies; these mercenaries were members of the military order for the length of their contract. Its members included Italians and Poles, some of whom were lay brothers, the only requirement being an ability to communicate in German. The Order also added secular vassals, local militias and crusaders to its armies. In short, it was a complex organisation.

After the conversion of Lithuania from paganism to Roman Christianity in 1386, the Order's mission seemed to have been accomplished. This led to discussions about what it should do next. One plan was to assist the Lithuanian Grand Duke and the Polish King fight the Tatars on the steppe, then assist them in wars against the Grand Duke of Moscow. Another was to shift the Order to the Danube frontier to assist the King of Hungary against the Turks; this was attractive because the king was also Holy Roman Emperor. However, all efforts failed totally—the Tatars beat the allied army, the offensive against Moscow failed, and the Turks were far too strong for them make a difference at such a distance from their Prussian and German estates. Then in 1410 the Polish King and the Lithuanian Grand Duke dealt the Order's army a crushing defeat at Tannenberg/Grunwald. The Order never recovered. But neither was it so weakened that it could not retain its hold on Prussia and Livonia.

By 1525, the year Grandmaster Albrecht von Hohenzollern secularized Prussia and made himself the first Duke of Prussia, there had not been many knights left there anyway. Many decades earlier the grandmasters had made a conscious decision to spend their money on mercenaries rather than to support a permanent force of knights; mercenaries could be hired for emergencies, whereas knights represented a permanent expenditure that lasted right through to old age. The Order's lands in Germany and Livonia, meanwhile, had become essentially autonomous—the *Deutschmeister* (German master, responsible for oversight of the convents in the Holy Roman Empire) making a strong claim to be equal to or, in important ways, even superior to the grandmaster (*Hochmeister*).

The Reformation divided the membership of the Teutonic Order sharply. Although most knightly members of the Order in the Holy Roman Empire decided to remain Roman Catholic, there were some strange regional variations—in Hessen there were an equal number of Calvinists and Lutherans, with only one Catholic knight, and the districts of

Thuringia, Saxony and Utrecht were completely Protestant. Elsewhere Roman Catholics dominated. The German master, Walther von Cronberg (1477-1543), took the title grandmaster in 1526 and made his seat at Mergentheim in southern Germany. For decades to come the military organization was a 'corporation of nobles' (*Teutschen Adels Spitale*), where younger sons of prominent families could spend a life as idly as the storms of the Reformation era permitted.

Cooperation was surprisingly good among Order members belonging to the three major confessions—Roman Catholic, Lutheran and Calvinist—because, as one said, 'we are *alle Cavallier*'. The emphasis was on being *Ritterbrüder* (brother knights) or *Ritterherren* (knightly lords). The major problems were the widespread confiscation by Protestant nobles of lands belonging to religious orders and bishops making their dioceses into secular states; monks and priests (and even entire chapters) left the Roman Catholic Church. Calls to the popes for a church council to give leadership to reform and to restore stability went unheeded—once the process of reform got started, the popes seemed to reason, it might not stop short of Rome. The Council of Trent (1545-63) took up the task, but too late and too slowly to reunite Western Christianity.

The grandmasters at Mergentheim slowly overcame the challenges of the time, including reviving the military function of the Order. They required younger knights to serve in three campaigns before becoming administrators of Order properties. To make way for these younger men, older officers were urged to accept employment from secular princes (especially the emperor); this usually meant administrative duties, but it allowed the grandmaster to save on expenses.

The knights of the Teutonic Order henceforth often served secular lords, but they were cautioned not to fight against the emperor or the Holy Roman Empire, and most were only willing to serve Catholic lords. With eighty-nine rising to the rank of general in various armies, they were clearly skilled at leading mercenary forces—the only kind capable of matching the armies of the Ottoman sultans, Protestant princes and French kings. It was widely believed that such celibate officers were more able to concentrate on command than secular officers with families. They may even have been chaste, though, given the culture of the times, that was perhaps too much to ask for.

The Priestly Corporation and the *Ritterorden*

As the scattered individual convents of the Teutonic Knights had drifted under the control of powerful local families, Catholic and Protestant observers had complained that the military order no longer seemed to have a purpose. They asked if the incomes and resources could not be better applied elsewhere.

There had been a proposal at the *Reichstag* of 1570 and again in 1576 that all young knights of the Order should serve one year on the Hungarian frontier, to defend Austria from Ottoman attack; this statement by the representatives to the imperial assembly demonstrated that they still considered *the German Order* an important institution, even a 'national' one. The emperor, too, wanted to revive the Order, but also to make it more responsive to his own needs. While the Order's knights successfully evaded that onerous duty, the proposal came up again in 1590, when the emperor's brother, Archduke Maximilian von Hapsburg (1558-1618) was grandmaster. The *German Order* had always felt a special affinity to the Holy Roman Empire, but only now was it able to revive the practice of electing grandmasters who could steer the Order's resources to imperial service. Maximilian had been a legitimate candidate to become king of Poland-Lithuania and had even led an army into Poland in 1588 to challenge Sigismund III for the throne, but was unsuccessful. Since the office of grandmaster was more or less a consolation prize, Maximilian reminded everyone of his exalted family ties by minting Thalers—heavy coins more suitable for heraldic display than commerce—showing him in full armour; the reverse showed him not as a warrior, but a competitor in a tournament encircled by fourteen coats-of-arms—all Hapsburg possessions, not territories of the Teutonic Knights. This had been sourly anticipated by many of the knights, who had resisted the forced resignation of his predecessor and the ham-fisted methods used in Maximilian's election. Their support of a rival, Johann Eustach von Westernach (1545-1627), indicated significant resistance to the new grandmaster's policies. Wisely, Maximilian had named Westernach his administrator in distant Mergentheim so that he could concentrate on dynastic politics and impressing his hardline Catholic orthodoxy on his Protestant subjects elsewhere.

Grandmaster Maximilian had been given a command on the Croatian frontier. He had with him thirty knights and seventy squires—about a quarter of the total membership of the Teutonic Order. All horsemen were dressed alike in the traditional white mantel with the black cross on the shoulder, with crosses hanging from their necks and armour protecting their mounts' necks. A silver relief portrait of the grandmaster in this campaign can be seen today in the Order's treasury in Vienna; there is also a Turkish/Persian sword on display—a weapon almost certainly taken from a fallen foe.

For many decades the Christians were on the defensive in the Balkans, and had to rely on local frontiersmen to warn against raiders and to hold local strongpoints. These allies were mainly Croatians, but also many Serbs who had fled their ancestral lands. All were devout Christians—the former Roman Catholic, the latter Orthodox—and all hated Turks and their Balkan and Tatar allies.

For some time Maximilian was imperial commander of all troops in Hapsburg Hungary, but, failing to recover the rest of that kingdom, he retired to Mergentheim. A few years later he was named administrator of the lands of the young Duke of Tyrol, a task that was more complicated than anyone had anticipated—among his duties was guaranteeing control of the passes through the Alps, task which required him to deal with independent-minded local mountaineers. He, like all Hapsburgs before him, discovered that the Swiss, no matter whether Catholic or Protestant, insisted on keeping their self-governance and on profiting from that independence. Maximilian was sufficiently successful to be honoured with an imposing funeral monument in the city parish church in Innsbruck, but he never subdued the Swiss. His successor, Karl von Hapsburg, did no better.

One of the notable officers involved in these wars was Georg Friedrich von Hohenlohe-Weikersheim (1569-1645). Late in his career, in 1618, right at the beginning of the Thirty Years War, he became commander of the cavalry of the 'Winter King' of Bohemia. Thus, he had first served an arch-Catholic prince, then the Protestant elector of the Palatinate. The Catholic victory in the 1620 Battle of White Mountain ended his rise toward greatness; records indicate that in 1634 he left his family estates to the Teutonic Knights—perhaps under compulsion.

In 1625, in the midst of the Thirty Years War, the Order turned to its aged, but competent functionary, Johann Eustach von Westernach. His ancestry was relatively modest by the Order's standards, but his experience in military operations against the Turks, as an administrator of the imperial army in the early years of the Thirty Years War, and as manager in Mergentheim, made him the logical opposition candidate to the emperor's most prominent general, Johann Tserclaes, Count of Tilly (1559-1632), who hoped to use its resources to finish off those Protestant princes who still remained in rebellion. Westerbach argued that the Order should retain its traditional independence.

Westernach's election effort was complicated by his family's mixed background of Protestantism and Catholicism and his own tendency to favour pragmatism over ideology, but the alternative was to submerge the

Order in the imperial army. His election did not end the debate, however—in 1627, the last year of his life, Westernach proposed that the knights make a choice, either to put their resources fully into the Catholic army facing the Swedish king, Gustavus Adolphus, or take more responsibility for protecting the southern frontier of Austria so that imperial troops could be transferred to the more important struggle in Germany. Should the former be adopted, he said, there was a possibility that the Catholic army would occupy Prussia and return that land to the Order; the implications of the latter was that the Order could avoid offending its Protestant members. However, because the Order's German properties had been ravaged by Protestant armies and brigands of all religious persuasions and none, Westernach had little ability to raise a substantial force for either field of combat.

Many of the Order's knights fought in the Thirty Years War. Not surprising, since this was a war that came to all parts of Germany; any individual who tried to stay at a distance discovered all too quickly that the war came to him. But we know little about their actions. As Helmut Hartmann says in *Von Akkon bis Wien*, there were many comrades in suffering, but no chroniclers.

The Order's material losses were made good relatively quickly once the war ended in 1648, but afterward the Order that had once been open to nobles of middle to modest means slowly evolved into the *Deutschritterorden*, an assembly of wealthy knights from the most prominent families of Germany; appropriate to this new role, it was commanded by a member of the house of Hapsburg, with his headquarters in Vienna. As it became little more than a neo-chivalric organization, its members proudly appearing in their outlandish costumes at state and religious festivals, but had little else to do. Only the expectation that members perform military service prevented order from descending completely into farce—a perpetual *Karnival* show.

In the future the knights usually fought as officers of secular regiments against Turks in nearby Hungary and the Balkans, and against what were perceived as French wars of aggression. Their soldiers were much like those of other princes, driven to enlist by a combination of reasons that makes it difficult to say that they were clearly mercenaries or not, but also impossible to categorize their motives as solely religious or patriotic. Certainly, recruiters would have been well advised to stress the opportunities for travel.

The story that follows is complex and often unconnected to the fate of the military order, but it explains why European expansion was delayed for a generation. Yet these years were important for the development of new military technology and new methods for employing it.

Ludwig Anton

The military role of the Teutonic Order revived with the enlistment of this well-born young prince. Born in 1660 to the Elector of the Palatinate (Pfalz-Neuburg, a scattered collection of territories, mostly east of Nuremberg, but with the principal residence in Heidelberg within sight of the Rhine). Ludwig (Louis) Anton was destined for a religious life—he was only two when his father petitioned the pope for permission to cut his hair to a tonsure and to dedicate lands for his support, and he was only eight when he received permission to join the military order. Imperial support for the family ambitions was guaranteed once Ludwig Anton's sister married Emperor Leopold I in 1676. At age nine he entered the Order's main chapter at Mergentheim, where he was dubbed a knight and then coadjutor (assistant and heir apparent) of the Grandmaster.

In 1681, aged twenty-one, Ludwig Anton was named colonel of the Neuburg Regiment (*Churfürstliches Leibregiment zu Fuß*); that is, he raised the troops from his family lands, regions long famous for supplying mercenaries; and two years later, at the siege of Vienna, he demonstrated his courage and his competence. Immediately afterwards he served in the battle of Párkány where the Polish king, Jan Sobieski, destroyed the Turkish army retreating from Vienna. The next year Ludwig Anton was named Grandmaster and Imperial Field Marshal.

His regiment was at all three sieges of the Turkish fortress at Buda overlooking the commercial centre at Pest on the other bank of the Danube. The citadel was on an imposing hilltop, with government offices and Turkish baths. In the first siege the losses were terrible—a French observer estimated that 20,000 Christians perished, two-thirds from inadequate hospital care. The Turks were even worse off, but their religious fervour, their simple habits and their fear of punishment made them formidable enemies. In the successful storm of the fortress, the Neuburg regiment lost 1,700 men.

Ludwig Anton led his regiment at the battle of Mohács (1687), a bloody encounter of two large, well-led armies. The wild Turkish attack in the opening minutes almost overwhelmed the Christians, but the coalition troops held, firing volley after volley into the oncoming masses until the multinational Turkish army fled the battlefield, leaving behind as many as 40,000 dead and wounded men and its commander. It was the first battle for

Max Emmanuel of Bavaria, whose coolness and good judgment were universally praised. He and Ludwig Anton were quickly transferred to the Rhine to fight against Louis XIV, but his regiment was soon back into the Balkans, where it participated in the 1688 siege of Belgrade; by that time its numbers had been reduced to fewer than 600 men.

One of his recruits from this time was Count Guido von Starhemberg (1657-1737), a famous warrior who had served in the garrison of Vienna during the 1683 siege, personally preventing the explosion of the powder magazine, an accident that would have been fatal to the defenders. He had fought under Prince Eugene and commanded the Hapsburg forces in Spain before assuming responsibility for defending the Austrian frontier.

As Louis XIV's armies stormed across the Rhine in 1689, burning the grandmaster's ancestral seat at Heidelberg, Ludwig Anton became a leader in the resistance to the French invasion; the destruction in the Palatinate became the stuff of legend—German Protestants fleeing as far as Pennsylvania in America and Berlin in Prussia, and the ruins of Heidelberg have impressed tourists from the time of Goethe to today. Louis XIV's intention was to deprive his enemies of a base for invading Alsace, but the destruction of cities that had surrendered without resistance left the population without winter shelter or food. Public reaction was outrage. The French thus became 'the hereditary enemy' (*Erbfeind*) long before *Die Wacht am Rhein* was written in 1840. The German response was more than resistance to French aggression—it was opposition to tyranny and religious intolerance.

Louis XIV had badly overplayed his hand—he lost England in 1688, when William III of Holland replaced James II; henceforth, the financial balance of power was against him, money essential for raising and sustaining armies flowing more easily to his enemies. Louis also made his most important ally in the Holy Roman Empire into an enemy by attempting to impose a favourite churchman as archbishop of Cologne, a post the Bavarian Wittelsbachs looked upon as a family possession; then his efforts to conquer Cologne by brute force failed. French and Bavarian politics were also at cross-purposes in Spain, where a son of Max Emmanuel was the heir of the expiring king, but he died under suspicious circumstances that allowed Louis XIV to arrange for his own middle grandson to inherit the Spanish crown. Louis XIV offered compensation to the Bavarian duke in the form of supporting his ambitions to become Holy Roman Emperor, which was hardly a generous act, since anything which weakened the Hapsburgs would be to France's advantage. This might have been a history-changing policy if Louis XIV's plans had stopped there, but his seizure of lands along the Rhine had angered even distant German princes.

Innocent XI (Pope 1676-1689), almost forgotten as a player on the European scene, disliked Louis intensely for not supporting the Turkish war and for insisting on the independence (i.e., royal control) of the Gallic church; that is, the French king admitted that the popes possessed uncontested spiritual authority, but he rejected their temporal rights in his kingdom. France would be ruled by Frenchmen—the king, the nobles and local bishops approved by the king before being ordained (a practice long conceded by the church).

This was important for Louis XIV because the Pope had used his influence among German and French Catholics to assist the Hapsburg cause. Louis took revenge after the Pope's death, successfully opposing his canonisation (which came only in 1956). German mercenaries deserted the French army, and during the campaigns in Germany French troops learned habits of looting and arson that punished local Protestants in the short run, but eventually undermined discipline and burdened men with loads of booty they were loath to abandon. German princes who had formerly mistrusted the Hapsburgs now joined in the anti-French alliance, and they had the new ruler of both Holland and England, William III, to provide money to keep their armies in the field.[1]

Ludwig Anton's regiment was present at the storm of Mainz, taking the fortress on the banks of the Rhine, then was transferred to the Italian theatre—making its way right into southern France—before being sent north to the Spanish Netherlands to assist in repelling yet another French invasion.

Such was the momentum of the French advantages in the military arts and unified command that Louis XIV's armies were not easily turned back. However, now the Germans were equipped with flintlock muskets (fusils) which were superior to the old-fashioned French weapons, and, more importantly, these new firearms could be equipped with bayonets, while the French still relied on pikemen. The French king, hearing that pikemen spent most of every engagement standing around—fearful observers rather than active participants—while the opposing troops were firing *fusillades*, ordered his generals to make this expensive upgrade; Louis XIV was already finding the war more expensive than his citizens could afford, but he refused to make peace.

Ludwig Anton personally had little involvement with the campaigns between the critical years of 1691 and 1694, when the greatest general of the Balkan wars to date, Türkenlouis[2], was in command; in November 1691 he was elected Prince-Bishop of Worms, a diocese which had been thoroughly devastated by French armies. His subjects needed a warrior more than a saint at their head; and the Pope obligingly allowed him three years to become a priest, a duty he fulfilled only at the last moment under less than regular circumstances. In 1694 Ludwig Anton was called to Liège, where, in a strongly disputed election for the vacant post of German master, he was taken ill and died. There was such a terrible epidemic raging that he was hurriedly buried, and afterwards no one could remember exactly where.

Ludwig Anton's life was short and turbulent, but he had successfully returned the Teutonic Knights to its roots. The military order might be only an arm of Hapsburg/Catholic ambitions, but it was once again at war against the enemies of the Church and of Germany. Perhaps as importantly, he was helping restore national pride. Louis XIV had been rightly contemptuous of German military prowess and the ability of German princes to work together effectively; he had cynically established judicial bodies (*Chambres des Réunions*) to determine what territories belonged to France—and, not surprisingly, the judges always ruled as the king wished, including a declaration that the Palatinate belonged to him, not to the Catholic Neuburg dynasty, because of the marriage he had arranged between Liselotte of the Palatinate and his own extravagantly homosexual brother. The brother, 'Monsieur', was a moderately good general, but Louis ceased to entrust armies to his command. This may have been jealousy, but it might have been royal suspicion that Monsieur was promoting men for reasons other than gallantry on the battlefield. Louis XIV may have been wrong in his judgments, but he was always certain of his opinions.

The French king did not respect the British army in the Low Countries— it was divided by religious allegiances, some officers were still loyal to the exiled King James, and many men and officers disliked their demanding Dutch generals. In invading Germany Louis had expected a short, limited war. Instead, he found that his bullying had brought a great coalition together—Austria, German princes, Spain, Holland and England, all states that had recently been at war with one another, and the armies commanded by the two great genius of the age, Eugene of Savoy (1663-1740) and John Churchill (1650–1722), later the Duke of Marlborough.

Franz Ludwig von Pfalz-Neuburg

When Franz Ludwig's father unexpectedly became elector of the Palatinate in 1685, he began to marry his fourteen children into the most important dynasties of Europe—among them the crowned heads of Austria, Spain and Portugal. Franz Ludwig (1664-1732) was a problem. He was the sixth son and, his father having run out of good places for boys, there seemed to be little left for him. Therefore, Franz was dedicated to the religious life almost at birth, received the tonsure at age eight, was chosen a church deacon at nine, and five years later became a canon in Olomouc (Olmütz) and dean of the cathedral chapter in Cologne. He became bishop of Breslau at nineteen upon the death of an elder brother.

Franz was present at the relief of Vienna from the Turkish besiegers in 1683—closer to the actual fighting, in fact, than Ludwig Anton, because his Bavarian and Frankish troops were in the centre of the line. Close to the emperor afterward, he moved swiftly up the clerical hierarchy—in 1694 alone he became Archbishop of Liège, then Worms and other posts, and soon afterward grandmaster. Throughout his life he was either fighting French armies or organising resistance to French diplomacy.

The war against the Ottomans brought the two confessions together— Protestants and Catholics were all Christians, after all, fighting against the primary enemy of Christendom. From 1529 to 1683, the Christians had been on the defensive; now they went on the offensive, and the advance was so swift that many expected they would even recover Constantinople. However, when Louis XIV sent his armies across the Rhine, the Balkan campaign had to be discontinued; it never regained equal momentum again. As the field of combat widened to include Orthodox Christians in the struggle against Turks and Tatars, some Teutonic Knights fought in the Russian army; others joined the Venetian forces, even though Venice was often hostile to Hapsburg interests.

Recent changes in military technology (flintlock muskets, bayonets, more mobile field artillery), in organisation (especially better means of supplying the army that allowed commanders to restrict foraging and to send camp followers away) and more dependable pay (by improving tax collection and making regiments permanent) resulted in high morale, pride in belonging to elite regiments, and accepting bits of cheap ribbon rather than expensive estates as payment for heroic service.

The steadiness of Christian soldiers now matched the enthusiasm of Muslim warriors. Only the Turkish Janissaries were better. This was because the Janissaries were trained from boyhood as warriors. Taken from their Christian parents as a 'child tax'[3], they were reared to be warriors— elite infantry—and bureaucrats. Sultans preferred to employ Janissaries because they could remove them from office or even execute them without offending powerful relatives, and they could order them to perform tedious bureaucratic tasks that proud Turks refused to do.

The Knights Hospitaller

This was the oldest of the military orders, founded in 1099 to defend the Holy Land, but it took its popular name, the Knights of St John, from the hospital order founded in Jerusalem in 1023 that provided its initial membership. After the loss of Acre in 1291, it was stationed in Rhodes, a strategic island that it fortified heavily. When Rhodes fell to Turkish siege in 1522, most of the knightly members perished.

The German branch of the Hospitallers (the *Johanniter Orden*) had the smallest numbers of any national group in the Order after the Reformation. Moreover, the membership was divided between Protestant and Roman Catholic confessions, making it difficult to form a united policy. Nevertheless, the Germans contributed significantly to the wars in the Mediterranean—the most difficult of all frontiers to tame.

The Order's piratical raids on North Africa were most famously led by Georg Schilling von Cannstatt (1490-1554), who devastated privateer bases later renowned as lairs of the Barbary Pirates. Cannstatt had begun his career at Rhodes in 1522, then represented the German convents at the meetings which in 1527 chose Malta as the Order's new base for attacking Islamic shipping and coastal towns. In 1541 his small navy joined Andrea Doria's expedition against Algiers. Had courage alone been sufficient to take the walls, he and his German knights would have done so, but they had to retreat after destroying most of the Muslim fleet. He returned to Germany in 1546, a critical moment in Charles V's effort to repress Protestantism, but he was not a major figure in the campaign that followed.

In 1571 the Order's naval vessels joined the fleet of Don Juan (1547-78) of Spain in defeating the Turkish armada at Lepanto, thus frustrating what seemed to be a swift expansion of Muslim rule across the Mediterranean. The Order was proud of its accomplishments in freeing Christian captives from Muslim slavery, but its own naval vessels were rowed by a thousand Muslims taken as prisoners-of-war or ordinary captives, and it sold many others on the Malta slave market. This eroded the morals of the noble members, many of whom began to live in luxury, and in 1581 the knights actually took one grandmaster, Jean de la Cassière, prisoner for trying to make them give up their concubines.

In 1580 Emperor Rudolf II attempted to bring the Knights of St. John under the control of members of his family, as he had done with the Teutonic Knights, but he was frustrated by the resistance of the knights and by the efforts of the popes to retain ultimate authority over all religious orders.

A Divided Legacy

The Knights of Malta were permanently divided by the Reformation. The core remained Roman Catholic and was centred in Italy and on Malta, but offshoots with considerable claims to equal status survived in several Protestant lands. All wore the distinctive Maltese Cross.

The Order's military role was reduced after the Ottoman threats to Malta diminished; the rich revenues that once poured in from northern lands dried up. As a result, there were fewer feats of valour. This resulted in a decline in the number of volunteers.

There were exceptions. One of the most important commanders of the Thirty Years War was a Spanish Hospitaller, Don Balthasar de Marradas (1577-1655), who had gone to Vienna in 1599 with an embassy led by a cousin. He served in imperial armies in Hungary and Italy, then in 1618, at the very start of the Thirty Years War, arrived at Vienna just in time to prevent a poorly organised Protestant offensive from Bohemia from capturing the city. Subsequently, he became one of the most important generals in the imperial army, leading the Spanish cavalry. Quarrelling with the great Catholic mercenary general Wallenstein, he became one of the four main conspirators in the successful plot to assassinate him.

The Peace of Westphalia in 1648 gave the Order's possessions in Protestant lands to the protection of the rulers of Brandenburg and Holland ('*Summus Patronus et Protector Ordinis*'), with some compensation to the grandmaster later.

Several knights fought at Vienna in 1683, others in the Turkish wars. Some joined in the attack on the Morea in Greece; others served under Prince Eugene. The 1694 expedition into the Balkans was led by Franz-Sigismund von Thun (1639-1702), one of the numerous talented members of his prominent family.[4]

There was a brief but close flirtation of the Order of Malta with James II of England, who shared their love of chivalry and their fidelity to the Roman Catholic Church; most importantly, each hoped to get something from the other without much cost. James even had his illegitimate son by Arabella Churchill (the sister of the great English general) join the Order in 1689, but when it became clear that James had lost the English throne, the grandmaster and his knights lost interest in the Stuarts.

In any case, the Order was more interested in the East than in Britain. With the Ottoman Turks as almost its only enemy, it was logical to establish a close relationship with Russia. Peter the Great hired officers and men from the Order of Malta to train his sailors, and in 1698 he sent his best general,

Boris Petrovich Sheremetev, as the head of a delegation to study naval tactics at Malta. Afterward more Russian officers were sent to Malta for instruction, and some became members of the Order.

The Swiss Guards in Papal Service

The Swiss Confederation was an unlikely nation—some cantons speaking their own versions of German, others French, some urban, others rural, and none possessing natural resources more important than the mountain passes over the Alps. They became unified through resistance to Hapsburg efforts to rule them, but their unity consisted mainly of an agreement to leave one another alone, especially in religious matters; thus, they considered themselves as a confederation, with the official name *Eidgenossenschaft* meaning an 'oath fellowship'. After their military skills attracted the attention of French kings and Italian despots, they put aside their local disputes for profitable employment as mercenaries; gaining loot from their neighbours was an attractive bonus. In 1500 the Swiss seemed to be unbeatable soldiers; by 1700, they were sought after largely for ceremonial services—as household guards they were efficient, almost incorruptible, and very colourful. Today their sole foreign employer of significance is the Vatican.

Military service was often the only hope that many young Swiss had for acquiring sufficient capital for a future career; in the past whenever they had taken employment for two or more lords, they worried that one Swiss unit would be pitted against another. Since Swiss rarely retreated, a confrontation would be unbelievably bloody. To avoid that, the Swiss made long term commitments to only a few employers—most importantly, the King of France and the Pope.

Swiss mercenaries first entered Italy in large numbers in the service of the French King, Charles VIII, in 1494, attracting such attention for their ferocity and loyalty that Sixtus IV (Pope 1471-84) opened negotiations with the Swiss Confederation three years later, going so far as to build a barracks near the Vatican and designate the church of St. Pellegrino for their soldiers' use. Still, it was not until 22 January 1506, that the first 150 Swiss, most from the mountain canton of Uri, entered papal service. They marched through the Porta del Popolo to be reviewed and blessed by Julius II (Pope 1503-1513). They performed so well that only six years later he gave them the honorary title of 'Defenders of the Church's freedom'. Probably they would have preferred more pay, but every employer knows (or should know) that a little praise now and then can ward off other employee complaints.

Julius II expanded the existing practice of making churchmen with military talents into cardinal-deacons (i.e., churchmen who were not priests, but were used primarily as legates, generals and administrators). As David Chambers notes in *Popes, Cardinals and War*, his successors were no soldiers. Leo X (Pope 1513-21) certainly was not; after his two nephews died (to be immortalised by Michelangelo, who designed and decorated their tombs), he reverted to traditional papal policy—protecting the Church's lands by expelling or assassinating the minor lords who had made cities their own. The Swiss Guard remained small, devoting itself to protecting the life of its employer.

Like British Gurkhas, these Catholic mountain men were the most loyal and most effective warriors their employer could possibly have found. In the modern world, too, some of the most dependable allies of advanced nations are mercenaries from rural districts whose motives for service are as diverse as their languages and folk habits.

Vestiges of the Military Orders Today

Military orders survive today, both as civic institutions and subjects of myth and popular imagination. They also live on in national pride—the Spanish soldiers who served briefly in Iraq in 2003 wore shoulder badges of the Order of Calatrava, unintentionally lending support to claims of Iraqi insurgents that the international occupation force represented crusaders.[5] An apparently indestructible mythology surrounding the Templars appears almost everywhere, commonly connected to the origins of the Masonic Order, most recently as part of Dan Brown's *The Da Vinci Code*. There was not much truth to any of this, but the myths, like others embedded in the popular imagination, fed on denials: if there wasn't something to it, why would anyone bother to prove it wrong?

Popes no longer have armies. Stalin is said to have asked rhetorically how many divisions the pope had, but John Paul II played a significant role in bringing down the Soviet Union, and world leaders still enquire about the views of the current pontiff.

The significance of the Catholic military orders for today is that they were Europe's first international army, the first to be organised on a permanent basis. If their effort were to be emulated today, there would have to be an institutional organisation with permanent bases and friendly connections with all the governments that support its endeavours. Also, most likely, it would have to advance the interests of those very governments.

The Point

Medieval political leaders—secular and clerical alike—had found it as difficult to defend distant frontiers as their modern counterparts. There was the constant danger of attack, the difficulty of providing supplies, and the high costs required employing special forces—the military orders. Only officers and men willing to take on the twin dangers of sudden attack and boredom allowed the Christians to hold onto the Holy Land as long as they did, and afterwards to defend endangered posts and even to expand royal possessions into Africa and Asia.

Whether similar organizations can arise today is not clear, but many Non-Government Organizations attract volunteers to service in dangerous regions, doing work similar to that of the religious orders that later took on a military role.

1. An example of England's wealth lies with the wreck of HMS *Sussex*, capsized in a storm off Gibraltar in 1694 while on a secret mission to the Duke of Savoy. In addition to a crew of 500, it was believed to have carried tons of gold coins to finance the war against Louis XIV; the duke, without funds to pay his troops, went over to the French.
2. Ludwig Wilhelm of Baden (1655-1707). His operations in the Balkans were almost uniformly successful, but his command of the Grand Army in the War of the Spanish Succession (1701-1714) had mixed results. Most importantly, he was able to defend his ancestral lands in Baden from being annexed to France.
3. Muslims were forbidden to enslave Believers. Since they could not do without slaves, they raided Christian lands and herded home formidable numbers. It is estimated that Tatars carried away a million Poles and Russians between 1550 and 1650. Balkan Christians provided the bulk of the Janissary numbers, which meant that there were always Janissaries who understood the languages of their subjects.
4. He is best known in Vienna for the palace Thunhof he built in 1694 according to the designs of Johann Bernhard Fischer von Erlach, one of the greatest architects of the era; it ultimately grew into the imperial residence of Hetzendorf.
5. After the conquest of Granada in 1492, the Order fell increasingly under the control of the kings of Spain. It was dissolved in a series of steps in the eighteenth and nineteenth centuries, a victim of inconsequentiality and Enlightenment thought. Its awarding membership to Farinelli, the most famous of the Italian castratti, is an ironic commentary on the lack of relevance to any military tradition by the middle of the eighteenth century.

Chapter 4

Africa – The Ultimate Frontier

Europeans living in the Early Modern era were ignorant of Africa because they not only considered it peripheral to their interests, but because they were acquainted only with the continent's outer margins. Europeans who had made it to China, to India, to the Ottoman Empire, were amazed by the rich and colourful cultures there, by the power of the rulers, and the self-confidence of their people; and they had eagerly brought back art and foods from their visits. Their response to Africa was very different; they found the native costumes, dwellings, and weaponry of the coastal peoples exotic but unimpressive. Had the Europeans not feared the tropical diseases, the unfamiliar jungles and dangerous animals, and the heat, they might have learned more, and been more impressed, but the African coastline lacked convenient harbours and the interior could not be penetrated by simply sailing up the great rivers; hence, they knew little even about the great Songhai Empire in the Niger Valley. Timbuktu became a synonym for an incredibly exotic place that no one could reach. Many attribute this lack of interest to racism, but ethnocentrism might be a better word. Certainly that word would be less confrontational and less judgmental.

Europeans did eventually confront Africa, but in ways very different from their earlier encounters with the New World or the Ancient East.

North Africa

Africa was a huge continent with much variety. There were rainforests, deserts, mountains, lakes, lots of insects, and people of every height and colour imaginable. And the native peoples had not always remained in the homelands of their ancestors, but migrated, sometimes slowly, occasionally very quickly, either to escape troubles or to find better lands. Scholars tell us that colonial boundaries were irrational, but that it would have been impossible to draw better ones, because nomads and farmers were not strictly separated; and some tribes had welcomed refugees to settle on their poorest land. Understanding this is particularly important in following the story of Muslims penetrating into Black Africa from the desert, and Christians pressuring the same peoples from the coasts.

The peoples of the Mediterranean and northwestern coastlands were not black, but a combination of native peoples (Berbers being the generic term to describe their languages and cultures) and Arabs. Europeans lumped all these people together as Moors, a term not used often today because of its lack of precision and because its Greek root means 'dark'. The darkness came partly from the intense sun, partly from the importation of black slaves, and partly from the looks that the Moors cast at Europeans.

Buying (or taking) black slaves over the past millennium had darkened the complexion of parts of the population, but the Ottomans who ruled the northern coastland were also importing white slaves—like the Circassians taken by Turks, or the Poles and Russians rounded up by Tatars, or Irish and Icelanders captured by Barbary pirates. The slaves came from diverse lands, some from the Caucasus Mountains, some from European borderlands or a few from distant islands, but others were prisoners-of-war or captured sailors; an ever large number came from raids on the Spanish and Italian coasts, so many that in the 1600s white slaves employed in raising sugar, rice and other crops in North Africa may have outnumbered the black slaves in North America. Sometimes the Ottomans made these prisoners into elite warriors, favouring them over natives because it was possible to punish or even execute them without offending relatives. Also, time out of mind Christian warriors had hired themselves out as mercenaries, often as personal bodyguards to Muslim rulers of the coastal states. Having no interest in the complicated politics, they could be trusted to concentrate on safeguarding their employer.

The thinly populated Barbary Coast (modern Algeria and Libya) was dotted with ports that flourished from trade and piracy, activities that were occasionally difficult to tell apart; and from time immemorial their captains had yielded to the temptation to capture ships belonging to European competitors. Crusaders had attempted to eliminate Islamic corsairs as a threat to Christian shipping and Italian and Spanish coastal towns; of course, they attacked Muslim ships and raided coastal towns, too. Each side claimed to be acting in self-defence or in retaliation, or to be performing great feats of arms as champions of their respective religions.[1]

Around 1500 two great warriors from one Muslim family changed the conflict from small scale warfare to a struggle involving all the major powers of the Mediterranean. Aruj (c1474-1518) was the elder brother, the emir of a small principality in Algeria. His father had been a Janissary (hence, most likely, of Balkan ancestry) stationed on the Greek island of Lesbos and his mother had been the widow of a Greek priest. When he was a young man he had been captured by the Knights of Malta and made into a galley slave—one of the worst fates possible since it meant a short lifetime of hard labour chained to a rowing bench, often exposed to the hot sun. After being ransomed, he took his revenge by attacking Christian vessels. His fleet was no larger than twelve galleys, but his captains struck hard at Spanish commerce and upset Spanish military operations against the French—once he captured a ship with hundreds of troops on board, presumably making all of them into slaves.[2] Having a flaming red beard, he was called Barbarossa, a name that his brother Khizr inherited after Aruj's death in spite of not sharing that characteristic. Little more is known of the first Barbarossa other than his dying in battle while opposing a Spanish/Berber army led by Charles V (1500-58), the King of Spain and Holy Roman Emperor who was conquering many of the cities along the Algerian coast.

Khizr (Barbarossa Hayreddin Pasha, 1478-1546), who at the time he met Suleiman the Great (Sultan 1520-66) commanded no more than 800 Ottoman soldiers, nevertheless received instructions to build a great navy. He completed this so quickly that he was given command. Soon he was famed even among his enemies—the legendary Genoese admiral Andrea Doria (1466-1560) called him 'the Great Corsair'. What made Barbarossa so dangerous was that the French king provided him bases in France that he could use to attack Charles V's lines of communication with Italy. Before Barbarossa retired to the comforts of Istanbul, he had made the Ottoman navy supreme across vast stretches of the Mediterranean Sea.

After the natural death of the aged Suleiman on campaign in 1566, while moving up the Danube toward Vienna, his successors stayed away from battlefields. Instead, they entrusted command to their grand viziers, who were experienced administrators and commanders. The sultans limited their activities to what they did best—harem politics and watching their grand viziers for signs of excessive ambition. Many of the grand viziers were technically slaves, taken in boyhood from their Christian parents and trained in their future duties—the best being selected for the most important duties. This gave the Ottoman sultans more talented commanders than Christian monarchs who gave out military positions only to high-born nobles.

It seemed, according to the dramatic narrative of Roger Crowley, *Empires of the Sea*, that by 1571 a divided Christendom could not expect to defeat the magnificent forces of the Ottoman grand vizier, Lala Mustafa Pasha (1500-80) who had the great advantage of being able to give orders and expect them to be obeyed. Catholic Europe was led by a hyper-cautious Philip II of Spain (1527-98), who could not forget the naval disaster at Djerba in 1560; Venetians remembered equally vividly the 1537 battle of Preveza, where the Holy League had tried to challenge Barbarossa—they blamed the defeat on Andrea Doria's refusal to come to their aid. Christian disunity had almost led to the fall of Malta in 1565—a siege of epic proportions—and made it impossible for Venice to hold Nicosia and Famagusta on Cyprus in 1571. The only good result from the eight-month defence of Famagusta, in the Christians' eyes, was that it cost the Ottomans 80,000 men they would have had only months later at the battle of Lepanto.

That famous victory reestablished European naval prestige briefly. The collision of two gigantic fleets—that of the Holy League (200 galleys and six large hybrid galleys/sailing vessels) being slightly smaller than the Ottoman force, but having more cannon—developed into an infantry battle on water, with the Christians having more men wearing armour and using firearms. One of the Ottoman squadrons was led by an Italian convert to Islam—Uluj Ali (1519-87), born Giovanni Dionigi Galeni in southern Italy. Captured by Barbarossa and, like many of his fellows, offered the choice between ordinary slavery and becoming a rich pirate, he chose to convert. Among the few Muslim commanders to survive the disaster, he was welcomed in Istanbul for returning safely with the giant banner of the Knights of Malta that he had taken from their flagship. Subsequently he became pasha of Algiers, then admiral of the Ottoman fleet.

The Ottoman sultan quickly replaced the lost ships, then ordered them to push cautiously westward along the coast, driving the Spanish from Algeria, deposing their native Muslim allies, and reaching almost to Morocco. This was the end of Christian hopes to conquer these coasts and the beginning of Ottoman rule.[3]

Morocco

The same weakness that made Algeria vulnerable to attack allowed the Portuguese to capture ports in Morocco—Ceuta in 1415, Tangiers in 1471, and smaller cities in the early 1500s. Prince Henry the Navigator (1394-1460) had seen Morocco as a jumping off point for explorations that would lead to the gold fields of Ghana. However, the heavy ships of the Mediterranean were unsuited to ocean travel, and their large crews consumed too many supplies. This problem was overcome by using a lighter sailing vessel, the caravel, which adopted the lateen sail used by Arab sailors; later this was combined with the well-known square sail to produce fully-rigged vessels that could withstand almost any storm. The next delay was caused by sailors' fears of unknown shores and winds—sailing south along the African coast was no problem, since Prince Henry's ships had a tail wind, but coming home against those same winds was testing. Nevertheless, in 1481 the Portuguese were able to build a fortress at Elmina in Ghana that Christopher Columbus visited shortly afterward; this post was profitable for both buyer and seller because it cut out the Muslim middlemen.

Moroccans, meanwhile, were experiencing Ottoman pressure from Algeria. Fortunately for them, they understood European weaponry well, a knowledge they applied effectively against the Turks. It was more difficult to resist the Portuguese aggression that began in 1576, because the Portuguese were not operating at the end of a long supply line. The new sultan, Abu Marwan Abd al-Malik, had just returned from exile to seize the throne, and his counterpart was Sebastian I (Dom Sebastião, 1554-78), an inbred, obstinate, gifted and ambitious young man.

King Sebastian was very aware that his captains were easily establishing trading posts along the African and Brazilian coasts and that his governors had repelled challenges to their domination of the Indian trade; in short, his captains seemed invincible. In contrast, Morocco appeared to be weak. A successful crusade there would bring Morocco over to Christianity (or at least make Portuguese exploitation possible) and open central Africa to European trade.

Under normal circumstances not even a prince as active and intellectually curious as Sebastian would have dared think so extravagantly, but he had come into possession of a rival to the Sultan, Abu Abdallah. The presence of Abdallah in his army, and a supposedly weak Abd al-Malik on the other side caused the battle of Alcazarquivir (Alcácer Quibir) to be known as the Battle of the Three Kings.

There was an important back story to the campaign. Abdallah al-Ghalib Billah (1517-74) had become Sultan in 1557 after his father was assassinated by Barbarossa's son on Ottoman orders. Immediately he had consolidated power by eliminating possible rivals—that is, killing his brothers. This practice was well-known in Islamic states because harems produced numbers of ambitious sons whose only hope to rule, or even do anything in life, was to lead a successful rebellion. However, he failed to capture Abd al-Malik, who had fled to Algeria and become a soldier for the Ottoman governor. When al-Ghalib Billah died, leaving power to a son, Abu Abdallah, instead of to a surviving brother—as custom required—Abd al-Malik raised a mercenary army from his Ottoman troops and seized power. When Abu Abdallah asked the Portuguese king for mercenary troops to recover his kingdom, Sebastian agreed to provide them, but only on the condition that he lead the army himself and share in the benefits of victory. Sebastian began to assemble his army in 1578, borrowing men from the king of Spain. Though Philip II subsequently signed a peace treaty with the Ottomans, the young Portuguese monarch pressed on. Sebastian believed that he had the resources to prevail, most importantly because of 2,000 Italians employed by Thomas Stukley (1525-78).

Stukley—a former pirate, mercenary, and possibly an illegitimate son of Henry VIII—was just the man for such a wild-eyed project. His original plan had been to land in Ireland, raise volunteers, then overthrow Queen Elizabeth. Stukley's career as an adventurer had begun during the reign of Queen Mary, when he had fought in the army she had sent to the Spanish Netherlands to support of her husband, Philip II. After Mary's death he entered the retinue of Lord Dudley, one of Queen Elizabeth's favourites, serving occasionally as a pirate. His activities in Scotland and Ireland are worthy of a novelist's talents, but it was his proposal to Philip II to overthrow Elizabeth and restore Catholicism to England that is best known. He was distracted by the battle at Lepanto, where he fought with distinction, then his plans to invade Ireland and England were delayed by the competing ambitions of more exalted personalities. It was only in 1578 that the Pope gave him 2,000 men for the Irish enterprise. It was not difficult to divert these men to the Moroccan expedition.

Stukley's men were well-equipped with muskets, and they had far more self-confidence than the situation warranted—they counted on a mass formation of pikemen to fend off the expected cavalry attack, then to push forward and break the enemy's infantry, which would have been shot to pieces by the musketeers. In addition, Sebastian had the usual assortment of German and Spanish mercenaries, but the bulk of the 23,000 Europeans in the royal army were Portuguese, the best his nation could raise. Awkwardly, the king could not bring many horses on his ships, but he had good European infantry and the horsemen raised by his Muslim ally, Abu Abdallah. Surely this army was sufficient to conquer any kingdom along the Atlantic or Mediterranean coast of Africa. This was especially true if their opponent was, as rumour had it, mortally ill.

Abd al-Malik had about 100,000 men, some of whom were anti-Christian fanatics, descendants of Moors expelled from Spain after 1492.

The two armies faced each other across a small river, the Christian-Muslim forces drawn up in a European-style formation, infantry in the centre, relying on their firearms to sweep the enemy away. It is not clear why Sebastian stood on the defensive, but that may have been the best choice considering the terrain and the unexpected numbers of horsemen in the opposing army. Sebastian commanded the Christian cavalry on one wing, with Abu Abdallah commanding the Muslim cavalry on the other. Abd al-Malik ignored the infantry, while using his superior numbers to surround Abu Abdallah, then closed in for hand-to-hand fighting. The Portuguese king led his horsemen forward, but disappeared quickly (his body was never found); Abu Abdallah was killed at some unknown point. Stukley commanded the centre of the line, which was holding out well until his legs were torn off by a cannonball. After that order broke down. His men found themselves fighting for their lives, flight impossible. When both kings and about a third of their men were dead, the rest of the army, perhaps 15,000 men, surrendered. Only perhaps a hundred fugitives made it to the coast alive; the rest of the Europeans became slaves.

Abd al-Malik had died, too, though no one had noticed immediately. The exertion of combat had been too much for him. He was succeeded by his imprisoned brother, Ahmad I al-Mansur (1549-1603).

The leaderless Portuguese kingdom collapsed, Philip II of Spain moving in to make himself king. It would not be the last time that Europeans attempted to establish footholds on the Moroccan coast, but there would be no serious effort to conquer the entire state until the nineteenth century.

Morocco and Songhai

The new Sultan of Morocco reflected carefully on the lessons of the battle of Alcazarquivir. His councillors were still confident in the superiority of their traditional weapons and tactics, but he had been impressed by the effectiveness of the Christian infantry. Al-Mansur imagined how the European weapons could be employed in the lightly populated centre of the continent, where the Songhai state had been recently shaken by civil war. Moreover, Moroccan trade with Songhai was being undermined by European merchants on the coast. Ships could carry so much merchandise that the Christians could undercut the prices of Islamic merchants, who had to pack their wares across the Sahara; and in the case of weapons, the Muslims would not sell them to their enemies at all.

Al-Mansur's informants led him to believe that Songhai would not be able to respond effectively to a well-planned invasion. In late 1590, a dozen years after becoming sultan, he announced to his council that he was sending an army of 3,000-4,000 troops and thousands of pack animals and their handlers on a four-month march across 1,000 miles of desert to the Songhai capital at Timbuktu. His commander was Judar Pasha, a European-born slave and eunuch; the goal was to acquire access to the gold mines and salt, so that he could pay for the European commodities his subjects desired—this had become increasingly difficult now that Portugal's Brazilian plantations were selling sugar cheaper than his subjects could. His force was outnumbered, but it included Turkish mercenaries and Christian bodyguards, matchlocks and cannon. The language of command was Spanish, a reflection of the importance of Iberian mercenaries in the campaign.

The Songhai Empire had been important since the early 1400s, stretching along the Niger River from the cataracts near the sea north and west for a thousand miles to distant gold fields. Its wealth came from trade, selling gold, ivory, salt and human beings across the desert to Morocco and to the Mediterranean coast. Fervently Islamic in faith, its orientation was northward. To the south lay forests, disease and paganism; it was much safer for Songhai warriors to stay in the drier but healthy regions of the Upper Niger River Valley, where the pasture land was more extensive than it is today.

The Songhai rulers were generally, but not consistently, tolerant toward the pagan practices of the southern people; as long as those peoples were divided, they were no danger, but could be exploited easily and cheaply. One ruler, Askia Muhammed I (reigned 1493-1528) had made the pilgrimage to Mecca with 500 cavalry and 1,000 infantry, establishing Songhai's reputation for being fabulously exotic and rich. This legendary wealth had attracted al-Mansur's attention, first for gold, then for salt—the exchange was often equal weight of one for the other.

Most of all, the sultan saw that the Songhai state was weak. Dynastic quarrels followed the death of each king; brutal efforts at imposing Islamic customs were resented both by desert nomads and farmers of the bush, all of whom believed in magic and who carefully treasured memories of past outrages. Vassal chiefs knew that their predecessors had been slain, their sons gelded and their daughters sold into slavery; and merchants resented the taxes. The royal processions were splendid and the king's army made a brave display, but Moroccan merchants could see that the Songhai Empire was a case of the least weak ruling the weaker.

The harem system had always encouraged jealousy and fear, and when the last great sultan died in 1582, the multiplication of potential heirs had reached its logical (and disastrous) outcome—civil war.

The Invasion

In late 1590 al-Mansur's hold on Morocco was at last secure. He had warded off European and Ottoman challenges, then expanded his kingdom into the interior, seizing some of the valuable salt mines that were central to Saharan trade. Overseas trade with Ireland, England and even Italy was prospering, and his enemies were involved in desperate wars on distant frontiers. It was an opportunity to break free of his financial troubles, those caused by the need to pay his mercenaries, by seizing the salt and gold of the African interior. Of course, his councillors were all against the expedition—it was a long journey over one of the more formidable deserts in the world, with almost no pastures and only a handful of water holes—and those were capable of supporting only small parties. He rejected this advice, heaping scorn on their caution and pointing out the advantages that gunpowder weapons and good cavalry had over men armed only with spears and bows. The numbers had to be small, he agreed, in order to cross the desert successfully, but if the troops were good, they could prevail. Conducting a siege without great cannons would be difficult, but the enemy, not knowing what they were up against, would probably come out to fight rather than watch their country ravaged.

The losses on the march must have been appalling, so it would have been wise for the Songhai king to have marched out to meet the Morrocans before they had recovered from their desert ordeal, but he did not; even his orders to fill in the wells had apparently not reached the nomad Tuareg chiefs—or they had disobeyed. Had that elemental step been taken, the Moroccan army might had died in the desert. However, the Tuaregs were Berbers; though they had little love for Arabs, they were always reluctant to take orders from anyone.

Fortunately for the Moroccans, the Songhai had not read Kenneth Chase's analysis in *Firearms* of the difficulties that armies face in a desert. The demands for water, food and fodder were so great that infantry usually had to turn back after two days, cavalry after only one. Had the army been supplied with camels, it would have done better, but it appears that the Moroccans were counting on using their horses in battle. The Moroccans must have been very relieved not to have to fight for each watering place along the march, but they probably did not worry about poison—nomads were not suicidal.

Judar Pasha's army met the Songhai host in March 1591 in the short and violent battle of Tondibi. The mercenaries had been greatly outnumbered, but their enemies lacked the will to fight. The Songhai king drove a herd of cattle at the northerners, but volleys of infantry weapons and cannon frightened the cattle, causing them to charge back through the king's forces, after which there was little organised resistance. Judar Pasha allowed his men to sack the cities and towns, after which he reestablished order and made himself governor, ruling from Timbuktu.

The victors were disappointed to discover that the fabled cities were collections of mud buildings, and that the gold had been taken away or hidden; worse, the gold fields were still far away, deep in Black Africa to the west. In Gao, the first city captured, the invaders found a Portuguese cannon that the Songhai warriors had not known how to use, a crucifix and a statue of the Virgin Mary. It was a fitting symbolism of Songhai military backwardness.

However, the Songhai king had survived the battle. From a safe distance he tried to pay the invaders to leave, but they refused—the gold he offered made them more eager to stay, not less. Nevertheless, the mercenaries saw little reason in holding onto their conquest, True, Timbuktu had an impressive mosque, learned scholars and some evidence of wealth, but the mercenaries had no use for places of worship or books, and they were forbidden to loot. Their numbers had been quickly reduced by illness, and the Songhai ruler continued to resist from his southern strongholds. Reinforcements were slow to arrive, and of the few sent, most were killed by Tuareg nomads. Meanwhile, chaos reigned—the king was removed by a brother, the peoples subject to the Songahi rose in revolt, and the mercenaries began to loot, rape and murder.

Judar Pasha's discouraging report on local conditions resulted in his assignment to a much lesser post, governor of Gao. His successor was Mahmud ibn-Zarqun, a eunuch, the son of a Christian. He stripped the houses of doors and doorposts to build two ships, then set off downstream to eliminate the last Songhai forces. A stroke of luck then came his way—civil war broke out among the Songhai. The new king had ordered his brothers castrated, whereupon they had joined the Moroccan invader. This allowed Mahmud to easily scatter the remnants of the Songhai army, after which he invited the king to a conference and murdered him.

That ended resistance in the north, but desperate Songhai in the south turned to one of the late king's brothers, Askia Nuh, who withdrew into the bush country, even into the coastal forest, where he proved himself a gifted guerilla commander. Aksia Nuh established bases in the swampy south and the rugged north where cannons and horses could not be used; and where malaria weakened the invading troops. Because the mercenaries' atrocities had by now appalled everyone, Askia Nuh was able to make common cause with ancient Songhai adversaries, while Mahmud found it impossible to exploit their many ancient animosities; as a result, Moroccan efforts to reach the gold fields failed. Meanwhile, the collapse of the Songhai had tempted every brigand in the desert to attack the caravans, so that trade with Morocco became more dangerous. Mahmud requested reinforcements, which arrived in 1593.

Victorious. Now What?

The decisive moment in the campaign may have been Mahmud sending one of his captains with 300 musketeers back to Timbuktu to protect it against raiders. The officer apologised to local leaders for past misdeeds and promised to keep his men in barracks after dark. The policy worked— open resistance ended, trade revived and exiles returned. He then led his men north against the desert raiders and, with local help, destroyed the worst of the bandits. More reinforcements allowed him to crush a dangerous insurrection in an outlying city whose inhabitants had more passion than political acumen.

This was not a policy that pleased Mahmud ibn-Zarqun, whose own efforts to pacify the south had failed. Wanting to take revenge on his enemies, not placate them, he began to massacre Timbuktu's leading families. Many who were not slain were loaded with chains and driven across the Sahara to Morocco. When news of this reached the Moroccan king, he ordered Mahmud removed from command. Mahmud, however, had already been killed in a fight against black pagans before his replacement arrived in 1595. Askia Nuh received Mahmud's head with satisfaction, presumably pleased by the proof that bows and arrows could defeat firearms. But that had no immediate effect on the war; Nuh retreated to his stronghold at Dendi, while a brother, Sulaiman, was put on the throne in Timbuktu as a puppet of the occupation army.

Clearly, the distant Moroccan sultan had misjudged the situation, and he was to continue to do so. This was easily done, perhaps inevitably, considering the inadequacy of information available to him. His effort to divide duties among his commanders provoked a civil war until finally Judar Pasha suggested that the army decide which of them should rule. After Judar Pasha's election, he poisoned his rival and then made all the appropriate gestures of loyalty and subordination to the sultan. In 1599 Judar Pasha returned home, rich with gold, slaves and exotic wares, ready to enjoy life in every respect except the founding of a dynasty.

The new *Arma* state was ruled by the army. Some soldiers had been Christian prisoners-of-war, others had been simple mercenaries; there were also Moors whose ancestors had fled Spain after the *Reconquista,* and Berber tribesmen. Most married local women, and when some tried to restrict alliances to their own races, reality struck home: where would they get women? That was the origin of a mixed race elite who eventually came to speak the language of their mothers and subjects. Since the army controlled the state, the reigns of the distant Moroccan sultans, which were often short anyway, made no difference. Civil war and rebellions prevented the Arma from becoming a powerful empire, but they had no dangerous rivals to threaten their existence.

Not even the weapons that Europeans supplied to coastal peoples threatened the northerners' vast state. As Chase noted in *Firearms, a Global History,* the savannah south of the Sahara was ideal cavalry country except that its diseases were deadly to horses—more so even than to Europeans, it seems, who could at least go indoors to escape the tsetse fly. And without cavalry to force infantry into tight formations, firearms were less than fully effective. The obvious strategy for Europeans and Arma alike was to recruit light infantry from the weaker tribes, relying on them to do most of the fighting, while the heavy troops guarded the baggage and artillery.

Edward Bovill notes in *The Golden Trade of the Moors* that by 1660 the Arma were so weak that Timbuktu had fallen to pagan enemies. Arising from the chaos was a black military force, the Bokhari, who became important in Moroccan affairs. They, like the white mercenaries, had no local connections and were, therefore, preferred as bodyguards to Berbers or Arabs. As for the politics of the Arma lands, it was complicated beyond any hope of summarising or reading with enjoyment or edification.

Slavery Supports the State

Al-Mansur had profited immediately from his conquests, but over the long term his invasion disrupted trade and pilgrimages, thus making his gains transitory and his losses heavy. His successors were not tempted to become involved in the politics of the interior, except to buy slaves who could be employed as bodyguards and elite troops. Trained in western methods and having no stake in local politics, their loyalty to their employers could be trusted; many were eunuchs, which limited their vices to those which disturbed the public least.

Although the Moroccan sultan had expected that conquering the Songhai kingdom would increase the slave trade across the western Sahara, it shifted to the coast, where tribes hostile to the new Muslim state were now selling prisoners-of-war to Europeans.

The practice of slave-raiding tore central Africa apart for many generations to come, but it mattered little to Moroccan sultans and their supporters how many villages were destroyed and how many perished during the long march north. Everyone was in the business of procuring and selling slaves.

Kanem-Bornu

This state lay to the west of Lake Chad, across the eastern caravan trail leading from the Niger River valley to Tripoli. Most of the inhabitants were farmers, but many were herders—an arrangement that worked to mutual satisfaction throughout much of the African interior until the Darfur crisis of 2003 revealed that the complicated mixture of races and religions had been placed under intolerable pressure by population growth and the encroachment of the desert on arable lands. This was not new, however— the conflict between nomad and farmer was a part of African history from time immemorial, most recently contributing to the 1984 genocide in Rwanda. Centuries before the Darfur crisis the danger of raids from the desert required farmers and artisans to live in walled towns, the fortifications made of unimposing but effective mud bricks.

Bornu had been just beyond the reach of the Songhai armies. Its horsemen collected slaves from the savannahs and jungles to the south, some prisoners being ransomed to their families and more kept for local use (some as soldiers). Everyone owned two or three slaves, often as concubines, some as eunuchs; one king acquired so much gold that he could make golden chains for his dogs. Since it was illegal to enslave Muslims, most prisoners were pagans. The best captives, mostly women and children, had long been herded north to the international market operated by Arabs, and to the west, to the kingdom of Songhai. Eastward from Bornu the road led to the savannah of Darfur, where it split into the 'forty day road' across the desert to Upper Egypt and the road to Sudan and the Indian Ocean. The horsemen who made the raids believed that they had no choice in the matter—they were always desperate for more mounts, and they could buy them only from Arabs who wanted slaves.

In contrast, neighbouring Arabs tended to ride camels because the tsetse fly multiplied during the rainy season, making horse raising impossible, and transporting fodder was expensive. The Bornu warriors, however, knew that horses were better than camels for war in the grasslands to the south. They used camels, but only reluctantly.

The most important warrior-king, Idris Alooma (reigned 1571-1603), conquered all the surrounding savannah with mercenary warriors, employing exceptional brutality. Once having pacified his state, however, he encouraged commerce, culture and education; he crushed banditry, required his subjects to live by Islamic law, and built mosques through the country. The high point of his reign was his impressive visit to Mecca via Tripoli and Egypt. In the course of his travels, he became aware of firearms. Purchasing some, he had Ottoman mercenaries train his palace guard in their use. In 1636 one of his successors obtained fifteen young Christians armed with muskets. These proved so effective that he soon acquired more. Details, alas, are totally lacking.

Similarly, we know little about the settlements the rulers established along the pilgrimage route toward Mecca. The journey took pilgrims through some of the most inhospitable regions on earth, so it made sense to have places where they could obtain food and water and could rest. This also served as a route for slaves, but only for small numbers. Therefore, the slave traders seems to have concentrated on specialised classes of humans—eunuchs, dwarfs, concubines, and artisans. Since runaways stood little chance of escape, care had to be taken only to prevent suicides among slaves driven almost insane by heat and exhaustion.

West Africa

When Europeans introduced muskets to the coastal peoples of West Africa, it affected the balance of power almost instantly—the northern horsemen now faced an enemy capable of resisting. A vicious cycle was set in motion: the coastal peoples were able to raid the Muslim-dominated regions to collect slaves, then sell those unfortunates to Europeans in order to purchase more weapons. More guns = more slaves = more money = more guns. Muslims struck back in combination with native allies, employing their own firearms in jihadist raids toward the coast. Africa being such a large continent, events in one part of the bush country were often not noticed elsewhere. Yet nothing happened in one area without it ultimately having a wider effect. The formation of new states, which was occurring everywhere now that the great empires had collapsed, was closely connected to slavery. Woe to those unable to defend themselves.

Meanwhile, across the Atlantic, slaves raising sugar provided Europeans with the money to buy guns from factories in their homelands, transport them to Africa for sale, and then pick up more slaves. They could use the sugar to make rum, which sold well, too. However, as competition reduced the price they could get for cloth and other products, and when African rulers demanded that merchants pay taxes, the slavers needed greater volume to keep profits high. About all that can be said in favour of the white slavers is that they had no interest in eunuchs, who had always been desired by Arab purchasers.

European observers were impressed by the courage of black warriors, but noted that this made them no more capable of defeating horsemen on the savannah than Europeans on the steppes of Russia or the Great Plains of America had been able to deal with enemies who struck swiftly, then retreated, or who could not be located at all. Nor, as Geoffrey Parker shows in *The Military Revolution*, were they interested in European weapons— sometimes wars were elaborately staged games, with few casualties; at others they were more interested in capturing slaves than in killing people. Since guns did not suit African needs, traditional weapons remained predominant.

The kingdom of Dahomey (now Benin) arose between 1620 and 1630 in response to slave raiding by coastal neighbours. Its people, the Fon, lived inland from the 'slave coast', in bush country easily penetrated by enemies. Only the terrible cruelties they inflicted on prisoners served to deter attack. King Houegbadja (reigned 1645-85) made the most interesting innovation in the military arts of the era by using female warriors as bodyguards. His capital at Abomey was eventually surrounded by an impressive mud wall six miles long and his palaces are now on the UNESCO World Heritage list.

When Houegbadja's eldest son died of smallpox in 1708, a succession crisis rose. Rather than having a ten-year-old on the throne, the boy's uncle, Dossou Agadja, seized power and ruled until 1740. Agadja expanded the role of the 'Dahomey Amazons' (the Europeans' name for them), employing them effectively in the 1727 conquest of the kingdoms of Savi, which gave him direct access to European traders.

While relatively little is known about these 'Amazons' before the nineteenth century, it seems that they were recruited from volunteers or women discarded by their husbands. They were not allowed to become pregnant, a requirement most easily met by abstaining from sexual relations. They trained rigorously and were equipped with the best weapons of the time—long-barrelled muskets purchased at the Danish post of Christiansborg. Their fierce habits made them greatly feared by all enemies, and their belief in voodoo made them resistant to the Islamic beliefs of many of their enemies or the Christianity of Agadja's trading partners.

Modern scholars, though usually eager to find women who excel in men's activities, minimise the importance of the Dahomey Amazons. The same is true of the elite bodyguard of Muammar Gaddafi (1942-2011), the Libyan dictator, which was composed of forty virgins. Perhaps that was seldom mentioned because his bizarre costumes, his boasting and his wealth reminded people too much of the larger than life, yet still mysterious rulers from Africa's past, a stereotype that might allow racist foreign politicians to excuse their meddling in African affairs.

The slave trade eventually led to the formation of a stronger state in Dahomey, but early on the arrival of competing Dutch, Portuguese, French and English slavers encouraged nobles to make themselves independent, then fight among themselves and against the king to establish their own local monopoly. Since there were simply too few slaves available for export and there was a reluctance to sell local criminals, Dahomey had to be strong enough to take prisoners-of-war to sell for weapons.

As the king made himself supreme, he tried to limit the trade, and thereby keep prices high, but that only encouraged Europeans to look for new clients. Eventually the king decided that it would be cheaper and more dependable to buy slaves from neighbours than to capture them himself; while his dependence on European-supplied tobacco, liquor and weapons made it impossible to break away completely from the trade in human beings, controlling the process helped keep his kingdom prosperous and free.

Just west of Dahomey arose the Ashanti kingdom. Formed about 1700 to protect its people from slave traders, it sold some slaves abroad, but employed others to mine gold. Here, as elsewhere, successful wars drove defeated neighbours into the waiting hands of European arms dealers— and later to ambitious colonial powers that were no longer content with mere commerce. The Gold Coast and the Ivory Coast became the Slave Coast, but later colonialists, embarrassed by the origins of their rule, brought back the older names. By then slavery had worn out its economic foundation. It never had a moral one.

Europeans and Africans

The number of European outposts on the African coast multiplied significantly after Portuguese power declined, but they changed hands according to the fortunes of war—Elmina fell to the Dutch in 1637; Gorée, founded by the Dutch in 1616, was lost to the French. All worked closely with native rulers—it was not yet time to rule directly. For many years this was a mutually beneficial relationship, the native rulers supplying slaves, gold and native products, the visitors bringing cloth, iron, rum and weapons.

French merchants established themselves in Senegal, English merchants in Gambia. Each fort was more a commercial centre than a military base. There was no way to end this relationship easily—Europeans selling products Africans wanted, Africans providing as best they could what Europeans wanted. Africans could not work together any more than Europeans could trust one another, and everyone who 'counted' believed the exchanges to be beneficial. All saw commercial prosperity and political survival in the trade of firearms for slaves, of European products for African ones, rum for rice, fish for local food to feed the merchants and the cargoes of slave ships. Also, eighteenth century Africa suffered repeated famines, creating massive disruptions that warfare made worse; then smallpox became epidemic. This was all blamed on Europeans, but Martin Klein, in Lamphere, *African Military History*, reminds us that Islamic slavery was less benign than it is usually portrayed.

An indication that there was plenty of blame to spread around comes from São Tomé, where the Portuguese founded a colony in 1490 to raise sugar cane on the African coast. It was never threatened by any African state because none had a navy. When it came to the mainland, even important African rulers were unsuccessful in efforts to face down the newcomers. The king of Congo tried to quash the slave trade in 1526, but he could not even manage to protest directly to Portugal. In the end, everyone came around to cooperating in selling people—after all, if they could not even fight the Portuguese without European weapons, why fight at all? Trade was so easy and so profitable.

Europeans stayed on the coast, especially in the harbours along the Gold Coast. They thought malaria was spread by bad air—the literal translation of the word; however, the real reason the interior was unhealthy was because mosquitoes preferred moisture and heat and disliked wind. Also everything Europeans wanted was found close to the coast—this meant, primarily, near ports, because whoever controlled the anchorages and warehouses controlled trade.

This made the Guinea Coast and the Gambia attractive to European merchants. The rivers there offered protection from storms and were deep enough for ships to sail close to potential customers, which were now independent states based on common languages and customs. These were sophisticated societies in which the military elite exploited the labour of the lower classes, but not so onerously that miners could not extract iron and gold, artisans develop attractive cloth, and farmers produce sufficient rice and other products for local needs. Salt was important for trade with the peoples farther inland, which offered their cattle in exchange.

However, in the mid-1700s Muslims noticed the growing prosperity. Their return to the slave trade complicated everything. The advance south and west from the Niger River Valley was not always crass militarism, but often the peaceful entry of Muslim merchants who then played local groups against one another much as the Christians were attempting to do.

There were relatively few Europeans involved—tropical diseases frightened off some and killed many who remained at the small trading posts. As a result, European commerce often fell into the hands of the children of the French and Portuguese who had married or cohabited with local women; the second-generation men knew both the European and local languages, and knew the people they traded with. However, Europeans with racist attitudes assumed that these mixed-race individuals were lazy, incompetent and dishonest.

By the 1750s, when a greater volume of trade seemed to require more expert supervision of the enterprises, European wars were disrupting commerce. Some native rulers turned to France, others to Britain. As prices for slaves rose and fell, new crops were exploited for sale—gum and indigo, ivory and gold. This attracted the attention of new Muslim states forming on their frontiers.

Contemporary Europeans—like modern scholars—understood this imperfectly. Those on the spot probably grasped local politics well, but had little overview; those at a distance were discouraged by the unusual names and customs, the confusing mass of information of questionable accuracy, and by racial and religious prejudice.

Diseases deadly to horses, uncooperative native rulers and the expense of mounting expeditions limited outsiders' ability to travel deeper into the interior, and when intrepid individuals did venture there, they either remained quiet about what they found or did not write about their adventures. The sole exception was Shabeni, a Moroccan merchant who was taken as a captive to London, where he told the story of his visit to Timbuktu about 1787. His account, however, did not become widely known until it was published in 1820. By that time a black American sailor named Robert Adams had already told the story of his more recent visit to that city.

The Congo and Angola

As the Portuguese made their way down the western coast of Africa in the late 1400s, they were frustrated at not finding good harbours. Then, once they found the mouth of the Congo River, they were unable to sail far upstream; worse, there was nothing that they could exploit easily—the climate was hostile, the languages and customs unfamiliar, and the only product they could resell at a profit was human beings.

The Portuguese crown established a base to the south, in Angola, but they still hoped to convert Congolese kings to Catholicism. Because conversion ran contrary to commercial and political interests, it demonstrated that Europeans were not driven entirely by greed. Natives could not grasp why celibacy was so good, monogamy so important, and why there were so many rules; also, why was the Christian god preferable to their own deities and traditions? The Portuguese kings and their administrators did not worry, however. Every missionary encountered these problems and usually they overcame them.

The uniformity of products across the region meant that there had been little incentive for trade between the fertile lower regions of the Congo and the interior before the Portuguese arrived, but once coastal rulers realised how valuable European products were, they hurried to obtain ivory, palm oil, salt and slaves from the interior. Portuguese arms and soldiers aided favoured allies in expanding their domains, and they returned the compliment—Angola was dotted with Portuguese settlements, each of which had to be fostered and defended. Angola was, as David Birmingham wrote in *The Cambridge History of Africa*, a small, aggressive trader-state equipped with firearms. As such states expanded, those on their frontiers collapsed, the people terrorised by slave-raiders and robbers. The wealthier and powerful grew even more so, while the poor and helpless were ever more at their mercy.

Europeans in Southern Africa

When Vasco da Gama (1460?-1524) rounded the Cape in 1498, he did not pause to make a settlement at the tip of the continent. Though the Cape's climate resembled southern Europe's, the coastline was dangerous and there was no suitable harbour; moreover, his goal was to reach India, which he quickly did. Captains who followed him tried to heed his advice to stock up on food and water before sailing onto the Indian Ocean, but they could not find such a place which was safe from attack by native peoples and Muslim pirates, and with a harbour that offered protection from storms.

Vasco da Gama thought he had found such a base on Madagascar, but, lacking gifts sufficient to impress the local ruler, he soon sailed on. His cannon-bearing caravels impressed Indian princes and frightened Muslim merchants, but although the Portuguese defeated impressive Arab and Turkish fleets, they could establish only footholds in India—the princes were reluctant to allow strangers to build fortified posts. Even in the East Indies, where they soon monopolised the spice trade, they found it wiser to work with native rulers than to supplant them.

While the Portuguese had swept Muslim fleets from the seas—even penetrating into the Red Sea and threatening Mecca—they knew that the Ottoman Turks still saw themselves as the protector of the Arab and Somali merchants. Unless they had a strongly fortified port on the continent, they would not be able to trade for East African products and slaves.

This fear proved illusory. Muslim merchants travelled overland to the African interior, using long-established personal relationships and their knowledge of Swahili to keep their markets open; they could have the slaves they purchased walk north to Somalia, carrying ivory and copper. Early Portuguese efforts to break into this monopoly were by individuals who penetrated into the interior with minimal official backing.

The Portuguese left Zanzibar, a traditional centre of trade, to the local chief. They would have liked a town at the mouth of the Zambezi River, since that would not only allow access to the kingdoms upriver, but it would be possible to sail from there straight east to India and back. However, there being no good natural harbour in the area, the Portuguese made their main base in Mozambique.

The Portuguese temporised, but they never forgot the dream of a commercial centre on the Zambezi, then penetrating deep into the hinterland, perhaps even reaching Lake Victoria. For decades, however, the unhealthy climate combined with native resistance (and, according to the natives, magic spells) discouraged all but a small number of merchants, soldiers and priests from going inland. These adventurers reported the existence of fabled gold mines, close enough to the mouth of the Zambezi for Portuguese administrators to imagine conquering them.

In 1569 King Sebastian, whom we have met before, sent Francisco Barreto (1522-73) with 600 musketeers, 200 native auxiliaries and some cavalry to take the gold mining region that lay east of the lands of the Monga tribe. A secondary motive was to revenge the 1560 murder of a Jesuit missionary whose success was resented by Muslim Somali merchants. Also, excessive enthusiasm typical of the time for Jesuits had led the missionary to demand that local king and his people abandon ancestral habits such as plural wives, men dressing and acting as women, and practising spirit worship.

Barreto was a capable soldier, trained in Morocco and with experience as a naval officer and administrator of posts in India; and he had Jesuit advisors who knew the country well. The expedition was a gamble, of course, but the Spanish had faced greater odds in the Americas, and they were now reaping the rewards for their daring. In contrast, the Portuguese had only the slimmer profits from their trade in India. The hold on Brazil was insecure; it was not even clear that the few outposts along the coast could be held if the Dutch or French attacked. The rainforest would not be easy to clear, most of the natives suitable for use as slaves had succumbed to European diseases, and sugar plantations using Africans were only beginning to show profits. It seemed more logical to put scarce resources into conquering the region today known as Mozambique.

In 1572 Barreto put his men aboard ships to sail up the River Zambezi and sent messengers to the Shona kingdom of Mutapa (Monomotapa in Portuguese), a successor state of Great Zimbabwe, asking permission to attack the Monga. The king agreed, on the condition that he was allowed to share in the booty. But Barreto did not like that arrangement, or perhaps he mistrusted the king. As he moved upriver he encountered a Monga army of more than 10,000 men blocking his way. He lost only two soldiers, according to his account, while killing and wounding an estimated 4,000 of the enemy, but the three days of desperate fighting persuaded him that he could not conquer the region with the men on hand. Retreating toward the coast, he put his troops into defensible forts while he himself hurried back to Mozambique to discipline an unruly officer. By the time he returned in 1573, his men—who had meanwhile massacred all the Muslim merchants they could find—were suffering so badly from tropical diseases that they were unfit for a new campaign. Soon he fell ill, too, and died.

Subsequent expeditions achieved little, because the gold mines were richer in rumours of wealth than in precious ores—these were clearly not King Solomon's mines. The missionary effort failed as well. However, coastal Mozambique had been opened to merchants and a handful of settlers. Despite great losses in a 1631 uprising, few of the Portuguese forts fell; the next year 300 musketeers and 12,000 native troops defeated the rebels. But without a major insertion of settlers, the Portuguese could only retain the most tenuous control of the region, and since the home kingdom lacked a surplus population for such a programme, that was unlikely. Consequently, commerce came into the hands of sons produced by Portuguese and Indian men who had married local women.

Mutapa did not flourish long, though initially the king profited from a heavy tax on trade. Quarrels among his successors led first one, then another to buy guns from the Portuguese, then to request direct military intervention. Eventually, it was impossible to tell who was hiring whom, but the Portuguese were too weak to take advantage of the chaos—trade cannot flourish when travel is unsafe and trading partners fall to rivals. Mutapa kings would declare themselves Portuguese vassals, then ignore orders; Portuguese trading posts dotted the kingdom, but control was weak. The foundations of the future colony were laid, but only a framework structure had been built upon them.

The Dutch and French

With Portuguese harbours not welcoming Protestant privateers, the Dutch had to look at places the Portuguese thought unsuitable. Considering that the Cape had the most European-like climate and soil in the whole region, it was surprising that it took even the Dutch until 1652 to establish Cape Town. The post grew slowly, but it was able to supply visiting ships with vegetables, meat and fresh water; after settlers introduced cattle, the base grew rapidly. That, however, led to wars with local tribes. The governors, lacking regular troops, relied heavily on local recruits with military skills learned in wars against Louis XIV.

The Dutch were frustrated by native men refusing to work for wages and by locally purchased slaves who easily escaped into the bush. The answer to the dilemma was to import slaves from more distant lands.

In 1685 the Dutch East India Company began an effort to attract settlers—Dutch, Huguenots, Germans, even Danes and Swedes. The only requirement was that they learn Dutch and be Protestant. By 1707 there were at least 2,000 settlers and one had already called himself an Afrikaner. Cattle farmers (*trekboers*) had already penetrated the first mountain barrier into the interior, turning natives into their labourers. Smallpox and cattle diseases crippled native resistance, after which cattle theft—each group stealing from all the others—became endemic. This angered the Dutch, who were not backward in the practice themselves, and it made the natives suspicious of one another. Bantu tribes became involved, participating in the subjection of the original native tribes and fighting the Dutch to a standstill, occasionally using firearms effectively.

By the time the British seized the Cape in 1795, the basic outlines of the future South Africa were clearly visible. The struggle over land, water and cattle had begun.

Meanwhile, the French made no effort to establish themselves on the mainland of southern Africa, but looked for island bases which could supply merchantmen heading for India. First they tried Madagascar, driving away the Arabs who had dominated regional trade. However, they discovered that the rest of the island was too populous and mountainous to conquer, and they could not prevent other European merchants from establishing themselves along the coast and selling firearms to local rulers. As native chiefs mastered weaponry, they also learned how to exploit European rivalries to make themselves powerful in different parts of the great island; this minimised French authority into the nineteenth century.

The French lost interest in Madagascar after they found two more suitable small islands, Bourbon (Reunion) and Ile-de-France (Mauritius). There the only significant worries were attack by British fleets and powerful cyclones (hurricanes). Pirates became important later, preying on the flourishing trade along the coast and on European vessels sailing to the Indies and India.

East Africa

Strong states were not present in East Africa when Europeans arrived; rather, the established states had already collapsed, leaving puzzling stone ruins. Post-colonial scholars have made much of this, even citing the ruins of mosques as proof of native genius. Earlier scholars thought that a mosque was proof of Arab influence, which shows how little they could foresee the direction that twenty-first century scholarship would go. Meanwhile, we have to work with what we know—that there was a slave trade here that was as great as or greater than that in West Africa. African tribes that could sell neighbours to Muslims on the Indian Ocean and Christians on the Atlantic were becoming powerful, and those which were too weak to do so went under.

Today we automatically deplore the institution of slavery, but at the time every major civilisation thought it was natural, just and inevitable. Even those Europeans who were sceptical about buying and selling people were willing to accept serfdom and tenant farmers. Africans do not seem to have thought the institution wrong. What they objected to was having their own tribesmen carried away for sale.

The resistance to slave traders seems to have been sporadic and ineffective. Aside from some gold, there were few resources other than captives that native leaders could have traded for weapons; not even ivory was that significant. With herding as the most important occupation in wide areas, rather than farming, there were few significant population centres for outsiders to conquer. As slavers changed from one local ally to another, each time to increase profits or put pressure on suppliers, it became more difficult for rulers to reward their most loyal followers, and it was easier for rivals to challenge them. Selling captives taken from local enemies

76

seems to have resulted in destabilising entire regions. When the slave trade dwindled in the early nineteenth century, this did not result in a restoration of stability before the Zulu onslaught began. When Shaka Zulu (1787-1828) developed tactics involving disciplined units and employing strategies that attracted allies and isolated enemies, the Zulus became powerful; they became ever stronger as they incorporated defeated peoples into their military system and moved south. The Zulu expansion is often credited with dislocating many peoples in South Africa, and most importantly in causing many Bantus to flood into areas eyed by British and Dutch settlers. Some modern scholars discount that story.

Shaka Zulu allowed a limited number of English missionaries and merchants into his lands, though it is not clear whether he wanted their goods and services or merely to counterbalance Portuguese and Boer influence. Clearly he was not impressed with Western weapons. These, he contended, fired too slowly to stop the rapid charge of his inspired warriors, but it might be noted that he never encountered a Western-style army of sufficient size to make the firepower of muskets and cannon effective.

The Portuguese in Ethiopia

The Portuguese did reach one of their goals—the kingdom they thought might be that of Prester John, a mythical Christian king deep inside Africa, cut off from the rest of Christendom by the Islamic states along the Mediterranean coast. At least, they considered Christian Ethiopia (Abyssinia) the plausible origin of a legend that had circulated around Europe since the crusades. Unhappily for the Portuguese, Ethiopia was too far in the interior for profitable trade. Indeed, the very isolation that had protected Ethiopia from Muslims made it also nigh on inaccessible to Portuguese merchants.

Portuguese soldiers and priests did make contact later, when invited by the mother of Emperor Dawit II (1501-40) to assist them against the Ottoman Turks. The Portuguese navy intervened effectively between 1520 and 1523, then sailed away—there were other opportunities for profit closer to their bases in southern Africa, India, and the East Indies. Since they left behind only a handful of priests, merchants and soldiers, they soon lost control of the Red Sea to the Ottomans. In 1529 a young Muslim prince, Ahmad Gragn (Ahmad ibn Ibrihim al-Ghazi, 1506-43), imam of Adal, occupied the coastal lands, then pressed inland, taking one fortified place after another and cutting Ethiopia off from the sea—hence severing

Ethiopian contact with the Portuguese. Ahmad Gragn's origin is obscure—perhaps Arab, perhaps Somali, perhaps from the Red Sea coast—but everyone agrees that he was the most dashing and capable commander of his generation.

In 1541, the new king of Ethiopia, Gelawdewos (1521-59), managed to send an appeal to Christopher da Gama (Cristovão, 1516-42), the son of the famous explorer. In response, da Gama brought 400 Portuguese troops, and, by fighting his way through Ahmad Gragn's blocking force, demonstrated the superiority of Western musketeers over archers. Ahmad Gragn then hired hundreds of Ottoman musketeers and in 1542 defeated da Gama, then beheaded him.

Da Gama's 120 surviving men, perhaps half his little army, rearmed themselves from depots and rejoined by Gelawdewos's forces, then went on the offensive. Ahmad Gragn, meanwhile, had dismissed most of his mercenaries, perhaps unable to pay them, leaving himself weaker than the Ethiopian-Portuguese army, small as it was. The Portuguese concentrated their fire on the remaining Ottomans, then shot down Ahmad Gragn. The victors soon fell out—the Jesuits offending the Ethiopians, the Ethiopians offending the non-Christian peoples along the coast. This allowed the Muslim forces to regroup.

Emperor Serse Dingil (1563-97) renewed the contacts with the Portuguese. Ceasing to rely on feudal armies, he took over the private armies of his governors and hired Portuguese mercenaries. He was able to ward off the Ottomans, but not able to recover the Red Sea coastline entirely. Pulling back from those endangered regions, he settled his people in the highlands to the west. At his death he left an infant son and powerful generals. It was easy to foresee who would prevail.

Portuguese influence decreased as the Jesuits insisted on the Ethiopians replacing age-old traditions with current Roman Catholic practices. This was the era of the Thirty Years War in Europe, and it is understandable that Western churchmen, especially the Jesuits, were dogmatic in matters that might have been overlooked in another era. Also the cost of maintaining the armies was too great for the Ethiopian economy. The emperors found traditional weapons sufficiently reliable, and without the trouble of pleasing a foreign ally.

As religious controversies and tribal loyalties continued to plague the emperors, they came to see that their foreign bodyguards—blacks, Turks, Arabs and local Muslims, all organised into regiments—were the one class of warriors they could rely upon. This lasted until those troops became accustomed to power, intermarried with local nobility, and began to see themselves as the nation's natural aristocracy. The emperors then turned to the rising tribe of the region, the Galla, drawing warriors from them. Eventually, power devolved to local warlords, who held sway until the mid-1850s.

The Galla were uncomfortable neighbours. When the Portuguese port of Mombasa was attacked by an Arab fleet, the Portuguese commander turned to a tribe known as Zambi. The name should have been a warning, since this was the local word for cannibal. The Zambi fell on the Europeans, reputedly eating them.[4]

In the end the revived Muslim enterprises triumphed. Muslim adventurers became powerful, Muslim merchants rich, and Muslim missionaries famous. Trade blossomed—some of it in human beings, so that eventually the total numbers of African slaves taken by Arabs and Somalis may have been slightly greater than the number taken by Europeans.

European View of Africa

Not surprisingly, Europeans were little interested in Africa except as a source of products. The vast continent did have its exotic aspects—such as giant bodyguards for minor rulers, and servants for lesser folk—but those were temporary amusements unlikely to distract European rulers from more pressing concerns—wars, trade, taxes, weather and disease—or lighter amusements—hunting, women, banquets and drinking. Also, some of the blacks came from the West Indies, a generation or more removed from Africa. What Europeans knew of the Dark Continent generally reflected what classical historians had written and what seamen encountered. That is, it was hot, humid, filled with deadly diseases and, quite possibly, sea monsters. True enough, for many years the coastline of West Africa was, unlike that of almost any part of Europe, jungle-like, dark and without towns where merchants and sailors were welcome. African art appeared satanic in every way, and the superstitious beliefs in magic and sorcery defied every effort by missionaries to supplant it. With drums, chanting, men and women dancing semi-nude around bonfires, their public ceremonies seemed more like a scene from Dante than anything in the visitors' experience.

That said, there were always a handful of specialists who knew more about the people and customs of limited regions than did any European into the twentieth century. Walter Rodney went even further in *The Cambridge History of Africa*—saying that popular travel literature made

Europeans of this era more knowledgeable about Africa than any until the mid-twentieth century. Of course, widespread illiteracy confined this interest to those with the money to buy books and the time to read them; and these individuals do not seem to have asked their black servants what they knew, and had they done so, they would have heard individual tales rather than an overview of customs and histories. Class prejudice discouraged such interactions, much as it did intimacy with white servants; and so it is not surprising that whenever European merchants or captains of sailing vessels encountered African music and religious practices, they found them unattractive, even uncivilised.

Anti-slavery efforts grew more intense as Europeans and Americans began to realise that the institution harmed whites as well as blacks. Moreover, middle-class Britons and aristocrats alike were repelled by newly-rich slave-owners from the Caribbean who brought their money and crass attitudes home. Nevertheless, when Europeans who went to the West Indies or Brazil for work came to realise that their chances of survival were low, they may have wondered what they were doing there, but they never wanted to take over the laborious work the slaves were performing.

Some Europeans who went to the West Indies were soldiers, some were overseers and merchants, and some were transported criminals and beggars; some were prostitutes, cooks, and household staff. But the reason all these persons were there was sugar. Other crops existed, of course, but as sugar became available to all classes in Europe, it became indispensable. Nations which had sugar to sell became rich, nations which had to pay high prices became resentful. However, nobody wanted to abolish sugar, and therefore the abolition of slavery long remained a noble dream—something for another generation.

The impact on Africa was less well known. Sailors visited the distant shores to carry away slaves, but they knew next to nothing of where their cargo came from, or why. With diseases racing through the tightly packed human cargo, the crews died in roughly the same proportion as the slaves. No sailor had the time or opportunity to interact with the prisoners—they were busy dawn to dusk and, when needed, through the night.

There were Dutch and French merchants who settled into trading communities along the African coast, married local women, and passed their businesses on to their descendants. These mixed-race children were invaluable for much of the 1700s, able to speak to both natives and Europeans until eventually they were crushed between the rise of Islamic states and European racism. However, they wrote little except letters to their business partners, who were not eager to share their knowledge with competitors, and the letters do not seem to have been very informative about local politics or customs.

Modern Scholarship

If Europeans seeking to buy slaves were responsible for the destruction of African states—one of the dominant *tropes* of pre-postmodern scholarship—then Europeans must accept considerable blame for later problems. However, today, scholars argue that Africans continued to dominate their own history, and that the handful of Europeans who visited their shores were essentially irrelevant. This presents some interesting intellectual puzzles for the scholar who wishes to be respectful of local interpretations of peoples' pasts.

Change is occurring so swiftly in the way historians look at the African past that whatever was true one day seems barely a memory the next. This is much like the growth of African capitals, which at a distance now look like any city anywhere. Yet it seems that in parts of the countryside poverty and lawlessness remain prevalent, and the crude military despots seem like time-warp stereotypes of tribal tyrants who lacked even a sense of how to dress appropriately.

Obviously not everything we knew before is wrong now, just as we cannot be sure that what we know now is so. The musical *The King and I* was set in Siam in the early 1860s, but what the king had to say was applicable everywhere and perhaps in every era:

> 'There are times I almost think
> Nobody sure of what he absolutely know
> Everybody find confusion
> In conclusion, he concluded long ago
> And it puzzle me to learn
> That tho' a man may be in doubt of what he know
> Very quickly he will fight
> He'll fight to prove that what he does not know is so.'

As sugar and other tropical crops became popular, more European rulers became interested in acquiring American colonies and in buying African slaves. As they learned they could play one African king against another, supplying their allies with firearms to protect themselves and to capture prisoners, they found this more affordable than sending their own troops into the tropics; at the same time they could harm their competitors for power in Europe. African kings learned to play the game, too. Those who were good at it prospered; those who were not, went under.

This same principle applied to the colonial era and the post-colonial era. Some Africans understood the game, others did not, some do not seem to have cared. The history of the Congo, with its reverse Midas touch (by which all gold turns to dross), reached its low point between 1998 and 2003, as armies from several surrounding nations and multiple internal militias fought for domination, with outside powers hoping either to end the conflict or profit from it.

The events of 2012-14 in Mali also illustrate why we need a deeper and more nuanced understanding of the interaction of politics and history in Africa—when jihadists and Tuaregs acquired weapons after the fall of the Gadhafi regime in Libya, they swept through Mali until French and African troops drove them back into the desert. This may not exactly parallel earlier Muslim penetration into Black Africa, but it is not irrelevant—as the advance of Boko Haram into Nigeria in 2014-15 confirms. Weak states cannot easily resist well-motivated, well-led attacks from the periphery, and states which have been poorly governed and are already divided by ethnic quarrels are especially weak.

The failure of the Arab Spring seems to suggest that rule by strongmen will persist for some time yet in North Africa and that this will affect all their neighbours. It seems to suggest, too, that the Ottoman Turks had good insights into the proper combination of institutions and administrators for governing diverse peoples scattered over a wide area. But we have to be cautious about assuming the past to be an accurate guide for anything beyond understanding how we got to the present.

Africa remained on the periphery of European consciousness into the eighteenth century, but by the end of the Early Modern era it was no longer an unknown continent. What Europeans knew may have been incomplete or even wrong, but what they saw most clearly was the reflection of their own military superiority, which they believed rested on a foundation of cultural and even racial superiority. That legacy, and the reaction to it, have created the continent that we have to work with in the future.

There are also lessons here for the interaction of the centre and the peripheries. Advanced societies took advantage of their superior technology and organisation, and African peoples had to react to this.

But Europeans were not alone in provoking resistance by tribal peoples. Moroccans and Ottomans did the same. And so, too, did every state and every tribe that attempted to impose itself on its neighbours. The temptations to attack weaker neighbours were too great—booty, slaves, power—and the penalties for failure too small. It would be a mistake to heap all the blame for the continent's current problems on one head, even if Europe had been ruled by one crowned monarch.

1. The success of Rossini's 1813 opera, *The Italian Girl in Algers* (l'italiana in Algeri) testifies to the long memory of Muslim raiders attacking Italy. Wisely, he staged the first performance in Venice, a city proud of its tradition of defending its naval empire and Christendom. At that moment, with Britain and France fighting the climatic battles of the Napoleonic Wars, the Barbary pirates had the rule of the Mediterranean Sea. After the 1815 Congress of Vienna, the European states agreed that joint action was necessary. Soon afterwards the British fleet forced the Algerians to cease piracy; the Americans had already taken steps to limit attacks on their trading vessels.

2. Voltaire introduced a similar episode into *Candide*. The old woman with one buttock told how her ship was captured when she was only fourteen. She had a good number of bodyguards because she was the daughter of Pope Urban X. However, like good soldiers of the Church, they threw down their weapons and pleaded for their lives. She was surprised at how swiftly the Moors stripped the women, then inserted fingers where she had never imagined they should. She later learned that this was an international custom, one even followed by the Knights of Malta, to search for diamonds.

3. Chase in *Firearms, a Global History*, contrasts the cost of a sailing vessel to that of a galley. Ottoman shipyards could turn out galleys more quickly than sailing ships, but it was more difficult to raise crews and supply them; also, Europeans had more experience with large sailing vessels. Geoffrey Parker, *The Military Revolution*, praises the impressive firepower and manoeuvrability of the galley. Moreover, a galleass mounting eight heavy guns fore and aft was more deadly than a sailing ship in crowded combats between fleets.

4. Today we are told that cannibalism, if it existed, was exaggerated. But contemporaries believed in it. Voltaire employed it in *Candide* to explain why the old woman could not ride a horse—she had sold to Janissaries who found themselves defending Azov against a Russian army. When the Turks ran out of food, they decided to eat the slave women. Killing her was unnecessary, they decided, since they did not need to eat all of her at once, so they took only one buttock for lunch. When the Russians stormed the fort, she was rescued, then made her way through Poland and Germany to Holland. It was a half-assed story, but it still makes us smile.

Chapter 5

The Collapse of Old Empires
The 1700s Around the World

In the 1500s it appeared that Portugal and Spain would possess all the significant overseas colonies that Europeans would ever acquire. Their favourable location on the southwestern tip of Europe, their knowledge of winds and currents in distant oceans, and the experience of their captains were augmented by royal support, the Church's financial resources, and the courage and resolve of their seamen. Spain's successes in overthrowing impressive empires in Mexico and Peru were paralleled by Portugal establishing a commercial empire stretching from Africa to Japan.

England, a latecomer to the contest for maritime empire, was first stirred into action by fear that the Great Armada would transport the Spanish army in the Low Countries across the Channel to overthrow Queen Elizabeth and the Protestant church. She responded by turning buccaneers loose on the Spanish Main; soon there were English pirate bases in the Caribbean. Then, as soon as captains began to capture slave ships and the Royal Navy took Spanish islands, the way was open to develop large sugar plantations. Finding a labour force, however, was difficult—Scots, it seemed, died too quickly in the tropics to make deportation pay. Therefore, the English had to take up the slave trade, with its huge cost in human lives. The costs were high even for pirates, whose fictional song, 'Yo-ho-ho, and a bottle of rum! Drink and the devil had done for the rest' catches the spirit of the Caribbean—live hard, fight hard, and die young.

The French, impelled by a similar fear of Spanish arms, allowed their pirates (mainly French Protestants known as Huguenots) to emulate English successes. Once victorious over an over-extended and exhausted Spain, the English and French fought over the sugar islands in the West Indies, then over colonies in Africa, North America and India.

In a sense these were wars over menus: sugar from the West Indies, spices from the East Indies, tea from India and China, and tobacco for an after dinner smoke. There was also coffee from the Ottoman Empire and chocolate from the Americas, rum for pubs—and for those who preferred something non-alcoholic, coffeehouses and tearooms. The immense quantities of gold and silver from Mexico and Peru spurred economic growth everywhere in Europe, but undermined Spanish entrepreneurs; moreover, the increased number of coins available to buy a limited number of commodities led to a destabilizing inflation. Governments desperate for more revenue debased their coinage, the French introduced paper currency, and Scots promoted a wild investment in a colonial project that failed spectacularly. While the colonial products were luxuries at first, in time upper class affectations became more widely accessible and, consequently, necessities. Thanks to the consolidation of states and the increasing security of travel and commerce, wealth was both increasing and dripping down to the classes of merchants, artisans and purveyors of material and spiritual comfort. Even farmers and peasants were doing better.

Better, of course, is a word that needs to be followed by *than*. Many people who lived on the edge of poverty or even slightly over it hardly noticed the changes; for them improved conditions only meant policies that forced them off the land into crowded and unhealthy cities. Malthus and Swift, who had both observed the growing poverty, knew that overpopulation was a serious problem. Surplus sons of impoverished peasants, without the prospect of inheriting land, provided manpower for the armies, the ships that carried the goods, and the work force in distant colonies. Those unfortunate enough to go to the Caribbean encountered heat, disease, rebellious slaves and dangerous European enemies. Life was uncomfortable and short. Even in North America's milder climate colonists were very cold in the winter, very hot in the summer, and they had to cope without the help that neighbours and occasionally the government had provided at home.

North America

After the Spanish destroyed the French pirate base at Fort Caroline (near St. Augustine in Florida) in 1565, subsequent French and English settlements in North America were made much farther to the north. There is a tendency among modern historians to ridicule the English colonists for having brought along soldiers rather than farmers and artisans, but the very real fear of Indians was less a reason for being well-armed than knowing how

Spaniards dealt with heretics who intruded into lands they might want to exploit themselves at some later date.

There were many misunderstandings of what the natives in the American woodlands were like. First of all, no one should have called them Indians, but Columbus believed that he had reached Asia, and the native peoples did not look or dress like Chinese; moreover, the name America was first used for the new continents only in 1507, when a cartographer got it into his head that a Florentine traveller, Amerigo Vespucci, had actually discovered the New World, when all that he had done was to demonstrate that these lands were not in Asia. As for what to call the tribal leaders, 'king' seemed appropriate at first, reflecting as it did a hope that the explorers had come upon a great kingdom, and afterward the title of chief, or chieftain, prevailed.

Modern misunderstandings abound as well. Everyone could see the different skin colours, but racism did not yet exist. If Europeans were confused and sometimes appalled by the customs they encountered, so too were the peoples the Europeans were meeting.

There would eventually be great nations in North America, but only after English colonists interacted with the native peoples on their periphery, then in bits and pieces occupied their lands. Within a century and a half of the first colonists establishing rude settlements on the coast there were over two million English-speaking peoples pushing up to the Appalachian Mountains and a few venturing beyond. These people were, as it were, on the periphery of the British Empire; and they were increasing unhappy about being treated as outsiders, an unhappiness that eventually led to the American War for Independence.

No one anticipated this when the first English settlements were founded shortly after 1600. The region between Chesapeake Bay and Labrador was not a *terra incognita*, since explorers and fishermen had visited the coasts often, but relatively little was known about the interior. Tropical crops such as sugar were impossible there, but the climate was good for familiar crops and animals which could feed Caribbean slaves, and there was a new crop, tobacco, that could be grown by slaves without the horrendous death toll of those used to harvest sugar cane. The early emphasis was on trade—mainly fur—and on catching cod for sale in Europe, enterprises supported not by royal aid, but by joint stock companies. Trade with the natives was often justified as a first step in converting them to Christianity; the Indians, however, were generally as resistant to English religious practices as they were to English clothing. What the Indians wanted was military aid in their wars against other Indians, or at least weapons that would allow them to seize their neighbours' hunting grounds.[1]

The Indians appreciated some Western technologies, and they soon became addicted to trade goods such as cloth, iron pots, rum and good tobacco. Wise men warned that European goods would undermine their society, and that contact would bring diseases which could destroy them. But few could afford to listen—once the Indians were involved in global commerce, they could not turn their backs on it. The losers in inter-tribal wars generally fled westward, sometimes pushing other tribes farther west and sometimes amalgamating with them. Since many tribes had moved great distances over the centuries, migrating west would have been no great hardship if the circumstances had resembled returning from their summer hunt to safe winter quarters. Now, however, there were no fields of maize waiting. Hard hit by disease and starvation, their women and children captured and enslaved, the refugees nursed a terrible anger. They sought allies who could perhaps help win back their lost lands or, at a minimum, save them from yet another mass flight westward. They found these allies in representatives of the kings of Spain and France.

The Spanish had trading posts and missions in Florida and along the Caribbean coast all the way to Mexico. The one gap in their chain of possessions was in Louisiana, where the French had built a large town at New Orleans. The Indians' principal complaint about the Spanish was their reluctance to sell them firearms—the king wanted to discourage warfare and encourage conversion.

The French, who had settled in Canada and Louisiana and along the rivers linking these places, limited emigration. This was partly to ensure royal control of the economy and guarantee that the Roman Catholic Church was not challenged, and partly to persuade the Indians that they were not intending to take their lands. The large reinforcement to the Louisiana colony by French refugees from Arcadia was allowed because they had been expelled by the British, who had renamed their peninsula Nova Scotia. These newcomers, known in America as Cajuns, spread through the swamplands along the coast; wherever war made navies too busy to search for pirates, they assisted buccaneers in robbing European colonists.

English kings did not provide the kind of planning and consistent enforcement that the Catholic monarchs proudly made central to colonial policy. They, like Parliament, saw America more as a convenient place to send religious radicals, the occupants of work houses, and petty criminals—the kinds of people the French kings would never allow to settle in their colonies—and to get needed raw materials—lumber, tobacco, and food for Caribbean slaves. As a result, although French fur traders eventually formed close ties with Native American tribes and spread along the Great Lakes and Mississippi River, the number of colonists in Canada remained small; in contrast, England's settlements grew in size beyond anyone's expectations. Apparently there were more undesirable Protestants in England than saintly Catholics in France.

The Americans, as the English colonists were eventually called (because it was too awkward for writers to list even the most important colonies on the mainland and in the seas roundabout), generally remained confined east of the Appalachian mountains, but many adventurous individuals considered the Indian lands to the west to be essentially empty—in short, farmers had priority over deer.[2]

Through these years Great Britain (as England and Scotland were known after the 1707 union) fought a series of desperate wars with France, relying on allied powers to tie down French armies in Europe while the British navy dealt with its French counterpart. Indian tribes, their numbers reduced by epidemics and intertribal wars, chose sides reluctantly, but the most important Indian confederation—the Iroquois—realised that British numbers would prevail over the French; with British weapons they swept their native enemies from the hunting lands in Ohio and Kentucky.

The Indian tribes thus evicted from ancestral homes found themselves with no good options. They lived with memories of ancient wrongs inflicted on one another, they had no common tongue to facilitate communication, and tribal and clan leaders had only limited ability to make individual warriors follow their decisions. Freedom was the boast of the warrior, but it was so extensive a freedom that it precluded the organisation of a modern state with a standing army, tax gathering powers and judicial bodies. Male pride discouraged commerce and industry—even farming was women's work. Men were hunters and warriors, but since they were responsible for feeding their families, they were reluctant to risk becoming crippled or killed. To avoid casualties they attacked by stealth and surprise, and they so strongly objected to pitched battles or storming battlements that Europeans incorrectly thought them cowardly. This put them at a disadvantage in fighting Europeans armed with muskets and cannon, who were not only more numerous, but also accustomed to risking everything in hand-to-hand combat. While the Indians did what they could to buy muskets, they could not produce these weapons themselves, and gunpowder and lead were difficult to obtain. Alliances with the French and Spanish helped, but the monarchs of those states believed that restricting the availability of firearms would reduce the number of wars.

The only way for Indians to stop the decline in population from disease, alcohol and war was to avoid contact with Europeans as much as possible, and to steal women and children from other tribes—not as slaves, but to increase the number of warriors; this encouraged the continuation of tribal wars, and those tribes which fled westward were not likely to join the British or the Americans who had supported their Indian foes. The French and the Spanish were natural allies, but the Indians remained minor players in the Great War for Empire that was known in Europe as the Seven Years War (1756-63), in America as the French and Indian War.

The long string of British successes between 1689 and 1763 ended only when a constitutional dispute with the American colonies led to Holland, France and Spain making a worldwide assault on British colonies and markets. Outnumbered even in the number of ships-of-the-line, Britain was on the defensive from 1778 to 1783, with a declining economic base. Imperial overstretch and overbearing attitudes, however, were matched by France's self-destructive desire for revenge.

This had been foreshadowed a decade earlier by Britain's own suicidal polices in America. At first it had seemed quite logical to ask Americans to bear part of the immense tax burden brought on by the Seven Years War. As Niall Ferguson noted in *Empire,* the average Briton paid 26 shillings a year in taxes, while the average American paid one; as a result, Americans seemed wealthier, hence better able to pay. Americans, in contrast, understood how British efforts to avoid inflation made it almost impossible to pay taxes in hard cash; their economy stressed barter and credit. Moreover, they believed that they had paid their share of the costs of the war in blood and suffering—contributions that British officers and politicians had mocked. In any case, given the nature of British trade policy and the practices of British banks, ready money was hard to come by.[3] However, the bone of contention was not taxation, but a constitutional principle that Americans summarised as 'no taxation without representation'. That is, America had no representatives in Parliament. British leaders haughtily responded that most Englishmen and Scots didn't, either, but that the elected members of Parliament represented everyone, which included all colonists; thus, even distant Americans had, in the words of the day, 'virtual representation'. Americans did not agree. More importantly, Americans resented being treated as outsiders, as a lesser people, more like Scottish tenants or Irish cottagers, than a swiftly developing society with scientists, artists and political leaders of talent and energy. This was the sticking point, where the pride of the parliamentary leaders and the army prevented compromises that would have defused the explosive situation—and, as some Whig leaders tried to remind the government, kept the rapidly growing American population loyal to the crown. Restraints would have changed British history forever, and probably for the better, but long term prospects were sacrificed for short term taxes that the government had little chance of collecting.

British arms were sufficient to win most of the battles in the ensuing war, but the number of redcoats in America was insufficient to occupy the vast region; and when European powers, both ancient foes and recent allies, saw this as an opportunity to embarrass the over-mighty Britons, they aided the rebels. The lesson: superpowers are always viewed with jealousy and suspicion. The British government, recognising that it could not afford to waste its army and navy on an area peripheral to its main interests, reluctantly made peace with the Americans.

In the future British governments would permit appropriate measures of self-government in the remaining colonies, more for those settled by Britons, less where Britons were few in number. For some colonies already existing—Ireland, the West Indies and India—the inertia of tradition was too strong for reform proposals to prevail. Resistance sometimes led to proposals for reform, which, since they failed to satisfy everyone, were followed by another revolution. Repression just required more repression.

Empires Tottering

France's loss of much of its empire—Canada and much of the North American interior east of the Mississippi, some sugar islands, most of its possessions in India—did not have the terrible effect that the loss of colonies had on Portugal. The impact on Britain was even less. The government had thought all along that trade with the colonies from Georgia to Maine was more important to the Americans than to Britain, a calculation that lay behind trade restrictions so onerous that in 1812 they led to a second outbreak of war. However, the loss of the mainland colonies was more than offset by gains elsewhere at the expense of France and Spain. Attention was soon drawn to the challenge by the new government of the French Revolution and then by that of Napoleon Bonaparte.

More significant than the political revolutions in Europe, perhaps, was the collapse or near collapse of empires elsewhere. The Ottoman Turks were staggered by repeated military defeats and economic troubles, but their state remained upright, thanks partly to the inability of European monarchs to decide how to carve it up. In contrast, the Mughal Empire in India lost all but its symbolic role in the political hierarchy. In China a tax revolt in 1794 acquired a religious aspect (the White Lotus Society) and became a serious threat to the Quin dynasty; although suppressed after ten years, the uprising was considered the turning point in Chinese history. Forty years later a somewhat similar uprising (the Taiping Revolt) took on trappings of Christianity and almost succeeded in overthrowing the dynasty.

Much of this is unfamiliar to today's European and American audiences, but that is no surprise. Every dynamic society has more important interests than reading about failed nations, no matter how relevant the lesson might be. Kipling wrote *Recessional* to remind his generation, 'Lo, all our pomp of yesterday Is one with Nineveh and Tyre!'[4] But who today reads the Bible well enough to know what Nineveh and Tyre were?

Even less was known about Africa, where discussions of the fate of Great Zimbabwe (11th to 14th centuries) can still generate more heat than light, and readers are more likely to be interested in the slave trade with the Americas than in the kingdoms which traded human beings for goods that could not be produced locally. There were winners and losers in the struggles for control of this trade—Congo and Ethiopia declined, Christian and Muslim traders did well, and mosquitoes spread diseases along the new trade routes. Yet much did not change. Pastoral peoples still coexisted with farmers and merchants, and much of the land remained unsettled. Here, as elsewhere, massive change came only with the phenomenal population growth of the twentieth century. Colonial rule meant law and order and better public health. Not even political disorder and the appearance of new diseases slowed the growth of nations did that did not even exist in 1500.

Wars over West Africa

For centuries Europeans had been as much victims as aggressors in their relationship with North African states, but in the 1500s new European weapons and the leadership of the Hapsburg emperors who ruled first in Spain, the Spanish Netherlands and important parts of Italy, then in Austria and the Holy Roman Empire, had blunted the Ottoman advance. After that, as we have seen, Spain and Portugal began to reorder the political, economic and religious arrangements in West Africa as well. Interior Africa was not yet greatly affected, and while scholars may disagree on what 'greatly' means, few will insist that Western ideas and practices penetrated very deeply in these years. Not even Western weapons had much impact in regions where they could be used only with great difficulty. African leaders, being intelligent, selected what was practical, affordable, and not likely to lead to rebellions which would cost them their offices and lives. They allowed small European trading posts to exist as long as this was to their advantage.

The system of co-existing European trading posts ended during the Seven Years War, when the British minister, William Pitt (the Elder, 1708-78), decided to wipe out the French colonies everywhere, to the fullest extent possible.

The French, realising their naval inferiority, abandoned India and soon left the Canadian garrisons to defend themselves; they concentrated their resources on protecting their sugar islands in the Caribbean. This meant leaving their African colonies practically undefended.

The French had three bases in West Africa—on the Senegal River, on the island of Gorée just south of Cape Verde, and on the Gambia River. Each prospered from sending slaves to the French sugar colonies in the Caribbean—the largest number was from Senegal, about 1400 annually. The British sent a fleet to attack these colonies one by one, in that order. Senegal fell quickly once the fleet made its way past the sand bars at the mouth of the river; the French garrison and civilians, given the option of going home, generally decided to stay with their native wives and families. Gorée was more difficult. Lying at the mouth of the bay of Dakar, it was a rocky outcropping of only eighty-eight acres, and heavily fortified. It required a second expedition, better armed, to overawe the garrison and its African auxiliaries.

Afterward, British troops settled in unhappily. In 1766 the commander of the British troops at Gorée was Charles O'Hara (1740-1802), reposted from his duties in Portugal. The son of Baron Tyrawley and his Portuguese mistress, Tyrawley had commanded the first British troops sent to Portugal in 1762. His force was made up of mutinous British soldiers who had been pardoned in return for serving—for life—in Africa.

No British officers and soldiers liked serving in the tropics, and the natives did not want them there. For three centuries Portugal, Holland and England had fought to control the trade in slaves and ivory, but as new sources of slaves appeared, it did not matter much that the French obtained possession of Goreé, the tiny island off modern Dakar. The mainland was held by chiefs (or kings, as they styled themselves) who periodically had moveable war booty to sell; and so many more slaves were shipped from the river mouths than from holding cells in Goreé (the infamous prison shown to tourists was not built until 1780). It was awkward for British officials to think that the only benefit of victory was to supervise the transportation of people to labour in the sugar colonies of the Caribbean, where many would perish from overwork and heat.

The West African coast is not as hot as most Europeans and Americans imagine, and the ocean breezes moderated the temperature, but for people raised in the British Isles and wearing woolen uniforms, the climate seemed unbearable. The humidity was high, and because there was no frost or freezing, there was no respite from the constant annoyance of flying insects.

The British returned Goreé to France in 1763, but retained possession of Senegal and the Gambia River. O'Hara moved to Fort James on an island in the Gambia River, where he was governor until 1775. His successors were men of incredible brutality, suitable perhaps only for managing (i.e., flogging) troops such as were dispatched to that hot and utterly unattractive rock, which was pleasant only compared to the steamy mainland; at least, it had sea breezes. Perhaps mercifully, few soldiers and merchants survived the tropical diseases until Senegal was returned to France by the 1783 Treaty of Paris.

O'Hara must have been pleased when the American Revolution broke out, because he was able to leave his unpleasant African post for a fort in New Jersey that protected New York City from attack by General Washington's forces. There he had relatively little to do except collect supplies and chase American cavalry, but he did it well enough so that when General Clinton sent an army to the southern colonies, he made O'Hara second-in-command. Together with Lord Cornwallis he routed the American forces in several hotly contested battles—he was badly wounded at the Battle of Guilford Courthouse, and his son was killed. Then Cornwallis was ordered to take the war into Virginia. That proved an impossible task, too. Ordered to retire to the coast, where his army could be taken aboard naval vessels and transported to New York, Cornwallis fortified the heights overlooking Yorktown and waited for the arrival of the British fleet. However, a French fleet drove the British ships away, then a series of confusing instructions from Clinton left the army unready to face a joint French-American force coming down from its positions around New York.

The fighting was once again fierce, but after French and American assaults took the forts on the bluff, the allies subjected the huddled British and German troops below them to a merciless bombardment. Cornwallis bowed to the necessity of surrender, but he feigned a cold rather than turn his sword over to Washington—that duty fell to O'Hara. Washington, however, realizing that this act was a calculated slight typical of Britons toward Americans, refused to accept the sword, instead pointing to a junior officer.

This was the effective end of the British Empire between Canada and the Caribbean. The war lasted another two years, but there was no changing the outcome: France had won, but had gotten little from its victory except a bit of revenge and a mountain of debts. Those debts would soon lead to the French Revolution.

Great Britain had massive debts, too, much more than those the government had used as a justification for taxing Americans. Now, however, the government found ways to manage the situation.

India

The Portuguese were the first Europeans to visit India, displacing the Arabs, who had dominated trade from the west, and Malays, who came from the east. But they were too few in number and too weak for Mughal emperors to worry about—they were nothing compared with traditional enemies north of the Khyber Pass. But in the end it was not Afghans and Persians, who for centuries had periodically overrun the rich lands of the north, nor the Hindu princes of the south, who prevailed in India, but a handful of British soldiers and administrators.[5]

What was life in India like afterwards? At first the British governed indirectly, giving suggestions rather than orders to the various Hindu, Muslim and Sikh potentates who continued to live in splendour. However, after the British government took over from the East India Company, everything but the pretence of independence ended. In Kipling's co-authored novel, *The Naulahka, A Story of East and West*, an American entrepreneur sassily asked the Maharajah for permission to build a dam so that he could mine for gold. All he got was a sulky, 'Go talk to the Government.' When pressed, the Maharajah explained, 'Nothing in the state is mine. The shopkeeper people are at my gates day and night. The agent sahib won't let me collect taxes as my fathers used to. I have no army.'

The American had little sympathy for the old man—the ruler still had his servants, his horses, and his opium. He became more disgusted when his native workers proved incredibly incompetent, and his anger boiled over at the extravagant marriage of the young heir to a three-year-old girl—the servants of the proud guests proving even more arrogant and demanding than their masters, and the throng of onlookers pushing toward the temple so strongly that the American could barely make his way close enough to glimpse the boy-groom dressed in gold and jewels, with the black diamond, the Naulahka, flashing brightest of all.

Meanwhile, the female missionary who had built the hospital found the local superstitions too strong to overcome. When the holy men warned that any women who allowed her to touch them would bear babies with tails like camels and ears like mules, her beds were soon empty.

The plans for gold mining proved similarly empty, as the Indians had predicted. Didn't everybody know that there was no gold in the river? Why did they think that Englishmen knew everything, even an Englishman who was not an Englishman? No one could understand these foreigners.

There were many twists to this story, its serialised publication requiring regular surprises that would keep readers buying the next magazine. It is awkward to read the story at one sitting. Nor is it one of Kipling's best efforts, but the novel presents many of the questions debated by modern scholars: was colonialism necessary to create a unified nation or did it distract India from its natural development? Were class and gender identities reinforced or were the seeds of change planted? How did Western racism express itself, and how did Indians react?[6]

China and Japan

Portuguese diplomats reached China in 1516, but they were hardly seen as equals by the administrators of the Celestial Kingdom. China was the centre of the world, and all visitors were by definition petitioners for the emperor's attention. Only five years later, however, the Chinese learned how dangerous even the handful of the Portuguese could be—hearing that the newcomers had conquered the strategic port of Malacca in the East Indies, which was technically an imperial vassal, they expelled the Portuguese from the empire.

The remainder of the century went badly for the Ming dynasty— Mongol invasions, the Japanese moving into Korea, pirate attacks, uprisings and horrible earthquakes. It appeared that the emperor had lost the mandate of heaven, which in 1644 was transferred to a new dynasty from Manchuria. The Qing dynasty reestablished Chinese faith in their superior values, this time reinforced by a strong military that occupied Korea and Mongolia, Tibet, much of Burma, and lands along the Silk Road leading to the Muslim world.

The Ming dynasty had already voluntarily given up commerce by sea— the emperor had abandoned a potential maritime empire to concentrate on expanding control over the nomadic tribes that lurked to the north and northwest, waiting to drive across the Great Wall again. Although ethnic Chinese considered the Manchus foreign barbarians, too, it seemed wise to assist them in crushing ancient nomad enemies first; and, in any case, there were very few Europeans anywhere near China yet. The Manchu emperors could safely ignore pale-skinned barbarians.

Japan was never completely isolated until 1635, when the borders were closed to Europeans wishing to enter and Japanese wanting to travel abroad. Before this, though the Japanese were extraordinarily proud of their culture and their race, they had been open to Chinese culture, especially religious ideas, and they had originally extended this welcome to Christian missionaries. What was different about Roman Catholicism was that converts were expected to give their allegiance to a foreign head of state. The ban on teaching Christianity ended the threat of a divided loyalty and also of the presence of sweaty foreigners who did not bathe often enough.

The Caribbean

Columbus's voyages discovered a New World. He didn't know it, of course. He thought he had reached islands off the Asiatic coast, islands that lay exactly where he had expected to find them and which seemed to resemble descriptions by earlier European visitors such as Marco Polo. Rather than fight over the new conquests, Spain and Portugal agreed to divide them between themselves, excluding all other nations. Thus, we have the West Indies occupied by the Spanish, the East Indies by the Portuguese. This tidy division of the world by a Spanish Pope awkwardly left Brazil in the Portuguese half. But the Spanish didn't care. Brazil wasn't worth quarrelling over—the riches of the newly discovered world were in the Caribbean.

Both Mexico and Peru had astounded Europeans by their wealth, while the ease with which a relative handful of Spaniards overthrew two great empires made other Europeans dream of finding a great Eldorado somewhere in unexplored country. More practical minds focused on the Caribbean islands' sugar and tobacco—products that all Europeans wanted and which could be resold in Africa, the Middle East, and even Asia. Also, sugar itself was less valuable than the alcoholic beverages that could be made from it.

There was a tendency to romanticise the New World. Voltaire made fun of optimism in *Candide*, but also of Rousseau's ideas by suggesting that a utopia could be found in America and a more just society in the Ottoman Empire. It might be noted that Voltaire loved the excitement of Paris, and only when royal edict made that city inaccessible, was he content with country life and extensive stays at foreign courts. Voltaire may have sent his literary creations to live near Constantinople, but, unwilling to shut up and disliking the thought of having a garotte around his neck, he did not visit Turkey. He may not have liked slavery, but he cared no more for Blacks or Muslims than he did for ultra-pious Catholics or overly-enthusiastic Protestants—he liked sugar in his coffee, both of which came from the Caribbean. However, he did not smoke. This set him off from so many contemporaries, who loved to spend hours fiddling with their pipes and flicking sparks off their clothing.

Neither did Voltaire consider going to South America to look for the El Dorado of *Candide*. Relatively few inhabitants of the New World could understand the witty remarks he made in French, and probably would not have approved of them anyway. He was a man of his times. He enjoyed the products of colonialism, even the Chinese ceramics and hard woods of Asian jungles, so he did not attempt to end the system that supplied them. He planted ideas that would eventually end colonialism, but he was patient enough to wait for future generations to act on them.

The periphery was definitely affecting the centre, and, as a result, old empires were falling. The twentieth century saw the disappearance of the great European empires, the collapse of empires in China and Japan, and the Ottomans in the Middle East. In their place we have seen the appearance of what some call neo-colonialism, the rise of ISIL (the Islamic Caliphate), and a bewildering number of religious-ethnic movements on the frontiers of newly independent states. One despot goes, another comes in. It appears, to use a trite phrase, that the only continuity is change.

But that may not be so. As the next chapter suggests, the most important continuity may be repetitions of the past. But the wheel of history, though it appears to come back to where it started, has actually moved a full revolution along.

1. An excellent overview of the strengths and weaknesses of the Indian way of life, the incredible diversity of languages, customs, and economies, together with the universal emphasis on individual rights and personal honour is in chapter three ('the Unyielding Indian') of Edmund Morgan's *American Heroes*.
2. English yeomen in the time of Robin Hood thought of the royal forests in the same way. Indian women farmed, too, but in the summers the tribes left their winter lodges to travel throughout the tribal domains, leaving the maize to ripen on its own.
3. In a somewhat analogous argument, scholars in India say that British tariff policies turned their land from rich to impoverished. British officials tended to blame overpopulation, religious conservatism and climate.
4. He continued, "If, drunk with sight of power, we loose/ Wild tongues that have not Thee in awe—/ Such boastings as the Gentiles use,/ Or lesser breeds without the Law—/ Lord God of Hosts, be with us yet,/ Lest we forget—lest we forget!'
5. See the relevant chapters in my *Bayonets and Scimitars*, which describe the process by which the British trained sepoy troops who made possible their victories over incompetent foes.
6. A prominent question discussed today is whether Kipling—or any other Westerner—could describe India accurately. Edward Said (1935-2003) mocked Western specialists trained in Middle Eastern languages, religions and cultures whose sympathies were still with Ancient Israel and their western homelands. Men and women trained in classic languages and mostly interested in enhancing Biblical studies through archeology and philology usually studied classical Arabic rather than the languages and cultures of the street; therefore, they were disconnected from the masses and the mass culture that was changing so profoundly. Since they had proudly called themselves 'Orientalists'; Said made that term distasteful and repulsive. But he begged the question about who could be trusted when well-informed natives disagreed.

Chapter 6

The Celtic Fringe
Overview

The 'Celtic Fringe' was once the periphery of English-speaking Britain. Most Britons know this, but it is worth reviewing the situation for readers elsewhere; moreover, there may be British readers who were asleep or distracted when this topic was covered in their classes. Moreover, what happened here was in many ways similar to the experiences of frontier peoples elsewhere in the world.

The British Isles holds four major ethnic groups, each arriving in a great migration or invasion—Celts (the Irish, the Welsh, and the Scots), then the Anglo-Saxons, Vikings, and Normans. Each new group took the best resources for itself, often making its predecessors into poor and powerless, angry outsiders. Even as the various ethnicities evolved into an English-speaking people, differences remained: Wales maintained its ancient language because its rocky hills were not attractive to outsiders; Ireland lost much of its fertile lands in the east to immigrants, but retained its language among the rock-filled western counties; Scotland's Highlands were wanted by nobody but the tax men, but in the Lowlands—the main agricultural region bordering England—English-speaking Scots made important economic and cultural progress.

Clan loyalty had been important in each of these peripheral societies. It remained important longest in Scotland, especially in the Highlands, where modern society had the least impact; it did not completely vanish in Ireland, but, as in England, local loyalty became more important than having a real or mythological clan ancestor. As for Wales, until recently the Welsh could not even agree on a standard form of their language.

The Celtic peoples in Britain, like every group living on a periphery, have a long and unforgiving sense of history. This occasionally leads to self-pity, often to self-delusion, but always to a sense of tragedy. Blame is laid at the feet of outsiders—angrily, as if surrendering ancient swords and shields—when the real problems were having too few warriors to drive the outsiders away and being reluctant to allow any local leader to organise the slender resources for a united resistance.

Wales was divided by geography, tradition, and political ambitions, and the leading families intermarried with the neighbouring English Marcher Lords. The ruler during the last years of independence was Llywelyn the Last (1223-82), whose alliance with Roger Mortimer (1231-82) did not save either one of them. Mortimer was also a grandson of Llywelyn the Great, but died just as he had celebrated a military victory that would have made him master of the country. This allowed Edward I (1239-1307), the Hammer of the Scots (*Malleus Scotorum*), to bring Wales inside his kingdom by building impressive castles, filling them with strong garrisons, and extorting heavy taxes. The 1995 movie, *Braveheart*, is fiction with some facts mixed in, but it caught the spirit of Edward's harsh methods and the Celtic resistance.

Edward made an accommodation with Welsh lords by naming his son the Prince of Wales, but it was 1536 before Welshmen were allowed to sit in the House of Commons. (The 1997 vote to establish a National Assembly and the existence of a Welsh sporting teams for international events suggests the people were not completely integrated into the English nation.)

Edward's imposition of English law, with its emphasis on the state's right to settle all civil and criminal matters, the growth of the money economy, restraints on the autonomy of the Welsh church, and the recruitment of soldiers for the royal army, undermined the last authority of clan leaders and the dominance of the Welsh language. Nevertheless, Welsh mercenaries insisted on being commanded by fellow countrymen and preferably by men of noble ancestry.

Intermarriage of the upper classes with noble English neighbours was common, but commoners remained separate; English was spoken in the towns, Welsh in the hills. Unlike the Irish, who in the era of the Reformation may have remained Roman Catholic partly to spite the Protestant English, the Welsh were as reluctant to use Latin as they were to acknowledge the Book of Common Prayer. The Bible was translated into Welsh, but their true allegiance was to non-conformist preachers—Baptists, then Methodists.

The English, far the most populous people and possessing the most fertile fields, the best climate, and the most advantageous position for trade with the continent, were not comfortable allowing the Celtic peoples to remain independent. This was not mere lust for power—the Welsh were cattle rustlers. 'Tammy was a thief' was a realistic assessment of the situation along the borders as well as a racial slur. However, the Welsh cannot be blamed for taking advantage of their neighbours, because even if there had been no taxes to pay, it would have been difficult to make more than a meagre living from their beautiful hills; even their splendid mercenary soldiers were infantry because few could afford horses.

English kings felt constrained to occupy the country, but they found the people too stubborn to subdue forever. It was a puzzle what to do with people who sing songs like *Rhyfelgyrch Gwŷr Harlech*:

> Men of Harlech, stop your dreaming
> Can't you see their spearpoints gleaming?
> See their warrior pennants streaming
> To this battle field.
> Men of Harlech, stand ye steady.
> It can not be ever said ye
> For the battle were not ready.
> *Welshmen never yield.*

Harlech is well-known for Owain Glyndŵr (Owen Glendower, 1349 or 1359-1415), the last native Prince of Wales, who resided there from 1404-9. Owain negotiated an alliance with France that allowed him to strike his English enemies both by land and sea; however, when the peace party prevailed in France in 1406, the tide of war turned against him. While seeking to avoid capture by English pursuers, he vanished suddenly, nobody knowing where he went, but everybody expecting him to return. Today he is a national hero.

Scots were no less stubborn and their alliance with France made them dangerous; Scot raiders and even armies came across the border regularly. The Border Reivers, consisting of both Scots and English, carefully avoided robbing their own kin and any powerful lord, but stole from one another as a matter of tradition. The rules of this irregular warfare puzzled Aeneas Silvius Piccolomini (later Pope Pius II, 1458-64) during his secret mission to Scotland in 1435. First, frightened practically to death by a storm at sea, he vowed to walk barefoot to the nearest shrine of Our Lady to pray. He had no idea how cold Scotland was, nor that the nearest shrine was ten miles from the port. His legs never recovered from the ordeal, leaving him partly crippled for the rest of his life. Second, when word came to a village he was visiting that reivers were on the way, he watched his hosts drive the cattle to safety and leave the women to protect the houses from being burned. When he asked if the women wouldn't be raped, he was stunned by the reply—yes, but the women wouldn't be hurt, and without cattle, we would starve. An Italian, he could not understand how this could be tolerated. However, being an Italian—and also one of the most brilliant and attractive literary figures of his era—he appreciated both the looks and the spirit of Scottish women; he fathered a child, but it did not survive. Fortunately, his autobiography (*Commentaries*) did, providing us one of the best accounts of life in Scotland and England in this period.

The Irish were separated from the rest of the British Isles by a sea, but a body of water is also a means of communication. This meant that the English could not ignore the possibility that a continental enemy could use Ireland as a base to attack them. In the late sixteenth century it was easy for English political and military leaders to imagine that Spanish forces would liberate their Catholic brethren, then invade England at the same time that an army was transported from the Spanish Netherlands. Everyone agreed that a Spanish army would make short work of English forces riven by religious and political division. Later, when the French replaced the Spanish as the chief danger, the dynamics of the situation remained the same.

Fortunately for the English, neither Spanish nor French monarchs could present the Irish with any acceptable political solution to their anarchic internal quarrels, whilst the mainland Catholic churchmen were similarly confounded by the ancient religious traditions practised on the Emerald Isle.

Geography Limits Options

Northern winds and short growing seasons made the British lands less prosperous than those of continental rivals, but history has repeatedly drawn England into a conflict with the richest and most populous of them—first Spain, then France. Because many Scots and many Irish perceived England as a dangerous enemy, they tended to see those nations as natural allies.

This, according to Brendan Simms in *Three Victories and a Defeat*, explain English foreign policy over the generations. The principal fear, he contended, was of domination by a continental power; fear for the survival of Protestantism was important in this, but not a complete explanation. Scotland's long association with France was joined in the 16th century by Spain's interest in Ireland. Royal policy was to 'shut the backdoors' to England, to prevent hostile armies from establishing a base anywhere. But royal policy as practised by the Stuarts was not popular—too conciliatory, and, when forceful, inept. Critics of the Stuarts found themselves awkwardly admitting that the king had the right to conduct foreign policy, while resisting the taxes he needed to do so effectively, then disliking it when he logically did nothing. This was less significant in Scotland, where the Stuarts had many supporters, but it explains much about the kings' failure to resolve the Irish question—the Stuarts considered Ireland to be less important than collecting taxes or art.

Military traditions in Scotland and Ireland reflected past politics, but can be understood only in the context of long-term poverty. War offered more than opportunities for revenge and gaining status; it was also a means of earning a living and perhaps becoming rich. Scottish and Irish mercenaries were active across Europe and throughout the British Empire. Indeed, it was remarkable that these lands could produce so many warriors, and warriors of high quality. Understanding why young men chose military careers cannot be separated from events in England and Scotland or the grand affairs of the Continent, but understanding local politics is even more important.

Diversity and Common Traits

In the 1630s Scotland and Ireland each had a parliament of its own, a state church, and an appointed royal governor. Each had clans (Scottish chiefs could summon up their members for military service, while Irish leaders relied on private armies of mercenaries, mostly local boys); each had an economy based largely on livestock and a tradition of stealing cattle; and each had traditions of feasting, drinking and fighting. Scots serving in private Irish armies honed skills that were useful later in European wars, where the pay was better.[1] Over both was a thin veneer of feudalism. And over that the sound of the pipes, summoning men to battle, to celebration and to mourning.

Both lands were sufficiently complex to defy efforts at explaining them simply. We grasp for some definition that clarifies more than it confuses. Kevin Kenny, in *Ireland and the British Empire* contends that contemporaries could never decide whether Ireland was a kingdom, a colony, a dependency or a nation. This ambiguity explains much about the failed efforts of successive English governments to establish a workable Irish policy. My friend and former student, Bruce Ogilvie, says that the Scots and Irish were 'essentially a similar people divided by a small sea, a bloody history and a strangely diverse language', and that their stereotyped and contradictory cultural images came from inter-family warfare and inter-regional rivalry, a hardscrabble rural economy and long dark winters. Lands of intense religiosity, they produced few saints in this era—Saint John Ogilvie (1580-1615) being the most important exception; a Jesuit, his only significant action was refusing to reveal the names of Scottish Catholics despite the most terrible tortures then known.

S.J. Connolly, in contrast, argues in *Contested Island, Ireland 1460-1630*, that the Stuart policy had been quite successful before 1640, at least in stimulating economic development that brought the Irish into a money economy. James I's colonisation policy was based on his experience in Scotland, where he had found resettlement effective in helping make an unruly kingdom governable. In short, Gaelic Scotland and Gaelic Ulster (the northeastern counties of Ireland) presented similar problems, which suggested similar remedies. These worked in the first case, but not in the second. Ulster, though no longer the scene of civil war, remains a contentious region to the present day.

Scotland seemed to be the simplest to understand—there were Lowland Scots and Highlanders—but clan loyalties made it very complex. Some Scots were Catholics; some were Episcopalians who recognized King Charles I (1600-49) as the head of the Church, with bishops determining doctrine and practice. Some preferred the simpler 'Low Church' style of the English Puritans; others were Presbyterians, the most radical being Calvinist Covenanters who believed that laity should control both church and state; then there were the sectarians. English was spoken widely, though some Scots must have been as hard to understand then as they can be today, and some spoke only Gaelic. Clan rivalries were fierce, pride was often overbearing, poverty often desperate, and ambitions were as great as desires to avenge past insults and defeats. Some Scots migrated to Ireland, where royal favorites made confiscated lands available for colonisation. Paying rent in a new land was better than starving at home.

Ireland had been under the control of the English parliament after 1494, when Poyning's Law limited local rights to initiate legislation and gave the crown a veto on parliamentary laws. In practice, however, local landowners and clan leaders made the law. Native Irish were the most numerous ethnic group, but many of the earlier English immigrants now considered themselves as authentically Irish as the majority who spoke only their ancient Celtic tongue; and Scots knew they were resented by those who had been evicted to make way for them, and by those who had been marked for eviction, but had been left in place because replacements had not yet been recruited.

Religion was divided along ethnic lines. Episcopalians (Church of Ireland) dominated the counties around Dublin known as 'the Pale' and some of the larger towns, but many of the 'Old English' were Catholic landowners who worked easily with the crown. In the 1630s the English lords, and their Irish counterparts, had won concessions by agreeing to pay taxes; by 1640 they looked forward to playing a greater role in their own governance. The vast majority of native Irish, however, were Gaelic speakers, Catholics who seemed to be in a state of permanent rebellion, determined to reverse past confiscations of land and discriminatory laws. But it was not as simple as a straightforward Protestant-Catholic dispute. Robert Foster, in *Modern Ireland,* reports that despite many of the Irish priests being trained in Salamanca, the Counter-Reformation arrived late; Jesuits coming secretly into Ireland hardly recognised the local Catholicism, so archaic and independent it was. As for inheritance of property and office, few outsiders could make sense of the rules—fluidity seemed to be the only constant. Contradictions abounded, observers saw what they wanted to see, and the Irish resented papal efforts to interfere with their local practices almost as much as they did English domination. Awkward facts, such as a twelfth century pope having given Ireland to Henry II of England, could be ignored by Catholics and celebrated by Protestants.

The Church of Ireland was, according to Connolly, not only alien, but predatory. Its financial problems were severe, but every effort to resolve them by collecting fines for non-attendance and setting aside lands for the support of priests and bishops made the situation worse. Language was an insuperable obstacle, since few English-born priests spoke Gaelic and few natives English; thus, one of the great advantages that Protestantism offered—worship in the vernacular—was sacrificed to a policy of forcing everyone to speak English. It was also under attack by its Puritan members, whose emotional meetings and insistence on calling the pope 'the anti-Christ' undermined efforts to draw the Irish away from the 'heretical' underground Catholic Church.

There were also newly arrived Scot Dissenters who were essentially Congregationalists (actual Presbyterians were still few in number) and English Puritans who were similarly unhappy at the high church policies of Charles I, who intended to force them to follow the Anglican forms of worship based on the *Book of Common Prayer* and to emphasize grace rather than predestination; when they abstained from attending state-sponsored services, they were fined.

As Muríosa Prendergast notes in *Mercenaries and Paid Men,* although the first sixteenth century Scottish settlers were mercenaries who fought in local feuds, they were quickly assimilated into local society; the second wave, in the 1560s—composed of 'redshanks' who changed employers often—

destabilized the country. A third wave of settlement brought as many 100,000 Lowland Scots to Ulster, and English reinforcements to the Pale. But instead of calming the island, the ethnic mixture was made more dangerously volatile.

The English response was to encourage Irish warriors to serve abroad. If these were already rebels in arms, even if they took service with a Catholic monarch, they were out of the country. If they could enroll them in Catholic royal battalions, they were also out of the country, but serving English political ends.

By 1640 Charles I thought he had moved toward stabilising Ireland. And indeed, the situation was much improved, especially for his Gaelic-speaking subjects. But in thinking that his main problems were with Protestant fanatics and banditry, he (and almost everyone else) underestimated the depth of Catholic anger.

Royal Absolutism versus Democratic Impulses

King Charles, having made a partial accommodation with the Irish, moved on the Scots in 1639, provoking armed resistance known as the First Bishops' War. Charles, having the larger army, expected an easy victory, but his opponents were led by Alexander Leslie (1580-1661), one of the most experienced commanders of the Thirty Years War. Leslie had entered Dutch service in 1605, then become a Swedish general, recruiting many Campbells to serve in Germany. In 1638 he responded to appeals to come home, then used his personal connections and his own money to equip and train Covenanter forces that totally frustrated the ineptly commanded royal army.

The time for a decisive battle not having yet come, both sides backed away from confrontation, agreeing in principle to disarm; but neither trusted the other. After this, Charles needed another army, but even his extraordinarily unpopular methods of extortion and his novel schemes for taxing the public without calling his exactions by that name were insufficient to his needs. Reluctantly, in the spring of 1640 he called the first election in a decade so he could ask Parliament for money. This was a mistake.

Parliament was unwilling to vote the taxes until the king changed his policies. When the king dismissed this 'Short Parliament', he found himself facing another war in Scotland—the Second Bishops' War. Defeated badly in only ten days, Charles could obtain a truce only by agreeing to pay the expenses of the Covenanter army which now occupied the north of

England—£850 per day. He had no money for that, much less to raise yet another army.

The problem was not a lack of potential recruits, but competition from continental armies which were aggressively recruiting mercenaries for service in Germany and Poland. This was especially true for Scots, who had made service abroad a rite of maturity—they would leave home boys and return as men. As for those Scots already serving in European armies, not all wanted to come back to fight in a complicated civil war that nobody had the money to fight properly.

Many had died of injuries and disease, and many chose to stay where they were, often marrying local women who were loath to move to a distant, dark land; they usually found some occupation or profession that offered better prospects than were available in their homeland. Their hearts may have been in the highlands, but their wallets were in Holland, Germany, Poland and Russia. Moreover, Scotland did not seem to be in great danger. Scots in Ireland were a different matter, but it was not easy to get Scots in the homeland enflamed over Irish problems until they had reached their own accommodation with King Charles.

As Irish Catholics saw the king's position weakening, they began to clamor for the restitution of their rights, then attempted to drive the Protestants off the lands that had once been theirs. Charles lacked any power to influence events except to encourage royal officials to keep the peace. Then he called another election in England, only to find that the parliamentarians of the late autumn of 1640—later known as the Long Parliament—were even less willing to give concessions than their predecessors had been.[2]

Meanwhile, to gain peace in Scotland, Charles had gone to Edinburgh, where he ennobled Alexander Leslie as the Earl of Leven and raised the 8th Earl of Argyll, Archibald Campbell (1607-61), to a marquis, then became so entangled in conspiracies that he was temporarily beholden to the Presbyterians. It was becoming obvious to all that the king was both incompetent and untrustworthy, but there was great reluctance to risk the anarchy that was currently playing out in Germany. Nevertheless, new armies began to form, each built around a core of mercenaries attracted home from the continental wars.

Wheels began to turn within wheels, local conflicts loosed by the weakening of royal authority. The Covenanters, believing the situation at home to be under control, demanded that the king hurry to the rescue of their countrymen in Ireland; similar sentiments were voiced by the Puritans in Parliament, who were momentarily the Covenanters' enemy. This caused

Catholics in Ireland, English and Irish, to take up arms before the Calvinists could put their inflamed rhetoric about 'papists' into actions; in the course of the next year, the 'Irish Confederation' formed an alliance with the king, then began attacking Protestant and even royalist strongholds in the north and east. Massacre and betrayal were common on all sides, but none of the armies was well-led or well-organised. A parliamentary army arrived, then a Covenanter army, and the Catholics already had their own forces. The alliances in this 'war of the three kingdoms' were so fluid as to defy all efforts to summarise them.

Irish veterans of the Thirty Years War flocked home, but aside from an occasional brilliant victory, they succeeded only in replicating the social disasters playing out on the continent. In *Mercenaries and Paid Men* Ciarán Óg Reilly tried to explain this phenomenon, asking why Irish soldiers did so well on foreign battlefields, but destroyed their own country. He blamed their willingness to fight to the death, an impulse that came from a desire for glory and a sheer love of war.

This thirst for total victory that made them favourites of foreign employers, but it frustrated each proposal to bring peace to Ireland through compromises. Scot and English settlers, other than those willing to become Roman Catholics, responded to Irish attacks with equal vigour and more success. The onset of the English Civil War opened the way to settle old scores, and for returning veterans to pursue ambitions of their own.

The most important of these soldiers was Owen Roe O'Neill (1590-1649), who had served in the Spanish king's Irish regiment for forty years, mostly in the Netherlands; 'Red Owen', as he was called, was the younger brother of the Earl of Tyrone. Though widely suspected of wanting to become king in Ireland himself, he probably envisioned nothing more than an independent Irish state, with himself as a leading figure. Complicating the situation was a papal nuncio of Italian birth and Jesuit training, Giovanni Battista Rinuccini (1592-1653), who opposed all efforts at compromise. Unpaid mercenaries, robbers, clan armies and city militias swarmed over the island, spreading panic ahead of their arrival, leaving death, destruction and famine behind them. Charles withdrawing his army to fight Parliament in England only made matters worse. O'Neill fought valiantly, but with inadequate forces against larger and more competently-led armies.

The English Civil War

The constitutional confrontation of King Charles I with Parliament became more serious in early 1641 when the king ordered the arrest of the House's leaders, then it became outright war in August 1642. Many of the shires were dominated by Puritans, hence sympathetic to Parliament, and when the Scots abandoned the alliance with the king, Charles authorised his supporters to raise money and conscript troops however they could. His strongholds were in Oxford and York, so when the allied Parliamentary and Scottish armies closed in on York in 1644, the king sent a relief army north under his nephew, Prince Rupert of the Rhine, the dashing son of Frederick of the Palatinate, the 'Winter King' of Bohemia. No one was more 'cavalier' than Rupert, no one less a 'Roundhead'.[3] This army represented a combination of the king's last money and best hopes.

Rupert, whose parents were exiles from their own lands, grew up at the court of William II of Orange. Early demonstrating an ability to master languages, mathematics, and the arts, his military career—notable for his reckless bravery—began at the age of fourteen. He made a good impression on King Charles during a visit to England, after which he had distinguished himself at the 1637 siege of Breda. The next year, serving as an officer in a company of Scottish mercenaries, he was captured by the imperial army and held prisoner for three years in Austria—resisting all efforts to convert him to Catholicism. When the Civil War began, he and his brother Maurice brought a company of Scottish mercenaries to the king's aid, and Charles gave him the command of the royal cavalry. His dashing leadership inspired the horsemen and almost won the war, but his arrogant manners offended prominent nobles around the king.

Rupert brilliantly marched around the allied position at Marston Moor on 1 July 1644 and disrupted the siege of York, but when he announced to the other officers that the king had ordered him to engage the parliamentary forces in battle and crush them, his hearers were disconcerted—the opposing army outnumbered them by 27,000 to 17,000, and it was led by the Earl of Leven, one of the finest commanders of the age, and Oliver Cromwell (1599-1658), an amateur who was proving himself equal to Leven. Rupert, however, insisted that his army contained better soldiers—professionals. That is, they were mercenaries with foreign experience. He also believed that he could catch the enemy coalition dispersed and unready for battle. Rupert's officers were not sure—there were many experienced men in the enemy ranks, too, especially Campbells who had served in the Swedish army. Moreover, knowing that the king's advisors usually counselled caution, they spoke against taking rash action now. Still, they gave way to the stronger personality.

Rupert put his men on a forced march to Marston Moor. Although he arrived at the allied camps too late to catch them by surprise and his men were exhausted, he ordered an attack before Leven could pull his scattered units together. At that moment some of his mercenaries refused to fight until they were paid. While Rupert negotiated, Leven put the Scots and Parliamentary forces into a line of battle behind a marsh, then, seeing that Rupert had chosen a strong position opposite him, he stood on the defensive. Not far apart, the two armies waited for reinforcements, watching each other cautiously. Rupert's reinforcements came in first, fine units from York. Although it was already late in the afternoon, Rupert announced that he would attack immediately. Again, his officers objected— the reinforcements were tired, as were his own men, and it was time for supper. Moreover, the commander of the York troops, James King, Lord Eythin (1589-1652), had long mistrusted Rupert's love of the wild attack; he spoke for fighting on the morrow. His was not a voice to be dismissed lightly. King had served in the Swedish army from 1609-1636, then in the army of the Landgraf of Hesse. At that time he had fought alongside Prince Rupert and quarrelled with him over tactics, now as then, considering the prince reckless and overly-daring. His counsel prevailed. As both armies began making camp, Rupert left the field, and his troops left their ranks. At that moment Leven ordered an attack. Cromwell was fortunate in that the opposing cavalry commander ignored orders to wait until the Parliamentary horsemen had floundered across the marsh, then been decimated by musketeers, before charging to meet them; unwilling to endure artillery fire longer, he rode through his own infantry, only to founder in the marsh. Cromwell's Ironsides scattered the disordered royalist cavalry, then swept through the gap in Rupert's lines and into the rear of the royal army. It helped that some royalist units preferred looting the campsites to fighting, while Cromwell's men concentrated on winning a victory, then pursuing the beaten enemy.

The traditional mercenary army composed of disparate units, unevenly trained and equipped, was clearly out of date; not even a solid core of officers coming home from the Thirty Years War sufficed to make up for its defects. Subsequently, Cromwell persuaded Parliament to reform the army along the lines of his troops—the 'New Model Army'. He standardized the composition of regiments of infantry and cavalry, cladding many in red uniforms; the state was henceforth responsible for pay, not the commander; and politicians were excluded from leadership positions. Discipline was emphasised, as was religious fervour. Cromwell's opponents, especially in Ireland and Scotland, were highly motivated, but they lacked discipline— a trait they would learn too late, but in the future apply effectively on foreign battlefields. It may have been Prince Rupert who first called

Cromwell's cavalrymen 'Ironsides', but it was a name that distinguished them from the 'Roundheads' who formed the earlier parliamentary armies—enthusiastic but undisciplined warriors.

Rupert continued to inspire and offend, leading his 'Cavaliers' to unlikely victories until 1646, when the king surrendered to Leven and made peace with Parliament. Unwisely, however, Charles believed that his bickering enemies were so divided that he could overthrow them one by one. Parliament sought to reduce the danger of renewed war by exiling the men most likely to assist him—most notably Rupert and his brother, Maurice. Rupert went to France, where he served in the English troops fighting for France against Spain; wounded in 1647, he returned to the court in exile, where he quarrelled with the queen's closest advisors—whose counsel hurried her husband to the block in 1649. As soon as Rupert recovered his health, he led an expedition to Ireland, where he operated more as a pirate than a soldier, then fled ahead of the English navy to Portugal, where he resumed his piratical activities until 1650, when the English fleet trapped his ships in the River Tagus.

In typical heroic fashion, Rupert escaped, to attack English and Spanish ships in the Mediterranean and on the African coast. In 1652 he sailed to the Americas, but found the colonists there reluctant to join the royalist cause—not surprisingly, considering that many Puritans had gone to America as much to escape royalist oppression as to improve their lot. In 1653, after Maurice was lost in a storm, Rupert joined Charles's court in Paris. He left for Germany in hope of finding employment, but found nothing to do except quarrel with those who should have been his closest friends and allies.

After the Restoration in 1660, Charles II gave Rupert a post in the Navy, where he served honourably in the wars against Holland and made important contributions to the exploration of the New World. His career was a fine example of the ways that personal, family and national ties intertwined with the great events of the times, especially in making nobles into quasi-mercenaries. In Rupert's case, he was able to make a career as a soldier while serving his family's interests. Not every exile was so fortunate.

Ormonde

James Butler (1610-88), the Earl of Ormonde, was among the most prominent royalist leaders who survived to enjoy the Restoration of the Stuarts to the throne. An Anglo-Irish nobleman of Catholic ancestry but Protestant persuasion, he had joined the hard-fisted administration of the

Duke of Strafford in 1633, and was deeply involved in the confiscation of Catholic lands and their distribution to English immigrants. When civil war broke out in Ireland in 1641, he successfully held off both Parliamentary and Confederation forces. In 1646 he almost brought the royalists and Catholics together, but was thwarted by the papal legate, Rinuccini, who had brought arms, ammunition and bad advice to Ireland. Frustrated by his feuding allies, Ormonde came to terms with Parliament, saying that he preferred the rule of English rebels to Irish ones.

The execution of Charles I in 1649 put Ormonde back in royalist ranks, this time trying to hold Ireland for Charles II (1630-85). The Catholic Confederation made him their general, but never trusted him. The massacre committed by Cromwell's besieging forces at Drogheda demoralised Ormonde's troops momentarily, but left the Irish with another bitter memory of Protestant oppression. In 1650 Ormonde's Protestant troops deserted en masse to Cromwell; following that, the Catholics rejected him as well, causing him to go into exile at Charles II's court in France.

Cromwell's army was no longer composed of psalm-singing Puritans, but of rough conscripts hammered into a truly professional army; he ended the war by using methods that memory and myth burned into Irish consciousness forever. Altogether, 7,500 soldiers were paid in Irish land, the original inhabitants moved west to counties where, as one of Cromwell's officials put it, there was not enough water to drown a man, nor wood to hang him from, nor dirt to bury him.

Ormonde returned to Ireland in 1661 as Lord Lieutenant, quickly making himself highly unpopular among all factions. His efforts to govern with moderation offended Protestants, his attempt to govern at all offended Catholics. In 1670, a year after being removed from office, he was briefly kidnapped by the infamous Colonel Blood, but managed to escape.[4]

In 1677 Ormonde returned to power, only to be criticised by the Irish for being too harsh and too English, and by the English for being too lenient and too Irish. In 1682 the king enhanced his title to duke, but never again gave him a significant role in the government. Although Charles II allowed Ormonde's enemies at court to attack him, Ormonde remained loyal to the Stuart monarch. James II's efforts to put Catholics in positions of authority, was another matter. The earl disagreed, but he died before the contest reached its climax in what Whigs called the Glorious Revolution.

Another Irish soldier who did well was the Protestant Murrough O'Brien (1618-74), whose military career had begun in the Spanish army in Italy. In 1641 he took command of the Protestants in Munster, successfully fending off all opponents. Snubbed by Charles I in 1644, O'Brien went over to the Parliamentary party; reinforced, he ravaged Catholic lands until the execution of the king persuaded him to change sides again. He almost saved the day when Ormonde was routed outside Dublin in 1649, but the desertion of his troops in 1650 doomed his cause. Four years after joining the court of Charles II in exile, he was named the Earl of Inchiquin, then fought in the French armies in Italy and Spain. During these years he converted to Roman Catholicism, a choice that made him unsuitable for high office after the Restoration. He recovered his estates, but aside from leading an expedition to Portugal was never entrusted with military power or administrative duties.

Whig and Tory

For a short period under Cromwell, Brendan Simms notes, England had ceased to be the laughing stock of Europe, but when Charles II became king, English foreign policy returned to its Stuart traditions—inept dithering in public, privately accommodating to French wishes. Parliament was pleased to have the civil war finally over and, once the surviving 'regicides' (the men who voted to execute Charles I) were beheaded, everyone agreed that the awkward episode should be forgotten; but Parliament was not happy that the kingdom's strategic interests seemed to be guided by whim and wishes rather than taking a stand against the more pressing international threat—at this moment Louis XIV, who was pushing into Germany. It was not a matter that anyone wanted to fight about, or risk going to the block for, but there were muttered private complaints, then public ones. Few were unhappy about the overseas gains in India and America, but there were warnings that victory in the Dutch wars would deliver the continent to the new national enemy—France. And what was Charles II doing? Sending troops to aid Louis XIV!

Charles backed away from his pro-French policy in 1678, redirecting the troops on the continent to support the Dutch. A less charming monarch could not have talked his way out of such inconsistencies.

The Restoration had banished Puritan restraints and returned the 'Merry' to England, but it could not end the rivalries between individuals, families and parties that are natural to human beings and which flourish in times of civil conflict. Charles II was able to balance the Presbyterians, the Episcopalians and the Catholics even to the extent of providing himself with mistresses from each party who could entreat favours of the king (usually at the moment he entreated favours of them). Two great parties grew up at this time, the Whigs (generally favouring Parliament and the army exercising power) and the Tories (favoring more royal authority). Left out were Quakers, Baptists, sectarians and Catholics, all of whom were barred from government employment—though some Catholics were managing to make their way into the army and into the courts.

According to Robert Foster, *Modern Ireland*, the last Irish guerrillas were known as *Toraidhe* (outlaws), giving birth to the name of royalist sympathizers—Tory. Thus, the name was not a compliment, and did not mean the most established ranks of the upper classes. The Whigs were dominant, but Tories like John Churchill, the future Duke of Marlborough, demonstrated through loyalty to Stuart monarchs that the party could be trusted to put nation ahead of religion.

Irish and Scottish Catholics who resented the system had few choices— to conform, to avoid making their opinions known, to go to jail, or to go into exile. Those who went into exile still often had only one means of supporting themselves—war. By becoming mercenary soldiers they could both earn a living and develop those skills that would be useful when the opportunity came to return home and assist their countrymen in expelling the hereditary English foe. For their generation there was to be only one great opportunity left—when Whigs invited William III of Holland to overthrow what they saw as the tyrannical government of James II.

The Revolution of 1688

Charles II had governed England cautiously between the Restoration in 1660 and his death in 1685, but his brother and heir, James II, did not. Already an aged man by the standards of the time, fifty-two, James felt the need for speed in returning the land to royal absolutism and the Catholic Church; and the birth of a healthy son, James Francis Edward Stuart (1688-1766, the Old Pretender), after many years of stillborn or short-lived children gave him more reason for haste.[5] James II's zeal, fanatics in his most intimate circles pushing him to ever more radical actions, and French gains in the war against Holland, so alarmed the Whig leaders of parliament and the military that in 1688 they invited the king's elder daughter Mary and her Dutch husband, William III of Orange, to occupy the 'vacant' throne. William organised the largest seaborne invasion in European history before D-Day. This was a mercenary army composed of myriad nations, including English and Scottish soldiers in the Dutch army. Once William was ashore, James lacked sufficient men to drive him away. More carefully put, perhaps, James lacked men he could trust to fight. Moreover, his fear of being seen as a French puppet made him refuse Louis XIV's offer of troops when they might have made all the difference. When James fled to France, he had every hope of returning to power again—and those who had betrayed him understood that, in that event, their necks would be severed or stretched.

Thus began the long internal contest of William III (his title in England luckily corresponding exactly with that in Holland) against those Stuart supporters known as Jacobites, a contest that intertwined with the wars against Louis XIV. There were two great battlegrounds—Flanders (in the Spanish Netherlands) and Ireland. The war in Flanders lasted until 1714, that in Ireland until 1691. Two famous sieges summarize the historical memory of this half-century—'Derry' for the Protestants, 'Drogheda' for the Catholics.

William III had many advantages in the Irish campaign. He had control of the seas; he could count on the Protestants in the Pale and Ulster who saw him as their only hope from destruction at the hands of enemies who had a different culture, a different religion, and often a different language; and he had a decisive advantage in the quality of his mercenary officers and troops—Dutch, Danes, Finns, French Huguenots, Germans, even a few Poles and Greeks. There were good English and Scot regiments, but not many; the royal army had long been so neglected that the English once again deserved the general reputation of being poor soldiers.

Louis XIV sent 8,000 men to help James. It should have been a larger army, but an act of exceptional cynicism—simultaneously declaring himself a defender of Catholicism and sending much of his fleet to the Mediterranean to tie down Hapsburg ships that otherwise could have been used against the Ottomans, then invading Germany to strike the emperor in the back—deprived him of the navy that could have prevented William from transporting an army to Ulster, and then of regiments that might have brought victory in Ireland.

Perhaps Louis was justified in his caution. A year later James, once again, demonstrated his political and military incompetence. In the spring of 1689, when the French navy had temporary control of the Irish waters, James decided against sending his Irish-French army to Scotland. It was his best chance to prevent William from establishing himself there, but James missed it, choosing instead to besiege Derry. Surely many sympathizers would have joined him in Scotland, men who doubted that the small force of Catholic Highlanders raised by the Earl of Dundee had any chance of success without a royal presence?[6] The doubters were wrong, at least in the short term. In July, Dundee, with the help of a few Irish volunteers, defeated a larger army of Dutch and Lowland Scots at Killiecrankie commanded by Hugh MacKay (1640-92). This was an unexpected achievement. MacKay was an experienced soldier—he had gone to France in 1660 in the army Charles II had sent to aid Louis XIV; in 1669-72 he had been in Venetian service, then back in the French army until witnessing Louis XIV's religious bigotry persuaded him that he was serving the wrong cause. After resigning his commission, he became an officer in a Scottish regiment of the Dutch army. In 1685 James II called this unit home, only to find the men unwilling to fight for him. MacKay had led the van of William's invasion force, then, as a staunch Presbyterian, had been assigned to command his troops in Scotland.

Killiecrankie was one of the Highlanders' finest moments. The charge of the Camerons had swept away MacKay's much larger army, which had no time to put bayonets into the muzzles of their weapons. But the costs were high—not as much in the number of clansmen falling, but in Dundee being slain. No similarly gifted general appeared to take his place, and a month later the Jacobite forces were beaten at Dunkeld. Though heavily outnumbering their opponents, the Jacobites were unable to bring this advantage to bear in the house to house fighting. With William's army approaching, the Highlanders chose to melt into the hills. Thereafter, the Catholic chiefs were ever less important in Scottish politics.

The Irish, meanwhile, were proving themselves even more inept fighters. They had exceptionally fine cavalrymen—the product of generations of comparative wealth and practice in the exercise of authority. The steeplechase, growing out of the practice of racing cross-country from one country church to another, was excellent training for such horsemen. Discipline, however, was lacking. While Irish horsemen behaved as though they were at a race, the infantry was prone to extremes of emotion—either their attacks were bold beyond their generals' wishes or they fled in panic. The troops' hunger for loot made it almost impossible for generals to conduct a campaign or pursue a victory. For James II, this suggested that he fight at the earliest opportunity, before his army melted away from desertions or took off on foraging raids; fighting at the head of undisciplined men was preferable to being unable to fight at all. But he knew that undisciplined troops would be easily cut to pieces in toe-to-toe fights against professional units, after which the surviving soldiers would desert. Whatever choice he made seemed fated to end badly.

William's campaign began in Belfast, which Lord Macaulay had described as the cleanest and most brilliantly lit city in Ireland, the only city 'in which the traveller is not disgusted by the loathsome aspect and odour of long lines of human dens far inferior to the dwellings which, in happier countries, are provided for cattle'. Belfast had been reduced to three hundred inhabitants, and while Ireland was a fertile land, it had been blasted by war—the population fearful, most hungry, many having fled their homes, many in prison. It was only a short march to the beautiful valley of the Boyne where James's army waited, and there was no reason to delay.

The Battle of the Boyne (1 July 1690) was almost over before it began, when Jacobite cannons, brought to the river's edge without being seen, opened fire on William's camp, wounding him in the right shoulder. Had the king not been able to rise and ride to all parts of his encampment, demonstrating that he was well able to command, the troops might have been too demoralised to fight. Already appeals such as one in John Gilbert, *A Jacobite Narrative*, had been addressed to William's men: 'Next to the honour of never engaging in a bad cause, there is nothing braver than to desert it … To call in multitudes of strangers and foreigners, of desperate fortunes and divers nations, who are contriving your slavery, together with the invaders of our country, the Danes … is so shameful that it cannot be honourable.' This argument would have had little effect on William's Dutch and Huguenot troops, but his death would have been fatal to his cause.

The French, having observed the quality of their Irish allies, were more concerned with protecting their route of retreat than to confront William's flanking force, and because James had left the field of battle when the mass of Irish foot ran away, there were fewer casualties than at many another great battle. Still, there were sufficient heroes on both sides for a mythology to develop around them. The Battle of the Boyne produced future British commanders such as Henri de Massue, Marquis de Ruvigny (1648-1720). A protégé of the great French marshal, Turenne, he was rewarded for his service in Ireland by being named Earl of Galway and later given commands in the Spanish Netherlands, Italy and Spain.

It is enlightening to read the words of the Jacobites themselves regarding their failure at the Battle of the Boyne. Though surviving documents are relatively few in number, John Gilbert's *Jacobite Narrative* presents clearly his party's vision of the world—Charles I was 'murdered' by Parliament, their enemies were 'mechanics' and 'tradesmen', and the noble leaders of the royal armies missed great opportunities to deliver strong blows against the Protestants and to rally royalist and Catholics against William III. He lamented that Jacobite commanders were mistrusted by their troops for putting them at risk foolishly: 'This is a frequent fault in commanding officers, who value the lives of their soldiers not so much as some men do their dogs.' Moreover, references to 'loyal men' (implying volunteers) were balanced by accusations of 'gaming, drinking and whoreing' that distracted the troops from mastering the skills of warfare. On the other side were foreigners, such as the 8,000 Danes led by the Duke of Württemberg[7], reinforced later by Germans, Dutch, French, Scots and Irish Protestants— 'well paid, well clothed, well armed, with numerous artillery'. These mercenaries outnumbered the Irish forces and the 'French volunteers' considerably, 50,000 to 35,000. James, so a prominent Jacobite reported, could have levelled the numbers by calling up 15,000 militiamen armed with pikes, scythes and occasional firearms, but he declined to do it. Better to fight with proper troops or, at least, troops that had proper weapons.

While religion was important in defining allegiances, it was not decisive for everyone. Protestants fought for James, and William's elite corps of Dutch Blue Guard (*Blaauwe Garde*) were Catholics.

The Battle of the Boyne was a one-sided affair, more a retreat gone wrong than a combat. James was not even a skilled commander, and the Irish had needed a genius. When the French sailed away, the Jacobite army dispersed into winter quarters (usually going home), while the army of William III continued its offensive until winter actually arrived.

Nor was James a skilful diplomat. Earlier, in 1688, he had refused the offer of a French army to help resist the Dutch invasion. It was a logical decision, since patriotic Englishmen would have been outraged to see French troops on the island, but it persuaded his patrons in France that he lacked the strength of will to be a king. The Irish, looking askance at James's brass coinage, concluded the same. When James's army reassembled in 1691, his generals argued over strategy and tactics; this resulted in an almost exclusively defensive strategy, hoping to wear down the Whig resolve. In the hard-fought sieges that followed the disaster at the Boyne, the Irish fought better, but were still not equal to the foreign troops employed by William III. Some talented Irish officers died in battle, others of disease, and their successors could not coordinate cavalry and infantry, nor prevent panicked retreats. Jacobites could only ask yet again, why were Irish troops so formidable on foreign battlefields, but so impotent in defence of their own country?

As John Gilbert sorrowfully concluded, 'Misfortune accompanied them in carrying on the war, and misfortune sticks to them in the conclusion.' The surrender agreement had allowed the French and Irish units to take ship peacefully and leave the island—the flight of the *Wild Geese*. William's generals agreed to respect the Catholic religion, to allow rebels to retain their lands and to practise their professions, and for a general amnesty. These promises were not kept. But neither did the Irish acknowledge William as the lawful king of the realm—the Jacobites now denounced their countrymen who swore the oath of allegiance to William and insisted that Ireland was a separate kingdom and that James and his descendants were their true kings.

Gilbert made two concluding observations. The first regarded those Catholic soldiers who agreed to serve in William's army. Initially, only 1,400 were to be retained, in two units; then all units were to be disbanded, after which five companies of one hundred men were raised and sent to the Hapsburg emperor, where all but a few quickly died of the plague and other diseases.[8] The second observation was that the King of France erred greatly in not supporting James more fully, since the alliance against him could not have been sustained without English money. Had he overthrown William III at that time, he would have prevailed everywhere.

As it was, Louis XIV had to take on all the rest of Western Europe, Bavaria and Spain excepted, and he lost.

Religious Fervour Run Amok

It has long been the practice to equate partisan feelings in Ireland and Scotland with religious affiliation. There is some truth to this simplification, as is true with all efforts to explain much in few words. But it is also misleading. Once again, a good guide is Lord Macaulay. Despite his distance from our own age and modern political sympathies, no one was better at explaining how complex and obscure passions interacted with the politics of William III's days.[9] The 'Glorious Revolution' had removed one religious hierarchy in England and Scotland without immediately establishing another. The result was an awkward situation, with many Jacobites refusing to take the oath of allegiance to William and Mary—thus earning the name *non-juror*. Radical Presbyterians also refused the oath on the grounds that no one churchman is superior to any other, causing Macaulay to believe that if William had been overthrown, they would have resisted James II with equal passion. Both parties defied William III, and each despised the other. Compromisers were called Erastians, thus equating the moderate Dutch theologian with their Dutch king. It was not a compliment.

To make matters worse, in 1688 William III had winked at the escape of James II, who had been taken prisoner briefly. This was a practical policy, since William had no desire to put his father-in-law either in prison or on trial. But it meant that many who hated James II's tyranny now regarded the new king as a traitor to both country and God. The 1689 Act of Toleration extended religious rights to Baptists, Quakers and

118

Congregationalists, but not to Roman Catholics. High church Episcopalians thought that his Parliament had it backwards, and several bishops, including the Archbishop of Canterbury, refused to recognize William as the rightful monarch. The Bill of Rights, which limited greatly what William could do as king, angered his enemies again by passing over James II and his issue in the succession in favour of Mary's sister, Anne, but it allowed the king to concentrate on the war in Flanders.

Scotland was not so easily managed as the English Parliament. Civil war there remained a distinct possibility, and the king's men were lucky in dispersing Jacobite resistance quickly. It helped that William was willing to bribe wavering lords into peaceable habits. As Macaulay noted, 'a sum which would hardly be missed in the English treasury was immense in the estimation of the needy barons of the North'; that is, small bribes by English standards were very effective in Scotland. After that the tendency of people to give way to the stronger party, and the fact that the majority of any population does not care what the outcome of such disputes is, made it possible for William to impose a compromise settlement that pleased few but satisfied many—he removed the 'non-juring' Episcopal bishops, thereby ending the primacy of that church in Scotland; he replaced the hostile Anglican clerics and gave religious supremacy to the Presbyterian church. By choosing the lesser of two evils, the king assured himself of domestic peace, even if he lacked universal love and respect—those came only after the first French attack on English soil made temporary patriots even of James's most fervent friends.

Lord Macaulay notes that James II had issued a proclamation filled with threats so vile that many of his adherents believed it was a Protestant forgery. James promised vengeance on a long list of enemies, with implications that anyone who served William's government in any capacity would be added to it. He said that he would, in effect, revive Judge Jeffreys's notorious judicial tyranny, only employing it more widely and thoroughly.[10] But this was not unexpected—there was no reconciling the Jacobites with each other any more than their leader was ready to forgive his enemies. As a result, practical men had to overcome their distaste for the new government and hope that time would eventually bridge the gap between the parties.

As the wrath of the Jacobite fanatics changed from attacking William III to accusing each other of crimes and errors, real and imagined, rabid Catholics, Episcopalians and Calvinists could not join together to oppose any monarch with a claim to Stuart blood until the Hanoverian dynasty came over from Germany in 1714.[11] George I (1660-1727) was a descendant of James I, a doughty warrior and a Protestant. But he was a foreigner. Worse, he was a German.

The problem was that James Francis Edward Stuart was by then a foreigner, too. His name was familiar and some prominent Jacobites had visited him in France, but he understood little about the people he claimed to rule.

To make matters even more complicated, the Pope supported the Hapsburgs against Louis XIV. This made the popes of this era into allies— once removed—of the new Protestant king from Hanover. James II and his son, the Old Pretender, remained on sufficiently good terms with the Popes to be buried in the Vatican, but not so close that the Holy Fathers would have rejoiced at seeing William III and Anne, the key figures in the anti-French coalition, in their tombs.

William's successes after the Boyne did not bring immediate peace, but they led to the Treaty of Limerick in 1691. As noted earlier, since William could not pacify the entire island quickly, and the divided Irish could not drive him away, it was agreed that the Irish army would sail for France; the understanding was that William would eventually withdraw most of his troops to Flanders, where they were sorely needed. Though this would not bring real peace to Ireland, it at least ended open warfare and the exactions that the armies were making on the civilian population.

The Wild Geese joined the earlier Flight of the Earls in Irish folklore and music—that sad longing for home that could never be satisfied, that combination of anger and fatalism that marked subsequent generations of emigrants. These memories fuelled unhappiness in Ireland until our own days, and deeply affected culture and politics in America and Australia and other lands.

Suspicion and hatred led to arson and assassination on one side, repression and retaliation on the other. William, seeing that the Irish soil was sown with the seeds of new resentments, resorted to traditional means of holding the country—encouraging loyalists to emigrate there. Soon Lowland Scots fleeing famine in their homeland were a majority in Ulster; most quickly lost their clan identity—all becoming simply Scots. Their situation being precarious, they expressed their loyalty to William of Orange and began calling themselves Orangemen. Because immigration had been only a temporary solution to their economic woes and they knew that the Irish would never agree to their living peacefully in Ulster, many of these immigrants moved on to America.

Ireland was not alone in having Jacobites. Many remained in England, some openly expressing their sentiments, some plotting secretly, and some in close contact with the 'king over the water' in France and with conspirators in Scotland. Crown officials kept track of potential traitors, though inefficiently, and made lists of exiles serving in the French army so that they could charge them with treason if they ever fell into their hands.

Scotland soon suffered an unexpected financial disaster. Much like the French public pouring huge sums into colonial ventures that promised huge returns—a failed promise that should have been a warning—in 1698 hard-headed Scots put perhaps as much as 20% of the moveable wealth of the nation into the Darien colony, then sent 2,800 settlers to organise trade between the Caribbean Sea and the Pacific Ocean. The Spanish attacked, the mosquitoes swarmed, and King William ordered his English subjects not to assist the enterprise. The fiasco left Scotland so economically exhausted that there was little resistance to the union with England in 1707.

Scots and Irish mercenary soldiers did not disappear as one might have expected. Instead, they became more important than ever—the Scots and Scots-Irish in the British army, Catholic Irish on the Continent.

Connolly, in *Contested Island*, notes dryly that as an economically backward area, Ireland was a natural recruiting ground for soldiers. Military migration was thus only one aspect of the long outward movement of people fleeing poverty and seeking opportunity. Irish soldiers, like Scots, entertained themselves with songs—mostly sad—that later became standard entertainment in pubs and models for later protest ballads.

Clan loyalties remained strong in Scotland until the disastrous defeat at Culloden in 1746. Eventually, realism set in. Scots settled for their own parliament, their own sports teams, and nostalgic tourists from North America. Until 2015, of course, when the vote on independence narrowly failed.

The Celtic Fringe of Britain is different from the tribal districts of Central Asia, but we think so partly because we are more acquainted with its history and culture. Emigrants from the British Isles remember the stories of their ancestors' trials and triumphs, often bearing grudges more fervently than the current generation living in the Celtic Fringe. Lastly, the methods adopted by Britons to subdue the peoples of Celtic Fringe are much like those we have seen elsewhere.

Machiavelli said that there were three ways a prince could subdue a conquered land: First, go and live there himself. That was a maxim that would work for any land with cities and creature comforts, but not wild frontiers. Second, establish colonies there. That was done in Ireland, with mixed results. Third, either pamper the natives or destroy them. Neither seemed practical, but historians are divided as to whether English policy tended too far toward one extreme or the other.

Machiavelli's general rule is to allow conquered peoples to maintain their traditions and religions. That is a maxim that the modern world should keep in mind.

Equally important is the difference between the ways that democracies and clans remember leaders who fail politically and militarily. In the former such men are seldom commemorated by statues and songs, but clans will forgive any charismatic leader and even make him the centre of the national mythology.

The Stuarts were handsome, cultivated, and well-spoken. That, in the eyes of Scottish patriots, more than compensated for their poor judgment, their stubbornness, and their bad luck.

1. We know much about the life of mercenaries from the memoirs of Robert Monro (c1606-c1680), who told of the adventures and sufferings of Scottish soldiers in Europe from 1626 to 1637. John Miller, *Swords for Hire*, covers Monro's career on the continent, but not his more controversial campaigns in 1640s Ireland as a parliamentary general.

2. Contemporaries (and some modern historians) attributed some of the blame for Charles's many disastrous political policies on his wife, the aunt of Louis XIV. Henrietta Maria (1609-69) advocated pro-Catholic and pro-French policies, a programme that would be remembered by her sons, Charles II (1630-85) and James II (1633-1701). A daughter, Mary (1631-60), married William II of Orange, and her son, William III (1650-1702), became king of England in 1689, but his claim on the English throne lay less in his Stuart ancestry than in his wife, Mary, being the daughter of James II. Another daughter, Henrietta (1644-70), married the bi-sexual brother of the French king, Philip; some contemporaries believed that Louis XIV was the actual father of her two daughters.

3. Timothy Dalton played Rupert (1619-82), in the movie *Cromwell* (1970). The movie takes liberties with chronology, events, the depiction of battles, and dialogue, but it has unforgettable portrayals of Charles I, Cromwell, Rupert, and the future Charles II. It won an Oscar for costume design.

4. Thomas Blood (1618-80), a veteran of Cromwell's army, had gone into exile in 1660, but later returned to England. Colonel Blood was a familiar figure in London's high society and at court, well-known as a scandalous and romantic adventurer. Ormonde should have been flattered to have been in his company, even for so short a time.

5. The role of James II's queen, Mary of Modena (1658-1718) was important, especially her admiration of Louis XIV's autocratic government and listening to Jesuit advisors. James escaped her forceful personality by the traditional means of keeping mistresses. One of these, Arabella Churchill, was Marlborough's sister. Their son, James Fitzjames, the Duke of Berwick, became a French marshal. The Tombses, *That Sweet Enemy*, note that Louis XIV's warning against efforts to overthrow James II was exactly what the king's enemies needed to demonstrate the existence of a secret Bourbon-Stuart alliance, when in reality James II was much more independent than Charles II had been. Louis XIV's revocation of the Edict of Nantes, stripping the Protestants of the guarantee of religious freedom, had brought a flood of refugees warning about the Sun King's ominous threats to Protestants everywhere. This managed to overcome a generation-long memory of commercial rivalry and war between Holland and England. That same act was very popular in France.

6. 'Bonnie Dundee' (John Graham of Glaverhouse, 1648-89) had served with English troops sent by Charles II to aid Louis XIV against the Dutch, then in the army of William of Orange; returning to Scotland in 1678, he was given the responsibility of suppressing the outdoor meetings of the Covenanters, a task he performed with such enthusiasm as to earn the nickname 'Bluidy Clavers'. The Tombses, *That Sweet Enemy*, note that French policy, now and later, was to create as much distraction to the English as possible at the lowest cost; that is, if English soldiers were tied down in Ireland, it would be difficult to deploy a large army on the continent. Both armies in Ireland were led by Frenchmen—Schomberg, a Huguenot,

for William III, Lauzun, a Catholic, for James II. Moreover, neither of the monarchs had complete control over his navy, which often behaved as though they were independent entities.

7. Württemberg had been ravaged by French armies in 1688 (and would be so again in 1692) Eberhard Ludwig (1676-1733) was an absolute ruler typical of the era. His small territory was sufficiently rich to keep him in palaces (Ludwigsburg), mistresses (he married one) and hunting masters, and to maintain an army that larger neighbours considered worth hiring.

8. Christopher Duffy, *The Army of Maria Theresa*, says that the 'Irish soldiers arrived in Austria like creatures from outer space'. Many were attracted to Prague, where Irish Franciscans assisted them in maintaining contacts with friends and family at home. Thirteen became field marshals.

9. Macaulay's lack of prestige today may be partly accounted for by his *History of England* (1849) being so little read, and partly because he believed in maximum freedom for the individual and minimum authority for the government. While he favoured Whigs over Tories and rationality over fanaticism, he did not hesitate to criticize early Whigs for their persecution of Catholics, their tolerance of slavery, and their easy adoption of the vices and corruption of their foes. No one ever had to puzzle out who were his heroes and who his villains. He was never at a loss for a strong opinion on any subject, or unable to pen a memorable phrase.

10. The Bloody Assizes of 1685 had condemned hundreds to hanging and burning, and many to transportation to the Indies as slaves.

11. Alexander McCall-Smith made fun of this characteristic in *The Unbearable Lightness of Scones* (2010). It might be said that no one can understand Scotland without reading Burns and McCall-Smith.

Chapter 7

The New Armies of the 1700s

The flintlock musket was the outward symbol of the new armies that were appearing in western Europe in the late 1600s; the weapon was expensive, but it was safer and more convenient than the old matchlock—it also allowed soldiers to stand closer together and thereby pour a heavier fire on opposing troops; it was also more easily fitted with the bayonet, which was soon considered the queen of battle.

Another symbol was the new uniform. Though the colour was far from *uniform* yet, the trend was toward outfitting the soldiers with identical shirts and pants, a stiff frock coat, heavy boots, and mitred hats. The hats made the soldiers seem taller, and they certainly required them to stand straighter—which made them more imposing to any enemy, and the improved posture gave them more self-confidence. Certainly they were better prepared for fighting in cold and wet weather, and when it was too hot, the frocks could be piled onto carts to be carried to the evening campsite, along with the knapsacks that soldiers carried until immediately before combat.

There were also more impressive fortresses, stout structures made of brick and stone, with successive lines of defence and well-protected cannon that could sweep each killing zone. Each fortress had barracks for soldiers and supply bunkers in case of siege or orders to outfit troops hurrying into the field. No commander in his right mind would order an immediate assault on such a place, and few wanted to leave his army half-unemployed and subject to disease and discontent while starving the defenders out. Still, since it was impossible to ignore fortresses, every campaign could easily end in a murderous assault on the most weakened part of the defences, a *storm* that might end in piles of dead and wounded attackers or the slaughter of defenders who were unable to escape or surrender.

Siege tactics were universally understood, so that once trench lines and tunnels had reached a point from which an assault was possible, any trained observer could judge whether or not the fortress could be defended successfully. At that time the defending commander would have to decide whether to sacrifice valuable soldiers in vain or to surrender the place and march away 'with honours'. The attacking commander similarly wanted to avoid losing men, and an essentially intact fortress was more useful than one which had been heavily damaged in pitched battle.

Improvements in artillery were obvious—better gun carriages, mortars for sieges, and heavy cannon for battering static defences. The largest of these weapons still adorn military museums in Europe and the Americas, and are found at many of the historic sites maintained for visitors and school children. Field artillery tended to be melted down and the metal reused.

Roads, bridges and canals were better, too. Though many were constructed to facilitate military operations, civilians did not hesitate to use them as well. Trees planted on the south side of roads allowed for travel in the shade, and public wells kept men and beasts from dehydrating. As transport costs went down, general prosperity went up. Government officials and economists realised that this commerce could be converted into tax monies that would subsidise royal expenses—the military, palaces and mistresses.[1]

There was also an equally significant change underway that Kenneth Chase described in *Firearms, a Global History*—a greater emphasis on discipline and drill. Earlier, few commanders had the time or money to train recruits fully—permanent forces were needed for road work, building fortifications, and guard duty; and when an army was needed, regular troops were supplemented by recruits and hurried to the battlefield with minimum additional drill. Training too often involved firing expensive gunpowder, exhausting horses, wearing out uniforms, and disrupting the peasantry. Therefore, as Robert Citino in *The German Way of War* and Christopher Clark in *Iron Kingdom* note, field exercises were rare. Even Friedrich Wilhelm von Hohenzollern (1620-88), the Prussian ruler known the Great Elector, was too budget-conscious to send his magnificently trained soldiers out to practise in the rain and mud.

There was also a new emphasis on developing a professional officer class. The most highly born nobles had always insisted on being given commands equal to those of their ancestors; even when still junior officers they were allowed to wear the most magnificent uniforms, prance on the best mounts available, and take their pick of the prettiest girls. Those who commanded regiments also received royal subsidies that allowed them to maintain their expensive lifestyles, even though this came at the cost of regimental preparedness; and kings looked the other way because they were dependent on the goodwill of the aristocracy. Often young nobles demonstrated great courage; however, they could be the despair of generals who wanted their orders obeyed, not merely followed when proud subordinates found them convenient and did not seem to be an affront to their status. Nobles tended to think for themselves on those occasions they chose to think, but they had a tendency to forget what they were supposed to think. Hence, when an opportunity presented itself for some damn-fool act of bravery, they did it. Self-control was rare. Moreover, it was not easy for them to identify with the soldiers—social classes did not mingle, partly because common soldiers tended to be, well, common; and partly because familiarity might breed contempt, making the soldiers doubt the officers' ability. Still, nobles made the better officers than equally well-trained men from the gentry or commercial classes because they had grown up expecting to give orders and to be obeyed, and soldiers generally accepted that as the natural order of the world.

Leading the way in by-passing the upper nobility and mercenaries was Prussia, a state whose rulers had never been reluctant to hire foreign officers and integrate them into the minor nobility. The Great Elector had employed the minor aristocracy known as *Junkers* as officers and administrators, giving them little choice in the matter—no more than he did the apple-sellers in Berlin to choose whether to knit or not while waiting for customers. Work, work, work was his answer to the region's lack of natural resources, just as hurry, hurry, hurry made the army formidable on the march and in the attack.

If middle-class youths or minor nobility in Germany or Russia had the potential to be good officers, this meant a potential lessened reliance on foreign mercenaries with military experience. There had always been an aura of suspicion about foreigners who were often both arrogant and ambitious, who did not speak the local language well and who did not understand the nuances of social conventions. This provided opportunities for young men such as Napoleon Bonaparte to receive the training they would then put to use after the noble officers fled France rather than risk a shave from the national razor—the guillotine.

Multinational Austria remained the most welcoming to foreigners, followed by the minor states in Italy where the rulers were often foreigners themselves, and Russia, where the boyars thought that every new idea was foolishness if not heresy.

Paralleling these trends was a growing awareness in all classes that everyone belonged to a nation rather than merely being subjects of a distant ruler. Historians tend to associate this process with the French Revolution, which made many Italians, Spaniards and Germans believe that they, too, were members of great nations. Oddly, in a sense, this awareness of national identity was appearing at the same time that a new international culture was spreading across Europe. As summarised in *Matchlocks to Flintlocks*, 'As France came to replace Spain as the dominant nation in Western Europe, the French language and French customs spread rapidly into the neighbouring states. To hold one's head up in polite society meant having it full of French ideas.'

This *Lingua Franca* made it easier for ideas to circulate. Some innovations in military theory and practice were widely accepted; some ideas, especially those connected with experimental science, were both exciting and safe; others, those associated with what we call the Enlightenment, had mixed receptions—traditionalists were outraged, while the younger set laughed at the humour without necessarily adopting the underlying philosophy. Life at the upper levels of society became less serious, even frivolous, to an extent unimagined before. Religion became formalised—with intellectuals and leaders of society making withering comments about institutionalised ignorance and superstition, the foolishness of the unwashed masses and ignorant country folk who still took miracles seriously, hypocritical priests and pedantic schoolmasters. Yet, when plagues raged through a kingdom, everyone prayed fervently and later raised monuments to God and His saints for ending the suffering. Superstition and credulity thus mixed easily with sophistication and cynicism.

To the extent that the Enlightenment meant abandoning old methods in favour of new ones to resolve practical problems, it had a profound impact on the military arts. First, there was the introduction of an effective supply system to replace foraging for food and fodder. Providing cooks and brewers assured that all units were fed, avoided dispersing soldiers every afternoon to look for food and fodder, and made it more certain that everyone would be present when roll was called the next morning. It also made the peasantry much happier, since there were fewer thefts and rapes; and villages which were not pillaged could be more effectively given lists of supplies to be delivered (or else).

John Lynn, in *Women, Armies and Warfare*, noted that this resulted in the almost total disappearance of camp followers. This made it possible for armies to become larger, since the resources once needed to feed and shelter women and children could support additional soldiers. Also, the sexual license that probably drew some men into military service was no longer present, making it easier to avoid quarrels over women and women's quarrels with other women. Wives and whores (cohabiting women) gave way to prostitutes, a somewhat easier class to discipline.

Officers began to look upon their commands as a way to make money—charging soldiers for uniforms, medical care, retirement benefits and other costs that often ate up much of their slender incomes. Soldiers no longer found desertion easy, and while recruits were often still technically volunteers, in practice communities were expected to provide their quotas.

The New Armies on the Frontier

The professional armies of the 1700s often found it difficult to defeat tribal forces in frontier regions. They enjoyed certain advantages—cannon that could shell fortresses that had rarely, if ever been captured, and greater numbers as well as more firepower. But it was not easy to get cannon into place before the enemy slipped away. Soldiers used to fighting in ranks were uncomfortable running after an escaping enemy, hampered by their clothing and gear and separated from their officers; also—like all human beings—they tended to panic when confronted by unexpected dangers.

Supplies were not always available. An army large enough to defeat a distant enemy might not be able to carry enough food, fodder and ammunition to sustain itself while penetrating the guerrillas' lairs, while one that was too small would be ambushed and destroyed. This was the Turkish experience with Montenegrins, in that army after army pressed into the mountains, past the piles of heads belonging to previous invaders, only to turn back in failure. If a Turkish commander was lucky he could bring the sultan a promise by the rebels not to harass his subjects in the future. Such promises meant little, but they might ward off the silken cord that was sent to strangle failed viziers.

Austrians used the Danube to float down supplies, just as the Russians did on rivers flowing to the Black Sea. Striking overland or into hill country meant proceeding without equipment, supplies, or foodstuffs that might soon be necessary.

Perhaps the best-known defeat of an army in this era was that of Major General Edward Braddock (1695-1755), the commander of British forces in North America at the beginning of what Americans call the French and Indian War. His career record was impeccable, as was his planning for the campaign to clear the French from the Upper Ohio River country where they had recently built a chain of forts. He began by asking for information and opinions from colonial governors, after which he devised a three-pronged offensive: one from New York toward the French fort on Lake Champaign; the Massachusetts militia against Fort Niagara; and himself leading two regiments of redcoats to Fort Duquesne at the confluence of the Ohio and Monongahela Rivers in Pennsylvania. Unfortunately, Braddock's only possible route lay through the rough mountains of the Appalachian chain that no British soldier had ever visited.

Braddock turned to knowledgeable Americans about what to expect in the heavy forests and narrow valleys. Could he, for example, take artillery and supply wagons? After all, it made little sense to reach Fort Duquesne without the means of blowing down its primitive walls.

He was told that he would have to build a road—Indian paths were little more than deer trails. Then he would have to rent horses and wagons. When Pennsylvania farmers proved reluctant to give up or even sell their valuable stock and equipment, Benjamin Franklin (a prominent newspaper publisher in Philadelphia, later American ambassador to France) persuaded them that if they did not offer what the British needed, Braddock would confiscate it. On the advice of the Governor of Virginia, Braddock made an aide-de-camp of a young officer, George Washington, relying heavily on his knowledge of the region and its native inhabitants.

Braddock hired many civilians to clear the trail, pulling out stumps and filling low places with sticks and dirt; relatively quickly he had a road over the most difficult passages, some sections corduroyed (covered with logs laid side by side). He managed to proceed almost within sight of his goal before he set aside his caution.

Braddock had been warned by colonials that the Indians were more dangerous than they seemed. Washington's own expedition to Fort Duquesne the previous year had ended with his camp surrounded and his men being picked off by sharpshooters until he surrendered; he achieved the release of his men only by signing a document in French that he could not read, effectively admitting guilt for 'assassinating' a French officer in battle. The episode was widely considered to have started the Great War for Empire, or the Seven Years War. All colonial governors had urged Braddock to modify linear tactics so that his men would not be shot down in their ranks without even seeing the enemy, but he apparently thought the Americans too cautious, perhaps even cowardly.

Braddock had been persuaded by the ease with which he had passed obvious ambush points that his redcoats had intimidated the enemy. When his van ran into waiting Frenchmen and Indians, it was quickly cut to pieces and he was wounded. As his panicked soldiers fell back on the main body, it was also quickly disoriented—a British officer giving the signal for volley fire was understood by the Indians as a good moment to take cover, then with the smoke still covering the disciplined line, to jump up, fire a shot, then take cover again to reload.

The Indians were, in truth, not extraordinary marksmen. The musket was not an accurate weapon even at the best of times, and long rifles were still rare. What the Indians excelled at was tracking and approaching a prey undetected. At close range a musket was much more effective than an arrow or spear, and the Indians knew how to get close enough to shoot, but without provoking a bayonet attack. All that saved Braddock's army was the Indians' reluctance to take casualties. If there had been enough Frenchmen to launch a final assault, the British expedition would have been wiped out. As it happened, George Washington arose from his sick bed to take command, organised his Virginians into a battle line behind trees and logs, and gained time for the redcoats to escape.

When Braddock was borne to safety, he gave command to George Washington, murmuring 'Who would have thought?' Washington ordered a retreat, successfully leading the army back over the road towards Virginia. When Braddock died on the fourth day of the withdrawal, Washington had him buried in the roadway, then marched the army across the site to prevent it being discovered and the body mutilated.[2] For the rest of Washington's life, he proudly wore the sash that the dying Braddock had given him, bearing it in every military engagement of his career.

The survival of the British and American troops was in no small part due to the Indian reluctance to pursue them. It was enough, apparently, to have driven the enemy away.

A year later, when a British column led by Henry Bouquet (1719-65) approached Fort Duquesne, his Scottish troops were so outraged at seeing kilts displayed along the road to mock them that their revenge would have been terrible. However, repayment for the massacre never came—the French withdrew, burning the fort behind them, and the Indians faded into the forest. The replacement, Fort Pitt, is today's Pittsburgh.

This behaviour was nothing unusual in frontier warfare. The best that 'civilised' armies could do in such circumstances was to attack whatever natives looked like those they were looking for.

By and large the British did not learn many lessons from this, nor did this harm them significantly—the rest of the 'French and Indian War' was fought between regular armies, with superior British numbers winning most of the battles. The Indians did not factor significantly in these combats—they were good scouts, but not highly motivated.

Who can blame the Indians for a lack of enthusiasm? It was clear that whoever won would be their new masters. The French were more likely to leave them alone for a while, but all the chiefs could do was muddle through—the long term prospect was dour. Even the Iroquois, the most dependable British ally, had little confidence that their future would in any way resemble their glorious past.

The British government made agreements with their recent enemies, but the Indians were doubtful that they would keep their hands off Indian lands or honour their promises to give payments to tribal leaders and permit them to buy gunpowder and alcohol at fair prices. Indeed, gifts to the tribes fell victim to budget cuts intended to help resolve the post-war debt crisis.

In one effort to honour promises to the Indians, the British government issued a decree forbidding Americans to cross the Appalachians, but since it would not station soldiers at the mountain passes to turn land-hungry settlers back, it was ineffective. This became another issue that made the American War for Independence popular among poor folk who saw those lands as their best chance for a better life. The Indians were too weak and too demoralised to do more than murder those who ventured too far into the forests—a practice that led Americans further to doubt that the British government had their best interests at heart.

Regimental Histories

We have good information about the organisation of armies in this era, but less about the individual units. For example, were ordinary soldiers taking increased responsibility to deal with comrades who slacked duties and avoided exposure to danger? This seemed to be the case to the extent that earlier even prisoners-of-war could be forced into the ranks to fight against their former comrades. But no longer—unlike mercenaries of yore, recent captives took every opportunity to get back to their comrades. As the influence of cliques of thugs diminished, pride in being a member of an elite unit—or even an average one—seems to have increased.

This was a new experience. By the ancient practice of accepting recruits from wherever a unit passed, or even compelling young men to enlist, most regiments had once been composed of a wide variety of nationalities. Even in the Swedish army—often regarded as the best in the period 1630-1715—only elite companies were composed of native Swedes; the rest of any regiment could be Poles or Germans or other locally recruited youths. Now the tendency was to recruit units from only a few regions, a practice that resulted in more homogeneity and greater unit cohesion.

This presented the Austrian monarchs with a serious problem. How could they make their multinational army as loyal to the dynasty as competing monarchs were able to do by combining love of country with respect for the ruler? Since it was difficult to assure unit cohesion when soldiers might not even be able to speak to one another, they needed a common language of command. Only German qualified.

Prince Eugene, himself an Italian reared at the French court, discouraged the enlistment of Italians. It was not a question of courage or competence, but of commitment—Italians tended to see through the foolishness of military life and, worse, they had little enthusiasm for the Hapsburgs. Eugene wanted German soldiers, but he was quite willing to enlist Bohemians, with their rich military tradition, because most Czechs knew a bit of German and were Catholic. German as the language of command also made it easier to work with allies from the Holy Roman Empire. Pressure to make Hungarians equal came much later.

There was also the matter of morale. After 1730 the Austrian army was beaten too often to go into battle with much confidence. It had been very different earlier, when Prince Eugene commanded victorious armies, but after the wars with Louis XIV ended and his successful siege of Belgrade in 1717, he retired to a pleasant life in Vienna (his Belvedere palace overlooking the city and his impressive *Stadtpalais* inside the walls) to collect art and books. The luxury of his later private life contrasted strongly with his austere practices as field commander. His reforms of the army had been rigorously practical. Dressing soldiers in grey frocks made it easy to see which units were his and which were the enemy's, even when thick white smoke obscured the battlefield, and the thickness of the frocks limited injury from spent projectiles; and since most soldiers reacted to incoming fire as if they were walking into heavy rain, concentrating on keeping their high hats from falling off prevented them from ducking their heads, a pose that was often followed by a panicked flight to the rear.

The Austrian army as a whole was weak, but some regiments were effective. This suggests that a study of armies at the regimental level might tell us much about the changes that were occurring in the 1700s. A good example of what can be learned is from the previously-mentioned Deutschmeister Regiment of the Hapsburg army.

The long-time grandmaster of the Teutonic Order, 1694–1732, Franz Ludwig, had little to do with the regiment beyond persuading his brothers to allow recruiters to raise troops in their lands in the Palatinate and Neuburg, but that was an important concession, because other, equally staunch Roman Catholic rulers would not have allowed recruiters to speak with their subjects. With the outbreak of war with France in the War of the Spanish Succession Franz Ludwig's two regiments of foot and a regiment of dragoons were withdraw from the Croatian and Hungarian frontiers, returning only in 1717 for the campaign that captured the great fortress at Belgrade, far to the south where the Danube makes its turn east toward the Black Sea.

The Deutschmeister regiment eventually came under the command of Charles Alexander of Lorraine (1712-80), one of the most important field marshals of the War of the Austrian Succession (1740-48) and the Seven Years War (1756-63). Everyone knew that he was competent but not brilliant.

Charles Alexander was not a lucky general, but no Austrian general did any better against Frederick the Great and Maurice de Saxe; he lost four times to the former and once to the latter, but he always reformed his army quickly and limited the territorial losses. He could be considered successful in one sense, in that Austrian soldiers who had given up the fight quickly between 1740 and 1746 in the First Silesian War had become warriors by 1756, when the second war with Prussia began. Austrian regiments then fought with such determination that the Prussians hardly recognised them.

This may have had little to do with Charles Alexander, and more to do with the greater popularity of Empress Maria Theresa and a new determination not to be humiliated again. In any case, Charles Alexander's position at the head of the army was secure. Maria Theresa was reluctant to give command to anyone outside the royal family, and even though he had only been married to her sister briefly, her only alternative was her husband, Charles Alexander's brother, who had no military talent at all. The empress's policy of concentrating power in the hands of the imperial family meant that there was little chance for another Eugene of Savoy to rise to greatness.

The office of grandmaster was a sinecure, to provide Charles Alexander incomes after he retired from imperial service, but it was also logical, since the new Deutschmeister Regiment had earned great fame under his command. This was officially the 4th regiment of the household troops, but its costs were covered by the Teutonic Order.

The Deutschmeister regiment was a well-dressed outfit. Standard gear for all infantry regiments included low-rimmed black felt hat with white brocade trim and regimental insignia, but the Deutschmeister soldiers were distinguished from other units by their pearl white overcoats with sky blue lapels and white buttons; they wore white neckbands, white shirts, white socks, white leggings (black in bad weather), black shoes, red leather cartridge case decorated with an eagle, backpack, flintlock, bayonet and sheath. Officers wore the same outfit—no gold or silver, and brocade permitted only when off-duty. They carried swords, daggers and pistols. Drummers and fifers dressed in red coats with blue shirts. The cavalry unit was also #4, *the Archduke Max cuirassiers*, with a proud heritage going back to the Thirty Years War; it was shot to pieces at the battle of Grocka in 1739, and during the Seven Years War was commanded by Johann Baptist Serbelloni (1696-1778), who was a member of the Knights of Malta and whose notoriously bad German was matched by his slowness in getting into the thick of the fight.

The regiment was ever more associated with the monarchy and less to the military order from which it sprang. Modern efforts to associate the Teutonic Order with Nazism run up against the fact that Hitler hated the Hapsburgs and nobles in general; he also hated the Roman Catholic Church, filling his earliest concentration camps with priests who objected to euthanasia; he mistrusted professional army officers, who repeatedly plotted to overthrow him; and his plans for National Socialism meant the creation of a new society that had no room for these artefacts of a culture that he declared were useless and dangerous.

Swiss in French Service

The Swiss connection to the French king that had begun in the fifteenth century grew even closer under Louis XIV; he employed them not only as regiments in the army, but also as his household guard. There were two units protecting the king, the *Cent Suisses* (literally the 100 Swiss), who were his bodyguards, together with the *Gardes du Corps*, of French birth; the *Gardes Suisses*, together with the *Gardes Françaises*, were responsible for guarding the palaces. There were also eleven Swiss regiments which served valiantly in every war, adapting to the technological changes swiftly— dropping the traditional Swiss pike for the musket and bayonet even though this meant accommodating themselves to a minor role in the larger armies of the 18th century.

Swiss regiments were often employed where Frenchmen were reluctant to serve. For example, they helped garrison the fortress of Louisbourg on the God-forsaken coast of Nova Scotia. This was a location beloved of fishermen, who could dry their catch on the rocky shores, but no one else. Even before the siege by American colonial troops in 1745, the garrison was mutinous, but it fought well enough that if reinforcements had been able to arrive by sea, the fortress would not have fallen. It was, after all, the French Gibraltar in the Americas; and it was recovered in the peace treaty!

The Swiss Guards could probably have thwarted the most violent excesses of the French Revolution if King Louis XVI had been willing to approve the timely use of force against the mobs raging through Paris and other cities. However, the gentle king was reluctant to allow the army to fire on Frenchmen. In retrospect, the outcome seems inevitable: on July 14, 1789, a Parisian mob, believing that a counter-revolution was underway, marched on the Bastille, once the east gate of the city, but later converted into a seldom-used prison. Its military function had long since disappeared except as a gunpowder depot and housing for some eighty invalid soldiers. The prisoners, it turned out, were not victims of royal anger, but a handful of common criminals, religious dissidents and prominent malcontents; moreover, it could hold only about fifty inmates.

The Bastille's evil reputation as a prison spoke more to popular dislike of royal absolutism than actual mistreatment—visitors were frequent, card games were allowed and there was even a billiard table. The food may have been more plentiful than tasty, but notables incarcerated there had fared well. Confinement itself, the isolation from the lively world outside, that was what made the Bastille feared; that and the knowledge that the king could imprison anyone for any length of time, without any judicial process (the infamous *lettres de cachet*)—the fact that this rarely occurred does not seem to have bothered anyone, certainly not to anyone who had ever heard the Marquis de Sade shouting down from the tower walks that the governor was intent on massacring all the prisoners. It was taken apparently as a matter of course that a governor would allow such behaviour; as was well-known, the Old Regime was not very well organised.

The Parisians' march on the Bastille was merely the culmination of a process that had begun days before. As Simon Schama described the events in *Citizens*, crowds celebrating the removal of the unpopular minister, Necker, had got out of control. The first attempt by the authorities to disperse the mob in the centre of Paris had failed, the cavalrymen retreating to the Tuileries—at that time joined to the Louvre to make one vast palace. The crowd then grew in size and began looting shops selling guns, swords and knifes, then bakeries, and finally tearing holes in the wall surrounding the city in hopes of attracting tax-free food from the country. It was at this moment, Schama says, that Paris was lost to the monarchy.

Still, it did not look hopeless to contemporaries. Although the king was informed that the French troops could not be relied upon, his German and Swiss units might be. This estimate was soon outdated—80,000 citizens marched on the Invalides, the military hospital and arsenal across the Seine. There they seized 30,000 muskets and the powder that had not been sent to

135

the Bastille. The foreign troops encamped only a few hundred yards away made no move to stop them.

The government, at last realising that the Parisian mob was dangerous, dispatched Swiss troops to hold the key points in the city. Thirty-two went to the Bastille, a number that could have held the fortress until help arrived, if the government had been willing to do so. A crowd of about a thousand gathered in front of the Bastille, warning the commander that they intended to arm themselves from the weapons stored there and that he might as well surrender.

The commander, Bernard-René de Launay (1740-89), had been born in the Bastille when his father had commanded the garrison there. His force— if it could be called that—consisted of about eighty aged veterans, some invalids. The Swiss reinforcements would be sufficient as long as the mob lacked artillery. Therefore, he refused to open the magazines as the leaders of the mob demanded.

The ensuing chaos was witnessed in part by Thomas Jefferson, then in Paris as the American ambassador. He described the storming of the Bastille, remarking that there were so many different stories of the event that none of them could be believed. What is clear is that the ropes to the drawbridge were cut during the negotiations. That allowed the mob to stream across. When someone began firing, the confusion turned into a battle royal, that is, royalist troops versus Parisians who were becoming republicans. Though the rioters managed to break into the courtyard, they made little further headway against the handful of Swiss troops until a unit of the *Gardes Françaises* arrived with two cannon. This elite unit had been plagued by desertions for months; now, in the critical moment, it went over completely to the people. The garrison, already out of water and realising that no rescue was coming, then reconsidered its situation and surrendered. As the troops tried to march away, however, the mob fell on them, lynching the commander and several soldiers. Most of the Swiss Guards, having taken off their uniforms, were mistaken for prisoners and 'liberated'.

Few realised that the Bastille was already on a list of fortresses to be demolished, to be converted into a public park. As the Parisians tore down the impressive building and carried away its bricks for private use, Louis XVI travelled from Versailles to Paris, with a tricolour ribbon on his chest to indicate his adherence to the revolutionary cause. Only a few months later a mob of women protesting the cost of bread (an event that should have been expected, considering the disorders in the countryside) made the royal family prisoners.

In June 1791 the king made an attempt to flee the country, to join counter-revolutionaries in the Holy Roman Empire. At a checkpoint near the border, however, he stuck his head out of the carriage window to ask what the delay was about. Since his profile was on every coin in France, he was easily recognised. As the armies of Prussia and Austria, supported by troops raised by exiled officers, pressed into northeastern France, the National Assembly became persuaded that unless the king and the remaining nobles and royal officials were dealt with, the Revolution would fail. However, the king was still protected by his bodyguard and the Revolutionary Army was at the frontiers.

By August 1792 the situation of the king was critical. Armed volunteers from around France were streaming toward Paris, singing *La Marseillaise* and looking for royalists to murder. One group ran in with the Irish regiment commanded by Theobald Dillon (1745-92), the last of the line of exiles to serve the French king; the Irish mistook the militia for Austrian troops supposed to be hurrying to rescue Louis XVI's queen, who was the daughter of Empress Maria Theresa. Dillon became separated from his men, was captured, then murdered and mutilated. Word of this atrocity spread to all the foreign troops, especially to the Swiss, who were now Louis XVI's last hope.

On August 10, 1792, a mob attacked the Tuileries Palace, the foremost royal residence in Paris. The palace was defended by 900 red-coated Swiss troops, but running out of ammunition, the best they could do was to delay the mob sufficiently until the royal family escaped. As the immense building was consumed by flames, the defenders who managed to stagger outside were massacred. Over six hundred died; about two hundred perished in prison or were later executed.

In retrospect, we can see that the Swiss mercenaries had not expected to be slaughtered in the brutal manner that soon became normal for 'the terror'. It was, as Schama remarked, the logical consummation of the revolution that had begun in 1789; bloodshed was not a by-product of the revolution, but provided the energy that moved it forward. Soon afterwards the National Assembly dismissed all Swiss troops and sent them home. The king was thenceforth helpless. Louis XVI thus lost his head twice—once in making poor decisions, the second time to the guillotine.

Swiss in Prussian Service

Because Prussia was a traditional French ally, King Frederick I (1701-13, elector of Brandenburg since 1688) was able to hire Swiss to be his household guard. Prussia being much colder than France, they may have shivered in their silk and satin uniforms, but they looked impressive; and Frederick I wanted to make an impression. After all, he was the first of his dynasty to acquire the title of king, and kings had to maintain a certain style.

His successor, Frederick William, immediately sent the Swiss guards home. He also sold the royal zoo, reassigned to the army the trumpeters and drummers who had announced his father's appearances, and reduced the salaries of all officers of the state (including military officers). He could have avoided this belt-tightening (a metaphor which accurately reflects a similar reduction in expenditures for royal meals) had he been willing to continue accepting foreign subsidies. But subsidies meant sending Prussian units to Italy, the Balkans and other foreign war zones. Frederick William wanted his troops at home, where he could make them into the best army in Europe. He continued to recruit mercenaries, even Catholic soldiers (for whom he provided chaplains and churches), but all recruits would be placed in units of the regular army, not in national formations.

Frederick William was tolerant in religious matters, giving refuge to 12,000 Salzburg Protestants who were told to convert to Catholicism or leave Austria, just as his father had welcomed many Huguenots who had received a similar warning from Louis XIV in 1685. What Frederick William would not tolerate was Calvinist Predestination (which was the dominant religious doctrine in Geneva), because he feared his recruits might conclude that they were predestined to desert. He settled the Salzburg Protestants in a distant province along what is today the Lithuanian coastline, a region that had been devastated and almost depopulated by war. Since any army proceeding from Livonia into Poland would have to pass through that region, it was not an altogether generous gesture.

Swiss in British Service

Swiss were not common in British units, except those in the Prince of Orange's Swiss Guards (*Regiment Zwitserse Gardes*), who accompanied William of Orange during his invasion of England in 1688.

Henry Bouquet, whom we met earlier, was a Swiss of Huguenot ancestry, consequently a man not only willing to fight French Catholics, but eager to do so. During the War of the Austrian Succession he served in the army of the Prince of Savoy, writing an account of his adventures that caught the eye of the Prince of Orange, who recruited him for his guards. He quickly rose to become the commander. In 1755 the British government, embarrassed by the defeat of Braddock's expedition, began to raise regiments of Americans. Realising that there was rich potential for recruiting among the German-speaking citizens of Pennsylvania—if they had German-speaking officers to lead them—someone suggested that Bouquet and a friend, Frederick Haldimand (1718-91), should be offered command of two battalions of the Royal American Regiment. Bouquet arrived in Philadelphia in 1756 and quickly enlisted over five hundred 'Pennsylvania Dutch' into the unit.[3]

Bouquet led the expedition that reached Fort Duquesne only to find its smouldering ruins. He had barely fortified Fort Pitt before Indians surrounded the place and demanded his surrender. Knowing that the Indians would never dare to attack, he said no. Eventually, he earned immortal infamy responding to the chiefs' demand for gifts before they would consent to peace negotiations by sending some fine handkerchiefs from the smallpox hospital. This probably had no impact on the epidemic that was sweeping North America. The very existence of a smallpox hospital in Fort Pitt's moat proves that the disease was already on the frontier.

For the next eight years Bouquet would be among the most important British officers on the frontier. So valued were his contributions that Parliament waived the rule forbidding foreigners the rank of brigadier general in promoting him.

The lesson of these wars seemed to be that European armies could not be beaten except when geography and poor leadership combined to make their virtues into disadvantages. However, since guerrilla forces usually cannot win a campaign without becoming a regular army, they are still at a disadvantage because regular soldiers require long training in specialised formations and modern weapons. Professional soldiers are superior to recruits or volunteers, and experienced mercenaries are the best of the professionals.

The use of irregular forces as scouts and to screen the main force from ambush and harassment was common even in Europe, where armies often surrounded themselves with a swarm of irregulars—Cossacks and Croatians being the best because they did not speak the local languages and despised unarmed peasants and villagers as less than real men. The same was true in America. Indians who could not afford to absorb casualties were kept away from redcoats and colonials on the march by a screen of friendly warriors who hated the Indian tribes opposing them.

---

1. Farm incomes were improving, perhaps in response to the slightly higher temperatures across Europe as the Little Ice Age (1350-1850) eased at the end of the seventeenth century.

2. In 1804 workmen discovered what they believed what Braddock's corpse. In 1913 the Coldstream Guards erected a monument at that location.

3. This unit was founded in 1757 as the 60th Regiment (Royal Americans) and was later filled out with recruits from Hanover (still ruled personally by King George III) and other German states. Awkwardly, none of these soldiers had any experience in frontier warfare. Its commander later became governor of Quebec, serving there from 1778-84, the critical days of the American Revolution after Burgoyne's invasion of New York from Canada had met disaster at Saratoga.

Chapter 8

Britain in America

The periphery is usually important only in reference to what is happening at the centre. As the ever-quotable Samuel Johnson (1709-84) once said, 'The noblest prospect which a Scotchman ever sees, is the high road that leads him to England!' To be more precise, Johnson meant the capital: 'Why, Sir, you find no man, at all intellectual, who is willing to leave London. No, Sir, when a man is tired of London, he is tired of life; for there is in London all that life can afford.'

If Johnson disliked Scots, that was nothing compared to his hatred of Americans: 'Sir, they are a race of convicts, and ought to be thankful for anything we allow them short of hanging.'

If his opinions seem excessive, that was characteristic of the times. Just as debates in the House of Commons were rarely noted for civility, newspapers and journals thrived on dismissive wit and scurrilous attacks. Dr. Johnson—the 'doctor' (*honoris causa*) came from Trinity College, Dublin (his alma mater, Oxford, believed that a Master's Degree was all he merited)—did not excel in public debate. He preferred long-pondered, long-distance character assassination in print. He was widely read.

Johnson was especially important in forming public opinion about America and Americans. They were incapable of self-government, he said, and slyly suggested that if they wanted to vote in a parliamentary election, they should come back to England and buy an estate. While accusing Americans of being interested only in money, he married a wealthy widow twenty-one years his elder. No children, of course. In short, the brilliant Dr. Johnson made the British public ready to believe the worse of the rapidly growing number of colonists across the Atlantic. He even managed to turn the average Briton's exclusion from representation in Parliament to an argument against allowing Americans to participate in their own governance; that such matters should be left to those who know better—the rich and the well-educated.

One backstory to Johnson's bile is that many thousands of Scots and Ulster Scots were leaving for America each year. The Scotch-Irish (as Ulster Scots called themselves after reaching the western parts of Pennsylvania and Virginia) were fleeing from rent-racking equivalent to what the hated Irish had long known. They had originally accepted farms on low rents, but when the contracts expired, they discovered that absentee English landlords now expected much higher payments. Johnson's patrons were not happy that the Scotch-Irish preferred to emigrate rather than work for next-to-nothing, nor that this reduced the number of potential recruits for the army and navy. It was even more infuriating to learn that the Scotch-Irish were settling on the frontier, carving small farms from the rocky hillsides, rather than working for wages on the tobacco plantations of the American aristocrats who owed them money. No problem, of course, since the plantation owners knew where to get workers who could not leave—slaves, often second generation chattels from Caribbean sugar plantations. Of course, that left the American aristocrats deeper in debt to the London banks.

When Dr. Johnson was asked why the Scots had chosen such barren land to settle, he replied, 'Why, Sir, all barrenness is comparative. The Scotch would not know it to be barren.' Johnson, who would rather have been quoted for wit than accuracy, knew that the low mountains of eastern America were more like the dimly remembered homeland in Scotland than the lush bottomlands of the coast, but even more importantly, the Scots could not have afforded bottomlands, while obtaining small plots among the rugged hills of the interior required only hard work and courage.

Few Scotch-Irish went to America as indentured servants. Most chose to work as labourers for a few years rather than be reduced to the status of servant for four to seven years, just to get free passage—the Scots were careful with their money, but pride came first. As soon as they had earned enough to support themselves until a crop came in, they moved to the frontier, often to join relatives. Once beyond the protection of the government (redcoats were stationed only in ports to guarantee the payment of taxes, not to protect settlers on the frontier), they encountered an enemy almost as dangerous as the Irish—Indians. Fortunately for them, the Indians avoided the diseases, the gambling and drunkenness associated with Americans by moving farther into the interior. Soon the forests were less filled by valuable animals—the newcomers, armed with newly popular Pennsylvania rifles, reduced the deer population far below the numbers of the seventeenth century, and even that of the twenty-first.

When Indians moved even farther inland to find game, they effectively invited more settlers in. While the Indians may have intimidated Americans accustomed to rural life in areas long since emptied of their native inhabitants, their threats had little effect on the Scotch-Irish—they had been schooled in the religious wars in Ulster.

As for the propaganda war on their morals and intelligence, the Scotch-Irish were generally literate enough to put Dr. Johnson in the context of their English landlords—they understood that no British government or British church would treat them well. If they were going to thrive in their New World, they had to do it on their own.

Scots Elsewhere

Once the 1707 Act of Union had cleared the way for Scots to move to England, they did so enthusiastically. They didn't always get the best jobs, but like minorities the world over throughout history, they found niche occupations. Usually, these were jobs that Englishmen did not want to do themselves. Government functionaries, for example, worked long hours for little pay, and they were expected to be honest—this was almost a job description for literate Scots.

Some of the best-paying government positions were in tropical colonies such as India, or in army units stationed overseas. It was no accident that James Fennimore Cooper's 1826 novel, *The Last of the Mohicans, A Narrative of 1757*, had Colonel George Munro valiantly defending an isolated frontier fort in Upper New York against French attack. The seventh movie bearing this title, made in 1992 and starring Daniel Day-Lewis, emphasised the Scottish connection both of the royal officers and of the frontier militiamen who were torn between loyalty to the crown and the desire to protect their families from Indian raiders.

As for India, Walter Scott referred to that colony as 'the corn chest for Scotland where we poor gentry must send our youngest sons as we send our black cattle to the south.' Those who could obtain a posting with the East India Company had the best chance of returning home wealthy—but no one with a name associated with Jacobite tendencies needed to bother applying. Those who simply enlisted in the army had neither hope of accumulating a fortune nor any expectation of living long enough to retire—the climate was hellish and diseases were deadly. Certainly their officers regarded these soldiers as the dregs of mankind, a poor sort of semi-human even for Scotland. Those who did manage to return home found the cold northern climate the unhappy opposite of their sun-soaked inferno.

However, those who did bring a fortune back to Edinburgh and other cities were able to fit in easily with well-to-do Englishmen who could admire their stories, their well-appointed houses, and even their reluctance to waste money on frivolous luxuries and wasteful habits. This contributed to the growing mutual respect between the upper classes.

Scots excelled at secretarial work, none more so than James Boswell (1740-95), who recorded practically every word the irascible Dr. Johnson uttered, even those denigrating Scots and Scotland, such as the famous definition of Oats in Johnson's *English Dictionary*: 'a grain, which in England is generally given to horses, but in Scotland supports the people.' So completely did Boswell bow to the scholar's impossible demands that one would hardly know that he had a separate distinguished career.

The British Army of the French and Indian War

There had been few British troops on the North American mainland until the Great War for Empire, as Henry Gipson called the worldwide struggle between Great Britain and France. This Seven Years War (1756-63), like earlier conflicts between those nations, should have been won by the more numerous and richer Frenchmen. But with Gallic frivolity French kings had never been able to decide what their national goal was—expansion into Italy, or into Germany, or the acquisition of colonies. The British Parliament, elected in part by an important commercial class, had no such problem. Parliament understood the paramount importance of the navy both for warding off invasion and for acquiring colonies that could increase the nation's wealth both directly and indirectly.

However, any military establishment is expensive. Britain's became even more so during this conflict, when the government provided huge subsidies to keep the armies of the anti-French coalition in the field. Much of this money came from borrowing—and the bankers wanted to be repaid.

The British army and navy, meanwhile, were also stretched to acquire more and better weapons of war because the peace treaty awarded important French colonies to Britain, and the French were rearming—it was no secret that they wanted revenge for the series of defeats stretching back three-quarters of a century.

No military establishment has ever found it easy to keep pace with challenges and change. It would have been easier to do if anyone had a clear vision of what the future would require, or if old methods, even old weapons, were indeed obsolete, or if new ones would work as well as hoped. But no aspect of military life is more difficult to change than the means used to supply and pay troops.

The British system had always been practical rather than logical or fair. It continued largely because those in power benefitted personally, but even they were not quite sure why this was so. Curtis, in *The British Army in the American Revolution*, reported that one parliamentary inquiry abandoned its reform efforts because it could not figure out how the system actually worked.

Each regiment had six fictitious soldiers on its rolls, some of the money going to a fund for widows of regimental officers, some to the colonel for regimental expenses, and some to the captains for company expenses. This can be excused partly by the inadequate pay. Curtis cited one estimate that a tailor lived on his wages better than a colonel, and that a common soldier barely had anything left after deductions for shoes, medical care, and repairs to his weapons, a kick-back to the paymaster, a contribution to the Chelsea Hospital, a payment to the regimental agent, and the cost of clothing.

Few officers married unless circumstances brought them to an heiress's attention, and long periods of separation were not good for a happy relationship. Nevertheless, parents continued to buy commissions for younger sons, and soldiers continued to enlist—even those who were sober when this happened. Many were reluctant to retire, both because they could not live comfortably on a pension and because they liked the military life. Being an officer was not a demanding job. There were drinking companions, willing women (for a price or a few compliments), and opportunities to gamble, ride horses, and otherwise pretend to be gentlemen.

Soldiers and Tax Collectors

Soldiers did not collect taxes themselves, but they accompanied those who did, both to coerce those who were unwilling to come up with hard cash and to protect the money until it was delivered to the Treasury.

Of course, government efforts to tax commerce immediately led to smuggling. As Michael Kwass showed in *Contraband*, taxes and the extreme measures taken to collect the taxes were very unpopular, and people rarely asked about the origins of anything they wanted, as long as the price was right. Smugglers avoided border posts, slipping goods from frontier regions into the borderlands, selling them to less conspicuous criminals who would find ways to get them past the customs guards at the gates of cities.

Efforts to collect unpopular taxes were rarely fully effective, which led some economists to argue that free trade would put smugglers out of business as well as lower prices for everyone. Few agreed—such a policy ran against tradition and logic. Surely the government should regulate trade, with the help of guilds, merchants and bankers—all of whom benefitted from their near-monopoly status.

In France only licensed vendors could sell tobacco and stamps. Small *Tabac* shops appeared there, then across Europe. But the evasion of salt tax was so common that the government required every citizen to buy an amount necessary for good health. Protests about taxes piled one atop the other, and the people's difficulty in paying them with good coins were part of the process leading to the French Revolution. Paper money seemed to work only in Great Britain, but the real problem, according to James Macdonald, was that absolutism was failing; not even the ruling class still believed in what it was doing, and since nobody trusted the king's ministers to repay loans, the financial crisis was insoluble.

In America the evasion of the sugar tax was so successful that Parliament lowered the tax, in hope of undercutting smugglers' profits, but squandered the goodwill by vigorous efforts to collect the lower tax. Colonial consumers recognised that the ultimate aim was to establish a precedent for more taxes later on. A national boycott made everyone aware that the colonies had to stand together, as they later did against the Stamp Tax; and the symbolic protest against the Tea Tax led to Americans becoming a nation of coffee drinkers.

At what became known as the Boston Tea Party, men disguised as Indians boarded ships with cheap tea belonging to the East India Company and dumped it into the harbour. Parliament was so outraged that it sent regulars to occupy Boston and then closed the harbour, effectively shutting the economy down. American militia units began to drill, and threats were made against anyone speaking on behalf of the crown.

This led eventually to a sortie from Boston to seize American weapons and gunpowder, then to a violent confrontation at Bunker Hill. Sending redcoats straight at the crude colonial fortification overlooking Boston was a mistake, but General William Howe (1729-1814) had assumed that Americans would never stand against regulars; he sent the Black Watch to chase them away.

Howe learned from the engagement not to attack American earthworks head on again—Americans lacked the training and self-confidence to take on British formations in the field, but they knew how to dig, and once in their trenches, they knew how to hold them.[1]

The British Army Adapts to American Warfare

The common assumption that the British army stubbornly held to traditional line tactics while fighting in America—and therefore lost key battles such as Saratoga—has been challenged by Matthew Spring in *With Zeal and Bayonets Only, the British Army on Campaign in North America, 1775-83*. General Howe's means of countering American earthworks was to manoeuvre so that when his men came in on the flank, the defenders had to come out and fight, or run away, or be slaughtered. Running was the usual choice. Militiamen's reluctance to stand firm against redcoats left George Washington in such fury that several times he threw his hat to the ground, yelling at the fleeing men, and courting death in their place.

Washington's response to the British flanking attacks was to build longer and more elaborate defensive lines, to replace his militia units with Continentals as much as he could, and to withdraw when he saw his men wavering. If he could get the British units to stop and exchange fire, his Continentals could inflict almost as many casualties as they took, and American riflemen could pick off the officers. This was something Howe could not afford—his men were both difficult to recruit and expensive to replace. America, in contrast, had a 'bottomless' supply of manpower, and at the war went on more and more men enlisted in the ranks of the Continental Army or state militias. Howe had expected loyalists to join him in large numbers. That did not happen.

Eventually, the British developed an effective response to the American strategy of entrenchment. This was to emphasise light infantry tactics that were rarely used in the European wars. Each regiment (roughly 400 men) was divided into ten companies, two being flank companies which served as light infantry; as the war went, more and more companies were trained to fight a more open order in ranks only two deep, to take shelter behind trees when necessary, and to move swiftly through woods. The critical moment came when the redcoats were forty yards away, when they would fire a quick volley and charge at a run with their bayonets. This almost always flushed the Americans out of even well-designed trench works. The speed and daring were intimidating, and the redcoats' practice of bayoneting the wounded and those who tried to surrender made them greatly feared. The redcoats were especially brutal toward riflemen, whose marksmanship killed so many of their comrades.

One problem, not mentioned by Spring, was that men in trenches knew they would be slaughtered once redcoats began thrusting bayonets down at them. Forty years before, Maurice de Saxe, the foremost French marshal, had his men build walls of logs or stone to avoid this fate. A fence of logs wasn't always practical in America, but every man knew how to use a shovel. (For more on this, read my *Bayonets and Scimitars*.)

The redcoats were not uniformly veterans, but they had an experienced core that brought recruits along quickly, and since recruits in America could not leave the army to tend crops or care for their families, within months they knew their business. As a result, they were much better trained than the Americans, and their belief in their invincibility made them confident.

This is important because although the redcoats won almost every pitched battle with the Americans, the war was lost from the beginning. Politicians and generals misread the depth of American dissatisfaction, and every effort they made to coerce the colonials antagonised them more. General Howe had rejected advice to make war on the American people because that would have turned the whole seaboard into a gigantic Ireland, where one-third of the army was usually stationed to keep the populace from rising. America was too big for that; the government could not afford it.

Since Howe and his successors could not afford to lose men, they preferred manoeuvre to frontal assaults. This frustrated junior officers and his Hessian allies, who yearned for a chance to finish off the Yankees in one great battle; all too often they watched Howe manoeuvre into a position to attack at dawn, only to find the well-constructed fortifications abandoned when morning came.

The redcoats adapted to the challenges of the American woodlands, the lack of roads, and insufficient local foodstuffs, but they were never able to finish off the American armies, which kept coming back at them until finally they were able to meet them on more equal terms.

Spring's account puts yet another end to the myth of the Minuteman being equal to a trained professional. 'Another end' is the way to say it because the myth keeps coming back again and again. Washington had proved that an effective army had to be trained and equipped in much the same way that European armies were organised, because there had to be a final battlefield victory. With French help he achieved this in 1781 at Yorktown. An America without an army would be at the mercy of foreign invasion and Indian attack forever. And foreign troops exposed to guerrilla tactics can become angry and vengeful in a hurry, much as the Indians already were.

Why Independence was Necessary

Too often historians think the American Revolution was about taxes. In reality it was because Americans refused to be reduced to second class subjects. Anthony Scotti, Jr's powerful short book, *Brutal Virtue, the Myth and Reality of Banastre Tarleton*, demonstrated this while trying to prove the opposite. The name Tarleton probably means little to readers outside of South Carolina, but few citizens of that southern state would fail to recognise it.

Movie-goers of 2000 might have seen *The Patriot*, starring Mel Gibson, in which the hero tried to remain neutral in the conflict, but was inevitably drawn in by Tarleton's misdeeds. This reflected Scotti's argument that patriotic propagandists used him to illustrate why Americans had to join the fight, but that Tarleton was really no worse than anyone else. This perhaps credits patriot propagandists too much. Those who knew Tarleton best either loved him or hated him; he was lucky not to have been hanged.

Another movie, *Sweet Liberty* (1986), made an additional point. A comedy written and directed by Alan Alda (who also had the lead role except when being upstaged by Michael Caine and Michelle Pfeiffer), the story centred on a small-college historian who had written a scholarly study of Tarleton's famous meeting with Mrs. Mary Slocomb, and who was frustrated by the director's efforts to turn that into a love story. When Tarleton came to Mrs. Slocomb's farm to burn it, he asked where her husband was and whether he was a rebel. She retorted, 'He is in the army of his country, and fighting against our invaders, and therefore not a rebel.'

The banter apparently lasted for most of the several days that Tarleton rested his men at her farm. She cooperated to the extent of feeding and housing his men, but probably not by sharing her bed. He responded to her courtesy by not burning her house and barns.

Every observer of the colonial scene agreed that South Carolina and Georgia were more loyalist than the other colonies. This was partly because the plantation owners with numerous slaves and the commercial class selling tobacco, rice and indigo saw themselves much like English nobility and merchant capitalists. However, without British armed assistance, the loyalists could not challenge patriot control of politics.

This changed when Cornwallis was sent to Charles Towne (as it was known then) with 14,000 redcoats and Hessians; after a long siege he forced General Benjamin Lincoln to surrender the city and his 5,000 men. It was the greatest defeat the Americans had suffered yet—the loss of an entire army.

Cornwallis set out to occupy the countryside, but he found it difficult to locate guerilla forces such as those of the Swamp Fox, Francis Marion. His answer to this problem was to recruit loyalists for a mixed light cavalry and mounted infantry body that he called the British Legion; he named as commander the brightest cavalry officer in the army, young Banastre Tarleton.

The British Legion became famed (or infamous) for its long, swift marches and deadly attacks. It would fall on patriot forces at dawn, slaughtering the sleepy men, or charge unsteady units so suddenly that the men would fly for their lives. Not that many got away. No man on foot can outrun a horse. Tarleton would demand that patriot regiments surrender, and if they did not, his men would kill everyone they caught. In short, like the French suppressing Algerian rebels between 1954 and 1962, his operations were a model of tactical efficiency, but a strategic blunder.

The green uniforms that the British Legion wore were a symbol of pride, but also of what was wrong with British policy. Britons chose to believe that all Americans were dirty, lazy and cowardly. Therefore, they were not worthy of holding government posts or being allowed to buy commissions in the army. They were not even allowed to wear red coats.

A far-sighted government would have made George Washington into a professional officer and rich Americans into aristocrats. But no, the government saw Americans as the equivalent of the Irish, the Scots, and South Asian Indians, that is, as a lower class of human being. When Americans complained that taxation policies and changing the royal charters were reducing them to slaves (something they knew something about), more than a few Britons thought that would be a good thing.

Benjamin Franklin had gone to London as a lobbyist for the government of the Pennsylvania Colony. World-renowned scientist, philosopher and humourist, honoured by British universities, he was nevertheless repeatedly humiliated by the government ministers. Before he returned to America he wrote a satirical tract, 'Rules by Which a Great Empire May Be Reduced to a Small One.'

The lesson is a hard one, easily understood but hard to apply when one sees the rudeness of frontier conditions and the seeming incompetence of the people there, but it is a manner of common courtesy—treat people with respect. This is especially difficult for those who consider themselves aristocrats, far above the common people.

Machiavelli warned princes not to make themselves hated. Cruelty is well used if applied decisively for a short period, then stopped. Secure your position and use your power to benefit your subjects. In that way your subject will be doubly thankful—first for having ended the violence, then for the benefits of peace and a few royal favours. The British lacked an army equipped to follow this path, so they began mildly and become more ruthless as the years passed. George III would have been better off if he had followed the advice of his Whig critics, to leave the Americans alone.

Military victories cannot win a peace alone. Without either a large occupation army or a sizeable number of loyalists who can take over the governance of the region, no outside army can hold a people down forever. There is always some other outside army and navy that will come to the aid of the rebels that inevitably arise.

---

1. Howe's career reflects the importance of connections—his father had been a colonial governor, his mother was the illegitimate sister of George I, which gave her easy access to the royal court; he was a member of Parliament, a distinguished veteran of numerous campaigns. He looked and acted like the perfect British officer.

Chapter 9

The Interior of Asia
China Moves Into Its Wild West

For many centuries the Chinese had worried about the nomadic peoples on their northern frontier—their Great Wall being history's most impressive effort to limit the depredations of barbarians, far exceeding the Roman *Limes* in length and quality of construction. However, they had not been able to eliminate the danger at its source—Mongolia. The problem was that rice-growing China raised few warhorses, and while the nomads to the north were willing to sell them from time to time, they delivered only inferior mounts; whenever the northern tribes were strong, they saved their horses for invasions.

The Great Wall had not been a cure-all, because whenever government broke down, the border garrisons were weakened, opening the way for charismatic barbarian leaders to ravage the northern provinces; the most famous invader, Genghis Khan, made himself emperor. Even the fall of the Mongol dynasty brought no respite. Chinese offensives into Mongolia failed for a lack of horses, grain, and enough silver to bribe tribal leaders; it helped that the Mongol khans had become dependent upon Chinese tea—though the government learned that an embargo was seldom effective enough to change nomads' minds when they had decided upon a plan. When Chinese farmers began moving beyond the wall to raise grain, and when silver came from the New World and Japan, the Ming dynasty had some leverage in dividing the Mongol tribes. The problem of dealing with these barbarians was so severe that one emperor put an end to the promising expansion across the seas so that he could concentrate on bringing food and horses to the garrisons along the Great Wall.

This changed in the mid-1600s, when a new dynasty, the Quin, came out of Manchuria to take Beijing, then, after a long war, much of the rest of China. Afterwards there were no serious attacks across the various extensions of the wall—partly because the Mongols had remained divided and weak, and partly because the Manchu state could be called Manchu-Mongol, and later Manchu-Mongol-Chinese. Even so, the Quin dynasty emperors, well aware of the potential danger from the north, abandoned the defensive strategy that had characterised Chinese policy.

First, however, they had to deal with Russian explorers and fur-traders entering the Amur River valley in the north of Manchuria. Peter Perdue, in *China Marches West*, says that the intruders were captivated by the grain-raising potential of the regions. After starving in their march across Siberia, surviving only by taking what they needed from already impoverished natives who were now fleeing whenever they approached, they saw the Amur Valley as the answer to all their problems.

The Cossack leaders of these expeditions, however, were unable to explain to their rulers in St. Petersburg why they should conquer the Far East; their tsars were fixated on the Turks, Poles and Swedes, and the advanced societies farther west. As a result, less attention was paid to the nomadic societies to their east than the powerful states to the south and west. The tsars and tsarina knew almost nothing of the Chinese, whose great wall kept the Mongols intellectually as well as physically barred from entry; they obtained what little information they had from steppe peoples who were themselves far from the Great Wall.

Similarly, the Russians had little knowledge of the Manchus, who were evolving rapidly into a centrally administered bureaucratic state on the Chinese model. The Manchus were almost equally ignorant of the Russian state, except that some Russians were entering their country.

The Manchus were better able to assess the value of the Amur region than the newcomers. Compared to the fir-filled taiga or the barren eastern steppe that the Russians had passed through, it seemed rich. But the truth was that the grassland was not an agricultural paradise. Had it been so, the Manchus would have exploited it themselves rather than invade China.

Still, should these Western intruders—among whom were experienced Cossacks—establish themselves there, then enhance their existing close contacts with the peoples of the steppe, the danger could become acute. A Russian presence in the Amur Valley, combined with remaining problems in Mongolia—within striking distance of Beijing—could not be tolerated. The Manchus first organised themselves to seize North China from the Ming dynasty, doing so with the Eight Banner army, each a multi-ethnic force headed by a warlord, then occupied Southern China. That done, they drove the Russians out of the Amur Valley, slaughtered a large Cossack force and its famed commander, then removed the farmers from the region so that there would be no grain to support any future Russian army; afterwards they invaded first Inner Mongolia, then Outer Mongolia—the very name indicating the Chinese view of the region. A defensive system, after all, is more effective as a shield for mobile forces that can strike an enemy than as a passive line of towers. The Manchus, a warlike race of horsemen who raised their own steeds, had no interest in defence, but would expand China's borders in all directions.

The offensive into the Mongolian steppe and desert was less difficult than past efforts had been—most Mongols had adopted a form of contemplative Buddhism that was incompatible with a raiding tradition; some Mongol tribes had long associated themselves with the Manchus, and many of those Mongols who insisted on remaining independent had already migrated west, taking their valiant warriors with them—even fighting with the eastern Mongols and each other. The most important of these western tribes was the Kalmyk (Torhus). Buddhists who looked to Tibet for spiritual guidance, they settled in Central Asia among Sufi Muslims who were inclined to welcome religious diversity.

About 1618 the Kalmyks began to move westward under pressure from an expanding western Mongol tribe known as Zungars (Dzungars). Fellow Buddhists they may have been, and closely related in language, ancestry and traditions, but nobody who survives on the great steppe could be a pacifist. The Kalmyks, disliking the alternatives of dying or submitting, made a long journey through southern Siberia—avoiding the Kazakh territories—to the plains to the banks of the Volga River and the Caspian Sea, where in 1630 they encountered the last Muslim herdsmen on the Kuban plain. After driving these peoples south into the Caucasian Mountains or west to join the Tatars, they agreed to serve as tsarist cavalry in return for peace and presents.

China Reaches Sinkiang

The emperor Kangxi (1654-1722) extended Manchu control deeper into southern China, where competing warlords fought over the remains of the Ming dynasty lands, then over the nearest tribes in Mongolia and even over Tibet; however, since the nomadic peoples could retreat ahead of his armies, he was unable to subdue every tribe on the great steppe to the west or even to supervise the eastern Mongols closely. In 1717, when Mongols advanced into Tibet, he moved to expel them. After retaking Lhasa, his generals attempted a partial withdrawal, ruling through the Dalai Lamas—a policy recommended by modern experts like Akbar Ahmed—but were repeatedly called back into the mountainous interior to deal with civil wars and invasions from Nepal in the south and the steppe to the north. Interventions, then as now, were necessary, but seldom decisive.

It was the great steppe leading westward—the old Silk Road—that worried him most. There was no maintaining peace on the frontier there or in Tibet without first pacifying the tribes between Mongolia and Turkestan, most importantly the Zungars and Uighurs. The region was mostly unsettled, a reflection of the nomadic practices of its peoples and the repeated conquests and assimilation of weaker tribes by stronger ones. Farmers, herders and merchants formed a complex society without densely populated cities. Long stretches of grasslands, mountains, deserts and swamps provided hardships for all travellers.

To overcome the challenges of space and tribal resistance, the emperor adopted a variety of measures that nineteenth century Americans would have recognized. The first of these was to develop an effective cavalry. The horsemen were not as good as Mongols, but there were more of them; this addition to good infantry, together with firearms and better supplies, allowed him to be victorious even in the most difficult regions.

Infantry could move faster on a prairie or steppe than one might think, and soldiers could keep going after horses were exhausted. The problems with infantry were two-fold. One was that they could be harassed by horsemen, and if brought to a stand-still and cut off from water and reinforcements, they could be destroyed. Second was that only cavalry could close swiftly for the kill. Therefore, successful armies had to be composed of mixed forces, preferably supported by artillery. A cavalry force that was defeated could always take refuge inside an infantry square until it rallied, then go out to fight again, meanwhile cannon bombarded the attackers circling around. This required discipline. If the soldiers fled in panic, all would be killed or enslaved.

Then the Chinese built forts at strategic locations, to control water resources and road junctures. Cannon at such locations intimidated the native peoples at the same time that governmental administrators provided law and order, something that merchants and artisans appreciated.

Good government, alas, was more often a hope than a reality. Although the Chinese occupied Sinkiang (now Xinjiang, meaning 'New Frontier') and areas even more to the west in the 1760s, the governors did not often understand the local people or their many feuds, and the Chinese immigrants brought in to provide food and other necessities were soon unpopular. Revolts broke out, each repressed brutally, but with the cumulative effect of making emperors wary of further expansion westward that would also have brought on a conflict with Russia, a great power already, on China's northern frontier. In time both the tsar and emperor realised that it was better to draw a firm line between their states, with each refusing to help tribesmen who remained stubbornly independent. Like modern independence movements cut off from weapons, money and places of refuge, the steppe nomads steadily weakened until eventually they had to agree to the terms of an overlord they had not chosen.

A better means of controlling the Mongols was to encourage contemplative Buddhism, which curbed the nomads' raiding instincts. Then, by occupying Muslim lands farther west, the Chinese could prevent Islamic missionaries from bringing in dangerous ideas such as the jihad. Chinese emperors were already worried about Roman Catholic missionaries. They did not need an Islamic problem, too.

Unfortunately, we know little about the composition of the Chinese armies in these frontier wars. Certainly many troops were Manchus for whom military service was a profession. Few if any were from the West, since European influence was still relatively slight, and the few Western soldiers that the Chinese saw did not impress them greatly.

The most important region in this westward expansion was Sinkiang, which lay along the ancient Silk Road that led to Persia and then to Syria. This was a relatively fertile region, despite the mountains and deserts that ringed it, and it was so large that many diverse people could view it as their home. The most important tribe at this time was the powerful Zungar (Dzunghar) khanate. Since 1717 the khans had sworn nominal allegiance to China—a tenuous relationship that was under stress from Chinese domination of Tibet to the south, secured only by rich gifts to the khans and a strong Chinese army ready to respond forcefully against raiders.

The emperor also tied the steppe peoples to the Middle Kingdom by trade. Khans who taxed commerce could distribute gifts among tribal and clan leaders, and so saw peace bringing more benefits than war. Next the emperor settled Han Chinese beyond the Great Wall, farmers who would supply grain and fodder to imperial garrisons and potentially even for large armies, while merchants would make Chinese products, especially tea, so popular among his new subjects as to be indispensable.

Unfortunately, the settlers brought with them smallpox and other urban diseases. Steppe peoples who had been able to avoid such deadly epidemics lacked immunity, so that when one member of a wandering group came down, soon everyone was laid low, and when no one was left to gather food, firework, tend the animals, and care for the sick, the death total would soar.

This was especially so after 1756, when a civil war broke out among the heirs of the late Zungar Khan. The Manchu emperor, Qianlong (1711–96), quickly exploited the opportunity. An experienced ruler, having governed since 1735, within three years he had totally defeated the Zungars, causing—according to modern estimates—the death of seventy percent of that people by war, smallpox and starvation. It was, in effect, a massive genocide. Then he moved many of the survivors east where Chinese officials could watch them, then resettled Xinjiang as best he could with Chinese.

The Kalmyk Migration

Modern scholars know more about these events three hundred years ago than almost any foreign observer of that time. Yet there is much to be learned from studying commentaries of that time—they teach us what contemporaries knew, suggest why decisions were made, and provide us an understanding of the intellectual climate in which decisions about frontier peoples were made.

Thomas Penson De Quincey (1785-1859) is recognised today for his 1822 *Confessions of an Opium-Eater*, but in his lifetime he was better known as a writer and journalist. A polymath who had demonstrated early in life extraordinary talents, he was prevented by poor health from doing more than commenting on society, politics and history. Still, his *Collected Works* amounted to twenty-two volumes.

His long article on 'the Revolt of the Tartars', appeared in a prominent magazine, *Blackwood*, in July 1837, and was almost instantly recognized as an adventure classic. He took the basic facts from a German article by Bergman, *Versuch zur Geschichte der Kalmüken Flucht von der Wolga*, whose narrative had been based on the recollections of a Russian prisoner, Weseloff. 'The Revolt of the Tartars' was, therefore, a third-hand narrative that reflected an obscure incident in the vast borderland between two advancing civilisations—China and Russia. The steppe tribes that roamed what is today Kazakhstan were caught in the middle. Hence De Quincey's subtitle: *Flight of the Kalmuck Khan and his People from the Russian Territories to the Frontiers of China*. This event, according to De Quincey, was perhaps the most romantic of any story in history, involving the mightiest of Christian thrones and the mightiest of pagan ones, a myriad of wills, the wild barbaric character of the migrants upon whom the national catastrophe fell, and the many open and hidden motives of those involved. There was first a conspiracy, then a great military expedition, and lastly a religious exodus. Against such a magnificent background, one equal in colour to the skies and mountains that framed the limitless prairie, what did mere facts matter?

The story began 21 January 1761, when Ubashi Khan (Prince Oubacha, 1724-75) succeeded his father as ruler of the Kalmyk people living on both sides of the Volga River. He had been only eighteen years of age when he first had a role in tribal leadership, not old enough to command the allegiance of the clan leaders of his widespread tribe and certainly unlikely to impress the officials of the distant tsarina of Russia who allowed the nomads free use of the Kuban plain in return for military service; and even when mature he lacked the domineering personality that impresses nomads. It was no surprise, therefore, that a rival was able to persuade the Empress Elizabeth (1709-62) to give him her blessing to assist Ubashi in ruling his scattered people. This started the series of events that led the Kalmyks to decide to leave Russia. Doing that, however, would not be easy.

First, the Kalmyks had been in the service of tsars and tsarina so long that memory of their having fled the attacks of the Zungars was distant folklore. Elizabeth and Catherine II (1729-96), their most recent Russian overlords, had plenty of infantry—conscripts from the peasantry—but those sturdy fighters were only familiar with draft animals; for cavalry they had their noble boyars, but those aristocrats insisted on returning to their estates quickly after each campaign was over. This meant that for a more permanent cavalry force the generals had to rely on Cossacks. These wild horsemen were, alas, undependable; they resisted every governor's efforts to control them and periodically revolted over issues involving pride and traditional independence.

As a result, military leaders had advised trying to replace them, or at least restrict their expansion, by asking more of the Kalmyks. As governors insisted that the tribesmen remain longer on campaigns, mass desertions resulted. This made generals determined to bring the Kalmyks to heel as well as the Cossacks.

Second, the Quin dynasty was not known for treating steppe peoples leniently. In 1756-7, only a few years before, the emperor had ordered his generals to kill all the Lamas of the 'Yellow Teaching.' This could only be done after destroying the Zungar leadership, which, as we have seen, they did by a combination of surprise, betrayal, and force. Such a policy of extermination was rare for the Quin emperor, but the Zungars had refused assimilation point blank; his response was to make their steppe into a human desert. Where once 600,000 nomads had lived, now not a tent could be seen anywhere.

For the Kalmyks this meant that a new homeland was available—actually their old homeland—if they could secure Catherine II's blessing to return there. They knew little about the lands in between, but one steppe and one mountain range were much like any other. Their ancestors, losers in the complicated wars of rapidly changing Central Asia, had come to Russia with only two usable skills—herding animals and making war. They had not seen any reason to learn how to farm or live in villages. This had meant that, since Russian generals always wanted more cavalry, they had enlisted for wars both in Europe and on the eastern steppe, where tsars were extending control beyond the horizon to the east. Now, however, they could see that this arrangement was coming to an end.

Once Catherine II began to settle wheat farmers in the Kuban in 1763, it was obvious that the wide plain was becoming too small to support the herds of the nomads. The immigrants known as 'Volga Germans'—Roman Catholics from the Holy Roman Empire—were introducing modern agricultural methods that increased production more than the traditional villages of serfs could do. While the empress seemed to be carrying out a traditional policy—encouraging enterprises that would produce more taxes—she was also reducing the danger of revolution by diversifying the population. Although Catherine II was angering Orthodox Cossacks and Buddhist Kalmyks by bringing in Roman Catholics who weren't even good Russians, she knew that ancient rivalries with the Muslims of the Caucasus Mountains and the Turks would make it impossible for them to acquire allies there.

Meanwhile, the Kalmyks were finding themselves ever more unwelcome in Russia. They had taken, in part, the Cossacks' main reason for existing—military service for the tsar. But more fundamentally, all herdsmen—Cossacks, Kazakhs, Kyrgyzs and Kalmyks alike—hated manual labour, working at lowly jobs in the towns and being treated as an inferior form of life. The Cossacks arguably suffered less—they at least spoke Russian and understood what was going on. But they all resisted as best they could.

No cattlemen anywhere have ever been known to be unduly sensitive to farmers' complaints about their herds trampling the grain. While the Cossacks giving up some of their horses and becoming farmers was nothing unusual—the Cossacks had always been men of the soil—for the Kalmyks this was a serious challenge to their entire way of life. A nomad was a man only as long as he was on horseback, and paying taxes to some Russian official would undermine the whole clan structure. Moreover, for a Kalmyk to become a farmer implied abandoning Buddhism. In the

Russian language the word for peasant was крестьян (Christian).

The religious situation in the Kuban was as easily ignited as a prairie fire, and as quick to spread. Everyone was aware of the wars that the Cossacks had fought against the Circassians and Chechens, and they anticipated the yet more fierce wars to come. But Catherine II, like most Enlightenment rulers, believed that she had the knowledge and the power to shape society as she wished, and that everyone would be better off for it.

This had resulted in a considerable reduction in Ubashi's authority. The Kalmyk clan leaders were already accustomed to considerable autonomy; after all, with the herds scattered over a very wide area, it had been impractical to refer all minor issues to the khan. When Ubashi was required to submit all his decisions to review by a council of tribal elders, it became possible for a rival, Zebek-Dorchi, to challenge him. (We do not actually know this rival's name, since Zebek-Dorchi means 'a legitimate claimant' to tribal leadership.) Soon the young upstart was the dominant figure among the clan leaders, a role that the tsarist governor seems to have recognised—and welcomed as weakening tribal unity. However, the government seems to have had an exaggerated view of what it could expect its new puppet to do. Clearly, there was no point in any Kalmyk leader asking permission to return to China.

When tsarist officials explained to Zebek-Dorchi what they expected him to do, he agreed to cooperate. But that was a lie. He saw what the settlement of German and Russian farmers in the most favourable areas between the Volga and Don Rivers meant—that more farmers would be coming soon. Already herders were being forced to take up lowly trades in the cities and forts; this would inevitably lead to conversions to Orthodox Christianity. But he could not defy the government, because the governor would give his new authority back to the old khan. Nor could he simply murder his rival—Catherine II was not a person to forgive such actions. But he could prepare the way to lead the Kalmyks back to their original homeland east of the Caspian Sea or even back to the Great Wall of China. To this end he began a correspondence with the emperor of China, who gave his approval to the proposal, then wrote a prominent lama of the Yellow sect, probably a Mongol (but often identified, probably incorrectly, as the Dalai Lama), who, presumably after consulting the stars and signs, set the date for the start of the migration in January 1771. All this had to be conducted in greatest secrecy, first to avoid tsarist officials taking hostages from among the families and then to make excuses for crossing the ring of forts that marked the frontier. If his intention was discovered, the garrisons could prevent their passing safely with their herds and wagons.

When Ubashi Khan learned what the tribal leaders had decided, he originally bent to their will, but over the months to come he made as much trouble for Zebek-Dorchi as he dared. He knew that he could not flee to the Russians because Catherine would not forgive him for failing to control his people, and the Kalmyks in the Kuban would probably assassinate him. Therefore, he accompanied the exodus, but did not cooperate fully with the Kalmyks' new leader.

The garrisons on the frontier were mostly Cossacks, Orthodox fanatics ready to kill Catholics, Jews, or Muslims, or even Buddhists like the Kalmyks. They were fierce warriors, completely at home on the limitless plains, and among the best horsemen in the world. There were also Poles, Germans, and representatives of all the oppressed people in the empire— the Russians had mastered the techniques of divide and rule, letting the subject peoples terrorize each other into submission.

Catherine II thus had good reasons to keep the Kalmyks in her service. If they were allowed to leave, why not others? Moreover, in 1770 Ubashi had led 40,000 cavalry to support the Russian army in its war against the Turkish sultan and had contributed greatly to the ultimate victory. However, the Russian court and army made no secret of their disdain for him and any of their other barbarian subjects. Insolence, contempt, and mistreatment—common features of imperial regimes—were typical of Russian officers and administrators. Since Western Europeans looked down on the Russians, the example may have been contagious; alternatively, it may have reflected the folk memory among Russians of the long and bloody oppression by horse-born raiders and conquerors from the south and east. It might have come simply from the difficulty of finding competent and humane men to spend their lives on a distant and backward frontier, but more likely it was hatred for the way that hundreds of thousands of their people had been carried away into Muslim slavery, and treasure uncountable had been handed over as tribute. It was pay-back time, even if the Kalmyks had not been guilty of those crimes and were not even Muslims.

If De Quincey alternated between 'Kalmuck' and 'Tartar', it is of no importance. No horde in that era was ethnically pure. Relationships were often symbolic; what was uniform was the lifestyle. Languages varied, but communication was not a problem—this was not the first time there had been a mass migration. A similar one had brought the Kalmyks west, just has earlier hordes—Goths, Huns, Avars, Pechenegs, Mongols and Tatars— had come through Russia into Central Europe. Many had followed the route back east when climate and politics permitted or required, and the route was strewn with the remnants of Turkic, Mongol and Caucasian peoples who had stopped along their migrations. Some of these peoples undoubtedly disliked the Kalmyk plans because they did not want anyone crossing their grazing lands, consuming the grass and spreading diseases.

Since Zebek-Dorchi had to consult with the tribes along his proposed route, it is no surprise that rumours of the exodus reached the governor, who first dismissed the idea, then became panicked. Zebek-Dorchi's plan had been for the Kalmyks to burn all their own dwellings—to discourage the faint-hearted from turning back—then to fall on all the Christian settlements in the Kuban. However, the ice on the Volga was too thin that January for Kalmyks in the Kuban to cross. Knowing that they would be massacred in retaliation if they attacked Russian towns and farms, they quietly returned to their homes. Thus, the exodus consisted only of the 200,000 Kalmyks living east of the Volga River.

The Russian army was soon on the trail of the fugitives—and a wide trail it must have been, beaten out by wagons, horses, cattle, sheep and camels. However, the Cossacks, regular army units and other nomadic peoples could not move swiftly, either, as they were burdened by a supply train and artillery; on the other hand, they had few civilians to slow them down, and no herds needing water and forage.

The Kalmyks had a considerable head start thanks to having made the first three hundred miles in a week. Exhausted, they paused at a river before moving on at an average of forty miles a day, a pace which was greater than the animals could stand for long. Soon sheep and cattle began to perish. Even earlier their milk had given out, making it impossible to feed the infants and younger children. As a result, it was the camels which saved the tribesmen, though they, too, were becoming gaunt. It was, after all, deepest winter in one of the coldest regions on earth.

The first confrontation was won by the heavily armed garrison of a fort at a river crossing. Fortunately for the Kalmyks, many of the Cossacks had gone to the Caspian Sea to fish, and the rest retreated under the renewed pressure of Kalmyk numbers. Nevertheless, the tribesmen could not take the fort, and since they could not pass by beyond cannon range, they and their herds were under constant shelling the five days it took to reach the opposite shore. At the very end news arrived that the rear guard, 900 men from one of the most powerful clans, had been defeated by a Cossack force and utterly annihilated.

The Kalmyks immediately increased the pace, fearing that the Cossacks would occupy the only pass through the mountains ahead. They gained time to cover that 150 miles thanks to a ten-day snow storm, during which they slaughtered many of their animals and feasted, regaining strength for the race to come; meanwhile each day some of the tribesmen made progress toward their goal. In early February they could see the mountains.

Their scouts, alas, reported that they had arrived too late—Cossacks were already in place—and soon other reports came in that hostile forces were approaching from every point of the compass. This new enemy—Kyrgyzs, Kazakhs and Bashkirs, all former allies well-known to them—deserved their formidable reputation both for valour and endurance. That made it all the more necessary to force the pass at once. But it was only when the Kalmyks attacked that they saw how small the blocking unit was; Zebek-Dorchi then led dismounted warriors around the defenders and came in from the rear at the same moment that the main body of horsemen struck from the front.

The battle quickly became a slaughter. The Cossacks had exhausted their horses and camels to get into position, and so the mounts lacked the strength to carry the surviving heavy riders through the snow to safety. For generations thereafter Kalmyks related the story of the battle as one of the most glorious moments in their national history.

There was still a formidable army plodding on behind them. Michael Johann von Traubenberg (1719-72) was a German-Balt with a reputation for moving as slowly as he thought. Governor of Orenburg, a Cossack outpost just north of the Kazakh lands, he was responsible for the huge region to the south. To maintain his family's status at the court, he needed a success in this expedition (or at least the appearance of one); on the other hand, he did not want to repeat the failure of the 1718 expedition to Khiva in the Uzbek khanate—the loss of the entire army of perhaps 4,000 men. The extremes of weather were formidable—brutal cold in winter, terrible heat in summer—so he was cautious about wearing out his men and their mounts.

Traubenberg followed slowly with his artillery as far as Orsk, counting on 10,000 Kazakhs and an equal number of Kyrgyzs to join him as soon as the spring grass was up. Both Turkic peoples were Sunni Muslims, but while their Hanfi legal tradition emphasised religious flexibility based on logical analysis of problems, they had each suffered Kalmyk attack when they had resisted tsarist expansion. Now the sides had changed—these warriors could earn pay and the tsarina's favour while dispatching ancient enemies. But spring was months away. So the best Traubenberg could do was send scouts to keep track of the fugitives, then follow along slowly with the main army. His scouts reported finding many frozen bodies of women and children who had vainly huddled around the campfires in hope of surviving another night.

By May the Kalmyk had covered 2,000 miles. Thinking themselves safe, they scattered throughout the rolling prairie so that their surviving animals could graze and they could relax. When envoys from Traubenberg caught up with them, their hopes of being able to negotiate a new relationship with the tsarina's government vanished—the only terms Traubenberg would accept were unconditional surrender. This was hardly rejected before Bashkirs struck, wiping out one isolated clan after another.

Once again the Kalmyks set off in wild flight, with their enemies trying to get ahead and hold them in place until the Cossack army could catch up. But the prairie was too broad to trap them long; and the Kalmyks, despite the desert heat and lack of forage, pushed on. In the summer both fugitives and pursuers reached settled territories. Both faced difficult choices—to proceed straight ahead meant encountering forces trying to prevent them from plundering, to go around meant starvation for men and beasts.

Our information about this summer crisis is sparse because our main informant about the winter march, a prominent Russian prisoner, had escaped and made his way back to Orenburg. De Quincey reports that when he rushed into his home, his mother was so overwhelmed by seeing her only son still alive that she fell dead on the spot.

As the two hordes approached the Chinese border in the early autumn, the fighting became ever more frenzied. As De Quincey put it: 'The spectacle became too atrocious; it was that of a host of lunatics pursued by a host of fiends.'

As it happened, that very day, September 8, the Chinese emperor, Qianlong, was visiting Xinjiang, hunting in a vast area made almost devoid of human population by earlier operations of the Chinese army. According to a Jesuit reporter, he was standing at the entrance to his pavilion when he observed a cloud in the distance, a cloud that became ever larger, rolling forward in immense billows. Quickly he summoned his military escort and huntsmen, who watched in consternation as they espied distant men thundering toward them, with faint cries of desperation and combat discernible. There were so few Chinese that they could be easily overwhelmed, but nobody dared move without an imperial command.

The emperor realised that the foremost party was the Kalmyk host, but he had not expected them to arrive for another three months and not in such furious haste. While the emperor debated with himself whether or not to retire towards his main army, he saw that the mass of horsemen began moving away at a slight angle toward a body of water, Lake Balkhash (Tengis). He was too far away to see well, but he was quickly informed that the Kalmyks, Kyrgyzs and Bashkirs had been ten days in the desert and were now perishing from thirst. With no thought for further fighting, the Kalmyks threw themselves into the lake. There they were slaughtered by their pursuers until the Bashkirs and Kyrgyzs also succumbed to the desire to drink. Then a desperate struggle began, with all sides trying to lap up the bloody water, to push enemies beneath the surface, and to gather in protective clumps of friends and relatives. Then the Chinese cavalry arrived and the commander of a nearby fort began lobbing cannon balls among those Bashkirs and Kyrgyzs who remained mounted at a distance. The Kalmyks then took their revenge on those dismounted enemies who had been abandoned by their fleeing kinsmen.

The emperor assigned the Kalmyks territories superior to those they had abandoned in Russia, but the losses in human and animal wealth could not be made good quickly. Moreover, Zebek-Dorchi was now thoroughly disgusted with the khan, an enmity that came to the attention of the emperor, who soon discovered that Zebek-Dorchi had been conspiring with various tribal leaders to throw off Chinese rule. The emperor apparently ordered the khan to deal with it, which he did at a banquet during the great assembly of the 'Tatar peoples'—an annual tradition dating back to the time of the Mongols—slaughtering Zebek-Dorchi and his fellow conspirators. Ubashi Khan was henceforth the undisputed ruler of the Kalmyks, but, with his people scattered to the five districts assigned by the emperor, he ceased to be important.

Ubashi Khan did have his revenge on his rivals—his partisans wrote the tribal history.

The Impact of Expansion on China

The conquest of Central Asia—together with other borderlands seized in Qianlong's ten great campaigns—almost doubled the size of his empire. The boundaries thus established have remained to the present day.

His encouragement of the arts and literature afforded us good insights into his wars, and contacts with foreigners resulted in additional first-hand accounts of China at the height of its power.

The later years of his long reign mark the beginning of that long downward spiral of imperial power. The taxpayers exhausted, the army stretched too thin, and, with the emperor unable to oversee the new territories personally, his administrators became warlords who made themselves as independent as they dared. When rebellions began among the Han Chinese peoples, the army was hard pressed to put them down; worse, each campaign weakened the empire. Manchu rule had been spectacular, but it was also unpopular. Soon Chinese control over Central Asia was challenged by a new power.

The Afghan Kingdom

Ahmad Shah Durrani (1722-72) had founded the first Afghan kingdom immediately following the death of the great Persian emperor Nader Shah in June 1747. Nader Shah, often called the Napoleon of Asia, had conquered Delhi eight years earlier (bringing back the famous Peacock Throne that then disappeared) and fought the Ottomans to a standstill, but he had bankrupted his country by excessive taxes and terrible punishments for regions that failed to meet his financial demands.

Ahmad Shah had been the commander of the Nadar Shah's cavalry— composed largely of Pashtun tribesmen—and was therefore the most important military officer left alive after the great conqueror had eliminated potential rivals by murdering the great nobles, his best generals, and even his own son. Realising that Persia was in too much chaos to control and that the Persians would not accept a rude tribesman as their ruler, he withdrew to Afghanistan, subdued the tribes there and founded the Durrani Empire. This was possible because he had left Persia with most of Nader Shah's treasury and the world's largest diamond, the Koh-i-Noor. The combination of money, charisma, and fear brought many tribal leaders to his side, and the subsequent conquest of rich lands cemented their loyalty. It helped that the British, Russians and Chinese had undermined important rival leaders and that the rest saw him as the best hope for evading foreign domination.

From his original base in Kandahar he expanded north to Kabul, then conquered the northern tribes (Uzbeks, Tajiks, Turcoman); his pressure on the Mughal emperor of India won peaceful possession of most of what is today Pakistan and Kashmir, but he had to return several times, finally sacking Delhi. Thus he had a state stretching from the borders of Persia into Central Asia, south to the Indian Ocean and east into India.

Ahmad Shah initially sought to drive the Chinese out of its western territories, but was distracted by wars in India. Challenged in 1760 by the Hindu princes of the Maratha Confederacy who had taken control of Delhi, he employed his larger force to encircle the 70,000 Indians and their 300,000 servants, then cut off supplies.

The starving Hindu princes tried to break the siege lines, employing their French cannon effectively, but when they advanced beyond that covering fire, Ahmad Shah's camel-mounted cannon cut the Maratha army apart, then his cavalry delivered the death blow. This Third Battle of Panipat was so bloody that the victors slaughtered the prisoners and tens of thousands of non-combatants. Anger had overcome even the desire to sell the captives as slaves.

Though victorious, Ahmad Shah had lost so many men that he could not retain control of India, losing the Punjab to the new Sikh Confederacy, Delhi first to his own appointed Mughal emperor, then to a revived Maratha army, and he had to cross the mountains quickly to put down revolts in Afghanistan. Ahmad Shah remained powerful—returning to the Punjab and to India—but he never consolidated his state properly. First, he was a war leader, not the builder of a state. There was no way he could create any loyalty that went beyond that owed to him as a tribal leader. Second, he suffered from either leprosy or a tumour that ate away his nose, then into his throat, lungs and limbs. By the battle of Panipat this ulcer had grown so large that he had to wear a diamond-studded mask; visits to Sufi shrines did not help, and when he died, his twenty-four sons fought over the inheritance.

Ahmad Shah had made less impact on the region than might have been expected. He did not, for example, interrupt the trade between Russia and China—the bricks of tea and loose tea became essential for that most Russian of all drinks, Chai (чай), served by brewing highly concentrated tea in a teapot, then diluting it with boiling water from a samovar. The tea road east more than substituted for access to Indian tea. After all, the English proverb is 'not for all the tea in China'. There is no mention of Indian tea until much later.

The Impact of Expansion on Russia

The Kalmyk exodus was followed by troubles familiar to Russia—a Cossack uprising in 1772 that began with the murder of General Traubenberg in January. He had been sent to head a commission investigating complaints about Cossacks transgressing on fishing rights and their unwillingness to pay taxes, but all he managed to do was antagonise people who already hated the tsarist regime. The aftermath of the brutal murder was described by Alexander Pushkin (1799-1835) in his novel *Marie, a story of Russian love*. Traubenberg's successor hunted down the murderers, executing those he could catch and exiling family members of those he could not. This contributed significantly to the events of the next year, when Yemelan Pugachev (1742-75) led a Cossack rising that threatened tsarist control of the entire Ukraine, Kuban, and Ural regions.

Pushkin was Russia's most brilliant poet, but he was a hothead in both his personal life and politics. Because his family was prominent, he was educated at the imperial academy and had access to the leading intellectuals of the capital. Making himself unpopular in the court for advocating fundamental social and political reform, he went south, living in the Caucasus and among the Cossacks. Then, like Byron, he went to Greece to help liberate that land from Ottoman rule; after two years he returned home, only to antagonise tsarist officials; this would normally have meant transportation to Siberia, but his family connections moderated that to internal exile at the family estate near Pskov, south of St. Petersburg. The Decembrist Uprising of 1825—the plot by army officers to establish a more European form of government—changed everything. The plotters and everyone identified with their ideas was executed or exiled. Afterwards Pushkin became acquainted with intellectuals who had been sentenced to live in the frontier regions impacted by the Kalmyk exodus.

In his twenty-ninth duel Pushkin was killed by a French officer—a conservative royalist who had gone into exile rather than serve the more liberal French monarch of 1830. The officer had seduced Pushkin's notoriously flirtatious wife and even married her sister (perhaps to have an excuse to visit the home more frequently). Life was much like an opera then, and Pushkin's stories made for good scores. His 1834 history of the Pugachev Uprising had made it famous in the West, and he had written *Marie* in 1831, shortly after his marriage, a romantic story of young lovers in the distant provinces of the east.

The Kalmyks generally do not come across in Pushkin's stories as heroic, but he admired their love of liberty and their natural dignity; in one poem his hero expressed his love for a Kalmyk maiden so deeply that he was almost ready to become a nomad himself. As for the Kalmyks today, they know that Lenin had their blood in his veins through his paternal grandmother. But all this came later.

In the nineteenth century the tsars resumed their drive to the south. The principal enemy was Ottoman Turkey, but it was easy for Russians to imagine that all Muslims were potential allies of a future Genghis Khan or the British. Paranoia prefers the companionship of nationalism and mapmakers to logic and balanced budgets. Thus, the publics of all nations involved endorsed proposals to make Central Asia their own.

For Russians there had been a tempting offer by Napoleon to join in a great expedition to take India from Britain. At the time, the benefits would have gone to France, but now that France was defeated and kept in check by its suspicious neighbours, perhaps Russia could carry out the project by itself.

The Impact on Britain

The British were aware of Russian daydreams. After all, British diplomats and merchants all spoke French—the language of the educated Russian—

and attended the drunken parties where tongues were loosened and boasting was applauded. With China losing influence in Central Asia, Russia was taking its place. Tsarist agents were in Afghanistan, which was falling into disorder under pressure from the Sikhs and Persians. Would tsarist armies follow?

The *Great Game* was soon on. What everyone had come to believe was that Afghanistan was so unstable that any major power could tip the balance toward any tribal chieftain it backed. So thought Britons in distant London, who had no idea what the mountains and deserts were like. In 1839 this faction appointed a governor-general (viceroy) who was determined to become famed for thwarting the Russian advance into the region. He rejected the advice of the knowledgeable veterans around him and sent an army to Kabul. Three years later only one Englishman made his way back to a British border post—the wounded survivor was allowed to leave only so that he could tell the story of the disaster.

Far from striking fear into hearts of oak—a naval term that reflected British priorities—the defeat prompted cries for revenge, and the Great Game became earnest. How long would it last is a question answered only in Kipling's novel *Kim*, 'When everyone is dead, the Great Game is over. Not before.'

The same could have been said about the complex spy and counter-spy operations in Central Asia that followed Lenin and Trotsky's plan to export the Bolshevik Revolution to India. The British won because they had better agents and more money.

Little had changed since the 1700s. China took itself out of the picture for a long while to concentrate on problems at home, As one famous historian wrote, China went to bed rich one night and woke up the next morning poor—it had crossed the demographical barrier between having enough food for everyone and starvation. This is slightly misleading, since the road to political collapse was not straight downhill, but paved with short recoveries, then more setbacks. China also found itself contending with Europeans on its borders—Russians in Manchuria, the British on the southern coasts—and the outdated military system was not equal to the task.

With the Persians weak, the Chinese preoccupied, and the Turks not interested, this seemed to have left only two contenders for hegemony in Central Asia—the British and the Russians—neither of whom understood the magnitude of the task they were facing. The reality was different—the periphery was stronger than either realised, and it remained so into the twenty-first century.

Postscript

The Kalmyks who had been left behind in Russia were moved to the Don River valley, where they lived peacefully alongside the dominant Cossacks. They fought against the Bolsheviks in the Civil War, partly because some of the prominent White generals had Kalmyk ancestry. When the imperial cause was lost, they clambered aboard ships that took them into exile. Many settled in Yugoslavia, where they founded the first Buddhist temple in Beograd.

The lessons are clear. Central Asia was never completely isolated, never a cultural or military desert ('backwater' seems an awkward term to use), but it was too weak to repel outsiders. Only the Mongols and Chinese had the resolution to pacify the regions by genocide, and today such a policy would bring international cries of outrage, followed by sanctions on trade, travel and communication.

Resistance in various forms thus made foreign rulers learn that they could rule only through native chiefs, and then only when they did not offend native pride and traditions. In addition, the geopolitical situation lent itself to some natives appealing to outsiders for help. Lastly, politicians and generals will continue to play the Great Game because the region is too important to abandon to rivals.

Chapter 10

The Periphery in Western Literature

Cities of the Early Modern Era (1500-1800) were so unhealthy that without a constant influx of newcomers from the surrounding countryside, many would have declined in size to insignificance. Generally these newcomers did not come from a frontier zone, but, because of local commercial ties, were already familiar with urban life; also, in an era of constant warfare a city was safer than a village or hamlet. Moreover, there were niches in each city economy that peasants could fill—house servants, for certain, carpenters, bricklayers, and clerks. Frontiersmen, in contrast, often lacked even basic social skills; they had only their strong backs and an ability to endure poor housing and poor food. As Benjamin Franklin advised colonial Americans, 'Let thy maid-servant be faithful, strong, and homely.'

Newcomers to cities probably understood the dangers of disease, crime and vice, but they still believed that life would be better in a town. Their motives for moving into an uncertain future varied—to find work or to escape wars, or unemployment or boredom—but they kept in touch with their rural relatives. This, in addition to the normal exchange of goods and services between town and country, meant that the folk tale of the City Mouse and his Country Cousin was familiar to every European and presumably to people in every other land and clime.

Literature built on this foundation, so that today we can read novels and poetry to understand partially what people thought and experienced. The insights we gain into their past is limited and biased, but it is the best we can do. Travel allows us to experience the impression that cathedrals, mosques, castles and palaces must have made on our ancestors. But while stones may astound us, they do not speak. Books do.

Schiller and de Staël

In the era of the French Revolution, 1789-1815, large parts of Germany were still wild and undeveloped—Grimm Brothers territory, Hansel and Gretel. It was the most important part of the Holy Roman Empire, but it was far from a unified state—Napoleon abolished the Empire after a thousand years of existence, replacing it with a French Empire that he thought would fulfill national ambitions for domination of Europe and also provide crowns for his brothers and sisters. When Napoleon was deposed, the Hapsburgs resurrected the tradition of the Empire, but centred on the dynasty's Austrian lands; many small principalities, bishoprics and free cities were awarded to the rulers that had most assisted in defeating Napoleon.

What unity the German people had after great disruption was based partly on language, in that every literate person could read High German no matter how confused they might be when confronted by local dialects, and partly on a collective memory of the horrors of the Thirty Years War (1618-48) and resistance to French invasions. While most subjects of larger states were proud of having come through the latest crisis with their rulers strengthened, many agreed with those in smaller states that Germany needed a strong leader who could keep the peace and protect the borders. Stories of the wars to preserve Germany from the fate of Poland—divided between Russia, Austria and Prussia—were central to the national literature. None was more central than Johann Christoph Friedrich von Schiller (1759-1805), who wrote *Wallensteins Lager* (Wallenstein's Camp) in 1798, a moment when French troops were occupying the most western German states; soon the French occupied all of Germany.

Madame de Staël (1766-1817) witnessed one of the first performances of *Wallensteins Lager*. Schiller was a German patriot, the foremost author in the *Sturm und Drang* (Storm and Stress) school, which emphasized the exaggerated emotion and action that she loved—romanticism run amok: 'It seemed as if we were in the midst of an army, and of an army of partisans more ardent and much worse disciplined than regular troops. The peasants, the recruits, the victualling women, the soldiers, all contributed to the effect of this spectacle; the impression it produces is so warlike, that when it was performed on the stage in Berlin, before the officers who were about to depart for the army, shouts of enthusiasm were heard on every side. A man of letters must be possessed of a very powerful imagination to figure to himself so completely the life of a camp, the spirit of independence, the turbulent joy excited by danger itself. Man, disengaged from all his ties, without regret and without foresight, makes of years a single day, and of

171

days a single instant; he played for all he possesses, obeys chance under the form of his general; death, ever present, delivers him with gaiety from the cares of life.'

We can see why her book *Allemagne* (Germany), published in 1810, made such an impression on contemporaries. Yet she was denounced on all sides, certainly by historians who knew something of the Thirty Years War, and all who believed that women should not involve themselves in forms of literature beyond their personal experience—which meant poetry and romances; women should certainly not analyze literature. Madame de Staël nevertheless prevailed. Nothing could stop an intelligent and self-assured woman in the Age of the Enlightenment, especially not a woman who was Swiss by birth, French by choice, and an international celebrity by avocation.

Goethe

Johann Wolfgang von Goethe (1749-1832) was perhaps the most famous all-around intellectual of his era—he was a political advisor, poet, scientist, and novelist. His books were wildly popular and his poetry is often credited with inaugurating the age of romanticism. He wrote two plays which had German mercenaries at the centre of their plots, *Goetz von Berlichingen* and *the Count of Egmont*. The former, written in 1773, was based on a minor figure in the German Peasants' Uprising of 1524-26. Luther's message of spiritual freedom had reached far beyond the bounds of his native Saxony, but in the hands of the lower classes it mutated into a call to eliminate all feudal bonds. Meanwhile, much of Germany was in the hands of robber barons like Götz von Berlichingen (1480-1562) who stretched their slender incomes by robbing passing merchants.

In the opening scene Götz met a runaway monk, Martin—dare we think Martin Luther?—who yearned for the life of a carefree, lusty noble. The conversation was broken off when approaching horses were heard. As Götz extended his left hand for a farewell clasp, Martin asked why he is not worthy of the usual knightly handshake. Götz then displayed his right hand, made completely of iron, the hand that was famed throughout the land, hated by the lords and loved by the oppressed. He had lost it in 1504 at the siege of Landshut, blown off by a cannonball. (Surviving contemporary iron hands confirm that such a hand could wield a weapon effectively.)

Martin Luther had little moral authority when the Swabian knights first rebelled against Charles V, but one can little doubt that he hoped that such

Protestant warriors would weaken the authority of an arch-Catholic emperor. However, when the peasant uprising of 1526 occurred, Luther was appalled; he considered class warfare contrary to the teachings of the Bible and certainly dangerous to the interests of his noble patrons. He denounced the rebels' excesses in his usual forceful manner, urging the upper classes to crush them without mercy.

By the late 1700s clerical enthusiasm was directed toward personal sins—excessive drinking (except when done by the nobility), adultery (except when done by the nobility), violence (except when done by the nobility), theft (except when done by the nobility), and so forth. There was an almost identical list of complaints about the clergy and the nobility, but those were being raised only by a small number of malcontents known as *philosophes*, most of whom were French. As it happened, time was on the side of these men and women. Their ideas—generally secular, scientific, romantic and rational—laid the foundations for the Enlightenment era. If the ideas and emotions were often contradictory, that was unimportant. Eras of intense intellectual development are marked by intense controversies and disputes, and disputes among modern scholars about what eras actually represented are just as intense, though rarely so bloody.

Of course, not everyone or every place was changed significantly by the theories circulating among the intellectual classes. Often enough, when the process of change disturbed ordinary people, they were just too busy getting on with life to bother thinking much about it. Fortunately for authors, there were always readers who enjoyed stories about distant and exotic locations; and fortunately for military recruiters, some young men wanted to see them.

Voltaire and Münchhausen

Human beings not changing much in their essential character from century to century, it is understandable that more people preferred to read for enjoyment than for mental stimulation. While writers such as Voltaire could combine the two, most of his contemporaries were much like modern polemicists—too angry to be funny. This left the field of literature open to an imaginative humourist who could create imaginary worlds based on travellers' tales and general knowledge. Voltaire's *Candide* was entertaining, challenging and funny, but he had never visited the distant lands he described.

Baron Munchhausen's Narrative of His Marvellous Travels and Campaigns in Russia took place in the eighteenth century against the background of contemporary wars. Several real-life Münchhausens had been associated with sixteenth-century Livonia, but these tales had nothing to do with them. The stories had apparently been accumulating for a very long time, all representing the fascination held by German travellers and adventurers with the exotic landscape of Eastern Europe, where the languages, music, and customs were so different from those of home. In the twenty-first century one is not supposed to remark that even an oriental or semi-oriental nation was ever exotic, and certainly not powerful and sensitive nations like Poland and Russia that were trying to imitate Western practices.[1] However, a post-modern reader is empowered to derive whatever message he or she gets from a text, no matter what the author intended. A reader is even permitted, under exceptional circumstances, to accept what the author intended—in this case that Russia was an interesting and exotic land.

The author, Karl Friedrich Hieronymus Freiherr von Münchhausen (1720-97), served the tsar in two Turkish wars, then retired to Hanover, where he told wildly embellished tales that were written out by a family friend, Rudolf Erich Raspe (1737-94), and published anonymously in London in 1785. The book was such a sensation that it was translated into German the following year. In 1798 a further eight stories were added by Gottfried August Bürger (1747-94).

The most famous fictional exploits had the baron riding on a flying cannonball, and once, during one of those typically ferocious Russian winters, when the baron at last found shelter, he tied his horse to a post and hurried inside. In the morning, he saw that the weather had made a swift change from very cold to extraordinarily hot; looking around for his horse, he found it dangling from the church steeple. The book quickly joined Swift's *Gulliver's Travels* and Voltaire's *Candide* as a popular imaginative masterpiece.

Swift

Gulliver's Travels appeared in 1726. Jonathan Swift (1667-1745) wrote this satire after his career as a political pamphleteer fell on hard times; essentially exiled from Whig London, becoming dean of St. Patrick's Cathedral in Dublin was the best his Troy friends could arrange. His most famous essay, *A Modest Proposal*, brought Irish poverty to public attention with its mock advocacy of eating the children of the poor.

In the land of the Lilliputians Gulliver was a giant, in the land of the Yahoos he was tiny. Each experience gave him a completely different perspective on everything. In Lilliput he heard a story that every reader would have realised applied directly to European affairs. Only the most persistently stupid could read about the eggs described below and not grasp that the reference was to contemporary religious quarrels: 'Besides, our Histories of six thousand Moons make no mention of any other Regions, than the two great Empires of *Lilliput* and Blefuscu. Which two mighty Powers have, as I was going to tell you, been engaged in a most obstinate War for six and thirty Moons past. It began upon the following Occasion. It is allowed on all Hands, that the primitive way of breaking Eggs, before we eat them, was upon the larger End: But his present Majesty's Grand-father, while he was a Boy, going to eat an Egg, and breaking it according to the ancient Practice, happened to cut one of his Fingers. Whereupon the Emperor his Father published an Edict, commanding all his Subjects, upon great Penaltys, to break the smaller End of their Eggs. The People so highly resented this Law, that our Histories tell us there have been six Rebellions raised on that account; wherein one Emperor lost his Life, and another his Crown.'

Swift was not given to laughter himself, a strange characteristic for a man who brought smiles to many a stoic face. His struggles with health, his frustrating searches for employment, his political career ending in failure—all these stood in contrast to his ability to make friends with leading intellectuals and writers, his deadly wit, his insights into the human condition and his conviction that he was serving the cause of human liberty.

Goldsmith

Oliver Goldsmith (1730-74) wrote his classic novel, *The Vicar of Wakefield*, in 1761-2, and found a publisher four years later. He began it as a satirical commentary on social customs, allowed it to become dark and melancholic, then concluded it with all problems resolved. One conversation concerned the vicar's lecherous nephew, who 'came to me with looks of real pleasure to inform me of a piece of service he had done for his friend George. This was nothing less than his having procured him an ensign's commission in one of the regiments that was going to the West Indies, for which he had promised but one hundred pounds, his interest having been sufficient to get an abatement of the other two. "As for this trifling piece of service," continued the young gentleman, "I desire no other reward but the pleasure of having served my friend; and as for the hundred pound to be paid, if you are unable to raise it yourselves, I will advance it, and you shall repay me at your leisure."'

This was not much of a favour—the death rate of officers and men sent to the Caribbean was horrendous. The vicar exclaimed to the young man,

'Thou art going to fight for thy country, remember how thy brave grandfather fought for his sacred king, when loyalty among Britons was a virtue. Go, my boy, and imitate him in all but his misfortunes, if it was a misfortune to die with Lord Falkland. Go, my boy, and if you fall, tho' distant, exposed and unwept by those that love you, the most precious tears are those with which heaven bedews the unburied head of a soldier.'

As the vicar later noted, 'The felicity of a soldier can never be called permanent.' The same for a reader—Lord Macaulay (1800-59), one of the most influential figures of his era, called the plot of this novel the worst ever conceived.

Scott

Walter Scott (1771-1832) wrote stories of his Caledonian homeland that became instant sensations both at home and abroad, spawning innumerable imitators. In Europe these romantic novels were long required reading in schools, but Scott's stories have retained their popularity without such artificial encouragement. The political context of Scott's novels has become less significant—while many Scots desire independence from Britain (i.e. England), few want a Stuart Restoration, the central theme of Scott's first novel, *Waverly* (1814). Real figures mix with fictional ones against the vivid backdrop of scenes that Lowlanders and Highlanders, and even distant Londoners could easily imagine. Certainly, anyone familiar with Edinburgh Castle, Holyrood Palace and Arthur's Seat will visualise the action easily. And the romance of the Highlands—hills, lakes, bagpipes, kilts and whiskey—has an enduring fascination.

The noble volunteers for the rising of 1715 were highly educated, quoting Latin at every opportunity, with occasional repartee in French and Italian.[2] The poor cottagers and herders who followed their clan chieftains, in contrast, were almost utter barbarians—the kind familiar to Romans and Normans as well as more recent English-speaking inhabitants of the North. James Miller, *Swords for Hire,* has a short essay on Scots in literature of the era. He particularly recommends Scott's *A Legend of the Wars of Montrose.*

Rob Roy appeared in 1817. Although Rob Roy McGregor was not the central figure of the novel and does not appear until half way through the book, everyone understood that the English merchant trying to recover a debt owed his father was merely a cover story for his effort to get into the Highlands.

Scott's stories were immediately popular both in his homeland and abroad. Everywhere imitators sprang up, each using his own nation's mythologised history as the background to exciting stories.

Similarly, Robert Burns (1759-1796) inspired imitators at home and around Europe, emphasising local legends, nostalgia and folklore.

Rudyard Kipling

Although Kipling (1865-1936) had been born in Bombay, he lived there only until the age of five. Nevertheless, he never forgot the India of his childhood, which seemed even better from the distance of his severe English boarding school. In 1882 he returned to India, beginning there his impressive production of novels and poetry, and seven years later returned to England via the United States. In 1892 he married in London an American, who, when she became pregnant, cut short a trip to Asia to return to her family home in Vermont. There he wrote some of his most famous stories about India, *The Jungle Book* for children, and the poems *Mandalay* and *Gunga Din*. In his *Barrack Room Ballads* was a bitter complaint about the public treatment of redcoats. Not long ago every educated person in the English-speaking world would have read the entire poem in school. Today that is no longer the case and Kipling is not even a well-known name.

> 'We aren't no thin red 'eroes, nor we aren't no blackguards too,
> But single men in barricks, most remarkable like you;
> An' if sometimes our conduck isn't all your fancy paints:
> Why, single men in barricks don't grow into plaster saints;
> …
> For it's Tommy this, an' Tommy that, an' 'Chuck him out, the brute!'
> But it's 'Saviour of 'is country,' when the guns begin to shoot;
> An' it's Tommy this, an' Tommy that, an' anything you please;
> But Tommy ain't a bloomin' fool - you bet that Tommy sees!'

Kipling's endorsement of 'The White Man's Burden' was not popular even before his death in 1936, and today it is usually mocked more often than it is read. Kipling would not have been surprised. He had no illusions about the task that Britons had taken upon themselves or about the mixed motives of the flawed human beings who carried it out. In *Recessional* he warned about overweening pride and dreams of glory.

The days of mercenaries were past, except in the colonies, when British power rested on the skills and loyalties of Sepoys and Gurkas. But attitudes toward soldiers hardly changed, even though today there are still occasional calls for the West to shoulder the White Man's Burden (without calling it that) in the form of aid workers, missionaries and investors, and from time to time military trainers and combat forces.

A Polish Artist and Novelist

At a time when the nation of Poland was divided by three occupying powers—Russia, Germany and Austria-Hungary—a painter and a novelist drew upon the most glorious episodes of the past to prove that *Polska jesze jije*—Poland still lives!—a line taken from its national anthem.

The painter was Jan Matejko (1838-93), whose speciality was gigantic canvases, the very size suggesting the greatness of the subject. His 1872 painting of *Bathory at Pskov* (*Stefan Batory pod Pskowem*) was a reminder that Poles were once accustomed to beating Russians in battle, not the other way around. In over 300 paintings he reminded Poles of a historic greatness that contrasted strongly with their nineteenth-century oppression.

The novelist was Henryk Sienkiewicz (1846-1916), whose books were similarly monumental. Most famous was the trilogy set in the middle of the seventeenth century, in the midst of Poland's greatest humiliations and triumphs, the second volume—about the foreign invasions that almost destroyed the kingdom—being appropriately named *The Deluge* (*Potop*, 1886). The hero was a Samogitian, that is, a Lithuanian from the most determinedly independent province of that proud eastern half of the Polish-Lithuanian state; the pagans there had been the last to succumb to Christianity, accepting it only when imposed by the combination of the Teutonic Knights, the king of Poland, and the grand duke of Lithuania.

In Sienkiewicz's mind, Lithuanians shared Polish culture fully, or should. Awkwardly, Lithuanians did not agree, nor did the many Russians, Ukrainians and Belarusians who inhabited the lands that Sienkiewicz's readers considered Polish. Together with *With Fire and Sword* (*Ogniem i mieczem*, 1884) and *Fire in the Steppe* (*Pan Wołodyjowski*, 1888), Sienkiewicz's novels became the most important single popular interpretation of Polish history; in translations and in film, this trilogy had a great impact on educated foreigners. He was awarded the Nobel Prize for Literature in 1905.

Germans, who were almost always portrayed as villains, were naturally offended by his novels. Hartmut Boockmann (1934-1998), one of the fairest of modern historians, said that Sienkiewicz's Teutonic Knights were portrayed as sadists, enslaving the native peoples, filled with hatred and arrogance. This, of course, was exactly the opposite of what the German public had been reading—that only cretins and sadists spoke Polish. This tells us much of the way the two publics saw one another in the long century following the extinction of the Polish-Lithuanian state. Only in recent decades have the historians of the two countries reached out to one another to find common ground in a common history. Boockmann, a German born in Marienburg (Polish: *Malborg*) whose family was driven out of their ancestral homeland by the Poles in 1945, was a major figure in the reconciliation.

Andrić

The great Yugoslav novel, *The Bridge on the Drina* (*Na Drini Ćuprija*) was written during the Second World War, when Ivo Andrić (1892-1975) was confined to his home by the Nazi occupiers. He was a Serb, but no one has written more sympathetically of Bosnians and Turks.

The centre of action was the little town of Višegrad on the Drina River, its sole claim to importance being that it lay on the principal trade route from Novi Pazar to Sarajevo. The ferry was slow, expensive and often interrupted by floods; therefore, Muslim traders had long complained about the delays. When a Turkish pasha visited the town in 1571, he ordered the construction of a stone bridge over the wide, swift river. The pasha, Mehmed Paša Sokolović (1506-76), had been taken from the town as a boy, part of the tax in children levied on Christian families, and enrolled in the Janissary Corps; thus, building the bridge was more than making Turkish trade more efficient—it was an act of beneficence to his home town. Sokolović had established a military reputation at the 1526 battle of Mohács that led to the occupation of most of Hungary, and the 1529 Siege of Vienna; he was grand vizier to three sultans, effectively the ruler of the Ottoman Empire until his assassination.

There was local resistance to building the bridge—a lack of enthusiasm and some sabotage—that frustrated the first architect. The second builder used more forceful methods, and succeeded. Andrić's description of the impaling of a saboteur is not for the faint-hearted.

Readers learn to appreciate the skills of Turkish architects and administrators, and the wisdom of the leaders of the various religious communities in the town who found ways for their peoples to live together in relative peace and comfort. But not in equality. That was too much to expect. Mutual respect existed, but not in super-abundance.

The bridge lasted for generations, but the hostel that housed merchants fell into disrepair when the Ottomans lost Hungary—the funds for upkeep had come from estates in the north that were back in Christian hands. From that moment on Bosnia entered into hard times. Christian armies invaded, but failed to occupy the region permanently, and later efforts by Serbs to throw out the Turks were repressed brutally.

When the Austrians finally occupied the town, they brought order, rules and the railroad. They erected fine buildings with Turkish architectural themes. But in the end they were just another group of interlopers, like the Turks, whose efforts were first ignored, then forgotten, by later generations.

Such is the fate of actors in history, and those who write about them. Literature lasts longer, but its influence diminishes year by year as new books—mostly trash or ephemeral—crowd the old ones out of the book shops and into the dark stacks of research libraries.

No one acquainted with Bosnia can think of this great bridge without being reminded of the better known 1557 bridge at Mostar (the *Stari Most*) that was destroyed in 1993 during the three-sided Bosnian War. The author remembers walking across it before the war from the Muslim side to the Croatian, to hear Croatian students sing. There was a common language, a common culture, and a common distaste for the self-management communism that was associated with Serbian domination. (Serbs, of course, felt differently about this.) Those were golden days, at least by comparison with the civil war that followed. As was occasionally remarked, there was more history there than could be consumed locally, and this history divided people rather than uniting them. The bridge was rebuilt in 2004.

Andrić received the Nobel Prize for literature in 1961.

The Moral of It All

Mark Twain wrote in his preface to *The Adventures of Huckleberry Finn*, that anyone looking for a motive, plot, or moral will be prosecuted, banished, or shot. He was combining humour and seriousness, something forbidden to most of us. Still, if anyone has to *look* for a moral in any book, it must not be very obvious.

The truth of the matter is that one tends to find what one is looking for. Therefore, it is no surprise that anyone looking for tribal peoples, clans, or mercenaries in literature will find them; those who are unaware of their importance will never see them. Similarly, it should be no surprise that the dividing line between clan-based cultures and peasants, or mercenaries and soldiers, became blurred—urban societies mistrusted them all, just as they hated the taxes and bureaucracy that made their comfortable states function. But changing any current equilibrium was not an easy matter. All of the impositions—taxes, rules, bureaucrats, armies—were part and parcel of the society of the times, and the clan-based societies did more than reciprocate the feelings that townsfolk had toward them. Hatred is stronger than disdain.

Still, to learn what people think (or could have thought) rather than just what they did, nothing beats a good novel. No one who wants to understand how attitudes are formed and sustained can ignore the novels, the folktales, and the mythology surrounding local heroes.

1. The fault may be linguistic. One can imagine an educated German who knew Latin, French and Italian, and maybe even English, recoiling from the multiplicity of new languages he would have to learn to understand what was happening in Eastern Europe. Especially frustrating were the unfamiliar consonant clusters of Slavic languages, different verbs for completed and uncompleted actions, and some consonants that no foreign adult could ever pronounce correctly. Fortunately, every educated person spoke Latin or French, and money could overcome any difficulty in communication.
2. Exile does provide opportunities to learn foreign languages and to appreciate the witty conversation of courtiers at the few courts which welcomed the Stuarts.

11

The Periphery Is Not Always Far Away

There is a borderland and a frontier. Both can be a periphery, but the first is less distant than the second—its population also acknowledges the authority of the centre, while frontiersmen often do not.

One might reasonably expect that the periphery is at a physical distance from the centre, but the mental distance may be more important. One can be an outsider—compared to the heavily populated core of a state—by simply living in a valley or on an island whence travel to the closest city takes time and effort. Isolation is a characteristic of the periphery that can create and sustain not only very different economic systems, but also very different values and attitudes.

In America the famous 'mountain pride' of the sturdy 'hillbillies' living in North Carolina, West Virginia and Tennessee is the stuff of legend—and a persistent frustration to do-gooders in the federal bureaucracy who want the people there to accept welfare and other government programmes. Odd, that in an era where idealistic young people praise self-sufficiency and locally produced foods, they criticize people who actually live by those principles.

Mountain folk prided themselves on being skilled shooters, good hunters and hard drinkers—a stereotype which, like the folk memory of fighting Indians, was passed on from generation to generation; consequently, even storekeepers, teachers and politicians today believe that these are their characteristics, too.[1] President Obama's comment to an audience of California millionaires about folks who grasp for their Bibles and guns was referring to men and women in the small towns and villages of the Allegheny Mountains.

Indians who had lived in these same mountains were similarly skilled in the use of rifles, but not as skilled as they would have been if they had had enough gunpowder for more practice at shooting; instead, they relied on their skill at stalking. Even so, tribes with firearms could drive native competitors westward and intimidate Americans who ventured into their lands. The Americans who first crossed the mountains were legends in their own lifetimes. Daniel Boone (1734-1820), who in 1775 cut the first road through the Cumberland Gap, earned a reputation as hunter and Indian fighter, then pushed ever westward until he crossed the Mississippi River into Spain's Louisiana Territory. He retired to a quiet life in the state of Missouri, but his ability as a marksman with the famed Kentucky rifle inspired generations of young men to dream of emulating his exploits.

Many of those who crossed the mountains were Scotch-Irish and Scots. They brought their stories, their music, and their pride into the Appalachians and the rugged hills that spread out into Tennessee. They allowed no one to dishonour them.

The famous Hatfield-McCoy feud was representative of conflicts between closely knit families in West Virginia and Kentucky, conflicts which lasted for generations, even long past when anyone could remember why they started. Often only a marriage could bring an end to such hostilities or at least a truce—much like the marriages of medieval dynasties—but sometimes, as the feud between the Shepherdson and Grangerford families in Mark Twain's *The Adventures of Huckleberry Finn* indicates, this was not enough. In fact, that love story was more like Romeo and Juliet. The utter backwardness of southern Missouri and all of Arkansas—where Twain's story was set—made politicians from the cities despair of ever changing either the conditions of life there or the attitudes.

Huck's 'pap' was an example of what happened when an uneducated person was degraded by drink, poverty and a belief that he was too good to have to work. Such a person was widely called 'white trash', but poor whites reciprocated by blaming everyone else for their problems—blacks, Yankees and educated folks. Real mountain people were generally too proud to sink so low, but some emulated what they admired in Indian culture—men doing nothing but hunt, fight, and relax. Work was for women. As for the non-standard English, frontier people of all nations develop their own dialects, some almost unintelligible even in neighbouring valleys. Habits that we call lazy or lacking ambition are also worldwide, and perhaps worldly wise—we are often told that we work too much and enjoy the simple pleasures of life too little.

Not everyone agreed with this. Indian women, seeing so many of their men destroying themselves with alcohol and gambling, married White and Black men who were available because so few of their women had come to the frontier; such men were good providers, and they treated their wives well. It is a rare Black family in Arkansas, Louisiana and Oklahoma that does not have some Indian ancestry, and Whites are known to brag about the ancestor who married an Indian princess.

History is full of such ironies. But this kind of counter-intuitive insight enlivens our study of the past and confounds the useful stereotypes that help us to make daily sense of a complicated world.

The examples go far beyond the American frontier and the wilds of Afghanistan.

Dithmarschen in Holstein

This North German community was an independent peasant republic until 1557. The Dithmarschers lived in marshlands recovered from the North Sea, clan members supporting one another in an epic struggle against nature and against well-armed neighbours to the east. Their determination to remain independent challenged the hegemony of both the landed nobility of next-door states and the cities of the Hanseatic League (two groups which were seldom in agreement about politics), and in 1500 they inflicted a military defeat on a huge Danish army that almost caused the proud Scandinavian kingdom to collapse.

The clan leaders were not quite nobles, but they were the wealthiest farmers of their districts. As such they could provide employment and protection to clan members, and though every male citizen had the right to speak at public meetings, they usually deferred to their hereditary betters. The clergy, both in the Catholic and Protestant eras, were more concerned about morality than politics; and the formal overlord—the Archbishop of Hamburg-Bremen—took his annual monetary gift and left them alone; the more distant Holy Roman Emperor rarely paid them any attention.

The clan system had its advantages, most of all in the practice of settling disputes by making payments for every type of injury. Not only did this ancient system of 'wergild' satisfy pride, thereby preventing feuds, but because every clan member had to contribute to the payment, each took it upon himself to restrain the most aggressive and drunken members of the clan from assaulting anyone. Elsewhere the payment might be called blood money.

Even their defeat in 1557 by overwhelming numbers of professional troops led by a competent general was a source of Dithmarscher pride—they had gone down fighting, and their spirit remained unbroken. Today they remain proudly different from other Germans, an attitude they pass on to immigrants and even to city dwellers looking for a country getaway in their quiet rural districts.

Dithmarschen was not an isolated backwater in those days, but had close contacts with the leading cities of the Hanseatic League. A glance at modern telephone books will reveal a surprising number of British first names.

America Between Myth and Reality

According to Ahmed and Kaplan, American policy has been fundamentally misdirected in recent years; by encouraging modernism (women's rights, religious pluralism, tolerance for homosexuals), it has challenged the moral values that undergird traditional societies. In their view, Third World resistance to the West comes not from religion or poverty or ignorance, but from perceived disrespect. As is sometimes said, Americans know the price of everything, but the value of nothing.

Such upsetting of traditional values is incomprehensible in any honour-based society. Even in the West aristocratic duels and bar fights did not begin over money, but over insults and perceived slights. The American philosopher and economist, Thorstein Veblen (1857-1929), remarked a hundred years ago in *The Theory of the Leisure Class* that the only significant difference between the upper and lower classes was that one had money and the other didn't. They shared attitudes and values that clashed with those of the rising Middle Class—a love of gambling, drinking, and combat as opposed to hard work, fairness and responsibility. Since Americans even then found it impossible to impose what were once called the Protestant virtues on their own society, they can hardly expect to impose them easily on foreign foes today. This is all the more so when we observe how thoroughly Americans (and other Westerners) violate their own professed values.

The sex and violence of Western entertainment media offend those who honour sexual purity as the highest value, while Western culture has encouraged women to behave as freely as men. One scene in *The Godfather* summarises this cultural divide: a distraught Italian-American undertaker approaches the local mafia head, Don Corleone, asking him to kill two boys who beat his daughter for refusing to have sex with them; the boys had been excused by the judge because they were from prominent families and the girl had been drunk. The undertaker made his request at the marriage of Don Corleone's daughter, a moment when no Sicilian could deny any favour asked of him. The Don, in true tribal fashion, rebuked the undertaker for not having come to him earlier, to offer him respect, then, when denied justice in the court, for asking him to commit murder. Is a

185

Don, he asked, just a common criminal? After agreeing to punish the boys for daring to attack an Italian girl, he criticized the father for not supervising his daughter properly.

When the undertaker tried to pay the godfather, he was told that this was an even greater insult. Was he an assassin for hire? The godfather rejected the money, saying that some day he would ask for a favour.

It may be an exaggeration to say that every important lesson in life is in *The Godfather*, but both the book and the 1972 movie tell us much about the honour societies that middle class sons meet on modern battlefields. It also applies to street gang members or skinheads; when we see these on a sidewalk ahead of us, we cross the street. In today's America, where every great city is governed by liberal Democrats, no one has figured out how to control the street gangs which are responsible for so much of the random violence and the local wars over the sale of drugs and other 'victimless' crimes; these petty criminals are bound together by a code of honour which makes them despise ordinary citizens and even the police.

Ironically, gun violence is worst in American cities with the strongest gun control laws—if a half-dozen of the large cities were stricken from the murder statistics, America would seem to be one of the safest countries in the world. The heart of the problem seems to be connected with the collapse of the traditional family structure—boys without fathers drift into a gang culture that provides structure and meaning. Every gang member wears tattoos and gang symbols as badges of honour.

These gangs represent no breakdown of civilised values, but the reinvention of a tribal mentality. Youths—usually racial or ethnic minorities—are attracted to cultural values that give them pride and purpose without requiring them to work or study. To understand this, read Veblen.

The habit of looking down on those who are less sophisticated and less well acquainted with city manners is universal. Europeans often worry about the immigrants among them, but they try to outlaw any expression of resentment or fear lest it lead to a return of right-wing parties or even fascism. Americans often find themselves regarded by Europeans as rural yokels who lack good taste and are even unable to learn a foreign language; those who do know foreign languages are appalled by comments that speakers assume could not be understood. In addition, as Britons put it during the Second World War, the major faults of Yanks were that they were 'overpaid, oversexed, and over here'. In short, we live on a Ship of Fools, where everyone dislikes everyone else but each has to form alliances that keep those below them in line.

There is also the resentment that urban societies feel about rural cousins who exercise power as a result of their military prowess—they cannot deny that they have to rely on these некультурный[2], but they don't have to like it. Kipling famously wrote about British civilians' disdain of 'Tommy': 'I went into a public-'ouse to get a pint o' beer, The publican 'e up an' sez, "We serve no red-coats here".'

Americans who feel their inferiority form a major theme in the novels of Henry James (1843-1916); unsophisticated Americans try to understand European culture, not having anything but money to offer in exchange.[3] Often, however, Americans make this backwardness into a virtue by thinking themselves more virile than their critics; even highly educated Americans who cannot imagine living west of the Hudson River are aware that not too long ago their ancestors faced warlike Indians and conquered a wilderness. One sees this in Hollywood movies, television programmes, and popular entertainment.

The popularity of American movies about the Wild West is widely shared by societies with a similar past, even, we are told, by jihadists. This perhaps reflects Huck Finn 'lighting out' for the territories to escape the tyranny of women and women's values. The mythical American West is a male society; the real American West honoured women who left every comfort behind to share the sufferings and hopes of their men.

Americans vacillate about whether their virtues can be shared with the rest of the world. Aware that a haughty mother country often disdains their history and culture, and that the French usually disdain everybody, Americans periodically retreat into what is called Isolationism. The fact that America is both a centre and a periphery explains much about its people's attitudes toward the world.

On the periphery of any organised society—in America the subject of Fredrick Jackson Turner's 1893 Frontier Thesis—small groups have to rely on themselves for economic survival and defence. The gun culture—as some call it—combines practicality (hunting, protection) with a defensive masculinity that is threatened on all sides by a changing world that leaves common citizens with little say on what happens to them, their families and their local communities.

This is a phenomenon that has appeared on almost every continent, and was particularly important in the early modern era, when well-ordered states were pressing their values and institutions onto peoples they had previously ignored. When encountering resistance, these states fielded large armies equipped with newer weapons and occupied the cities. Tribal peoples still held out in mountains and deserts, but usually they were no danger to the centres of civilisation, and it was often easy to deal with them by bribery or even hiring the warriors to serve as scouts or irregular troops.

Many of these people are living among us today, either as exiles or as economic immigrants, but have not left their habits of thought behind. A few—usually the second generation of immigrants—see governments and police as potential enemies, the mores of their host nations as abominations, and are frustrated that they do not prosper as well as white peers whose linguistic and social skills enable them to succeed better in schools and workplaces.

In short, they do not think they have been treated with respect. Their dignity has been offended.

The Age of Revolutions

Military history from 1500 to 1789 has lessons to teach the modern world, but the lessons are taught better as stories than as maxims. This is especially so for the conflicts in this book, which range from the well-known to the obscure, but each illuminating some aspect of our all-too-human characteristic of resorting to force to get what we want.

Alexis de Tocqueville looked back on that long era through the lens of the French Revolution, the cataclysmic event that affected the history of Western civilisation more decisively—though some might argue the point—more than any other. He is far better known for his two-volume *Democracy in America* (1835 and 1840) than *The Old Regime and the Revolution* (1856). This is because his observations about American character seem to be timeless, whereas the events leading to the overthrow of the French monarchy are useful only for analysing later revolutions.

De Tocqueville argued that feudal France was not dominated by the kings, but by institutions which limited royal power. These were sometimes national, but usually local, sometimes personal, and often communal or class-based. Cities, the Church and the Aristocracy strongly defended their rights against the crown, nullifying royal efforts to make changes in economic, political and military institutions, even when reforms seemed necessary and good. It was a cumbersome, inefficient and sometimes self-destructive process, but it protected people against an over-mighty monarch. When the kings, especially Louis XIV, made their authority supreme, those institutions fell into disuse. The result was only a marginally more effective central government and an increasingly wide gap between those who ruled at the top and those oppressed at the bottom.

Without the institutional buffers between the king, his courtiers and his bureaucrats, the nobles, clergy and burghers could only grumble that a few reforms could make everything better, even perfect. But nobody was willing to make loans to absolute rulers who could default at any time. Little did victorious revolutionaries of France foresee that their hope of creating a utopia would be frustrated by an inability to raise money once they had abolished the unpopular taxes; moreover, they were done in by the unhappy poor, the radicalism of the intellectuals, and the fears of exiles and foreign powers. Ultimately their choices would be between decapitation, despoliation or exile.

By this interpretation, by 1789 France had been boxed in, constrained so tightly by royal rules and regulations that only a violent explosion could release the tensions. Of course, no contemporary realised it (or none who counted). This is similar to events of recent years where the 'inevitable' uprising overthrows a moderate tyrant and replaces him with a person or system that is dangerous beyond previous imagination. Napoleon has many imitators. Some of them belong in the nut-house, but all have their admirers. (The difference between young women at rock concerts and men at political rallies is hard to see.) Tyranny does have a way of cutting through the clutter of institutions and traditions.

Great Britain, in contrast, retained sufficient ties between the classes that no revolution occurred. The British probably had equally callous tax collectors and administrators, equally snobbish aristocrats, and certainly the king was hardly better than Louis XVI, but somehow the common people did not see them as oppressors, and bankers were willing to loan the government money. Who could imagine George III (1738-1820) as a tyrant except distant colonials?

It may be, as Simon Schama suggests in *Citizens*, that the French kings were more easily mocked by scurrilous satires and rumours of sexual license than the English monarchs. But perhaps the English had become so accustomed to Jacobite attacks on the Hanoverian dynasty than they could dismiss all critics of their German kings as partisan hacks, Catholic malcontents or, worst of all, Scots. Actually, the Hanoverian dynasty was a pretty dull lot. George III had relatively little influence over his ministers and from 1765 on was periodically prostrated by mental illness.

The French, having lost three wars against Britain in a century, courted bankruptcy to win one; then, having managed to help the Americans achieve their independence, made a peace that brought them almost no advantages. Revenge was sweet, but it repaid no loans to bankers and other lenders who now wanted their money.

The Lesson, if There is One

There is, alas, nothing in these stories that suggest wars will end soon, much less the rumours of war. As Isaac Newton (1642-1727), the philosopher-mathematician-astronomer who lived through many of the events described here, wrote, 'I can calculate the movements of the stars, but not the madness of man.'

The madness of war—like the post-modern insistence that we can understand the masked reality of a society by studying the violence of its extremes—is perhaps best seen in the wars along the periphery, where the standards of Western morality and common sense tend to melt away.

Studies of the peripheries of the other great civilisations of the world are few and are written from a Western point of view. We know much about what Europeans thought of Turks, Mongols and Africans, but are only slowly learning what those peoples thought about Europeans. Partly this is because the alleged sins of European scholars—most importantly looking at 'the other' through a cultural lens—have been adopted by historians who reject everything else that Europe once offered. Honour requires total acceptance or total rejection.

This is something that the West does as well.

Romantic Roads and the Great Game

A periphery is rarely an area devoid of human life. First of all, there are few pure deserts in the world—Death Valley in California, the Gobi in Central Asia, the Empty Quarter in Arabia and areas so covered with ice that neither man nor beast can find sustenance. The rest are areas of thin population, with only hermits and monastic communities, or nomads and merchant caravans. The word also reflects cultural prejudices—the Great American Desert of the 1830s became what Kansas farmers of the 1970s called 'the breadbasket of the Soviet Union'. Soviet bureaucrats visiting this golden prairie at harvest time went home determined to plough up a seemingly similar prairie around the Aral Sea, but they decided to grow cotton, which required using river waters for irrigation. Ploughing the American Great Plains had seemed wise in the 1920s, when rain was plentiful, but ten years later, when dry weather returned, it became a Dust Bowl; the land recovered when much of the prairie was returned to grass. In contrast, Central Asia is still suffering from ecological disaster brought on by Soviet central planning; the Aral Sea, having almost completely dried up, is only slowly beginning to refill.

Sometimes the lack of population reflects an unfavourable climate, other times the people have simply fled out of fear of attack. Either way, people only enter these thinly populated regions to look for wealth, or spiritual enlightenment, or to cross for trade and war. These routes often have romantic names—el Camino Real (the royal road), the Silk Road—and some are pilgrim routes of major world religions.

Often this romanticism is connected with a river or a gap in the mountains. For Americans this could be the Cumberland Gap, through which pioneers ventured into lands of semi-nomadic Indian tribes to carve out new lives for themselves. For Britons it could be the Khyber Pass, where redcoats in pith helmets stood ready to fight Afghan raiders or, if the Great Game went awry, Russian armies. Rudyard Kipling's name is forever connected to the rugged landscape and the fierce warriors of this gateway to India. Whether Kipling's message is that of Gunga Din, the Ballad of East and West, or the White Man's Burden, the listener is compelled to think of the Northwest Provinces, not Tibet or Burma. The Road to Mandalay and Singapore were romantic and commercial, without heroic elements; both were also too hot to encourage physical exertion. Women there were unlikely to present a white feather to men who were reluctant to risk death in arid mountains.

We still await the historians who can inform us of the equivalent roads in China, India, Africa and Latin America. Or why Christian and Muslim societies made their roads so much more central to their literature and their self-image than other cultures did.

Meanwhile, memories of the Great Game grow dim. In the nineteenth century British politicians and generals feared that tsarist armies would penetrate first into Afghanistan, then through the Khyber Pass into India. That should have been perceived as the result of overheated imaginations, but the belief that Russians were supermen was deeply ingrained—and reinforced by the memory of the armies which had defeated Napoleon and the Ottoman Turks, operating with few supplies and incompetent leadership, suffering incredible losses, but almost always sending the tsar messages of victories. Also, there was a belief that Muslims and Hindus would acquiesce to new rulers as easily as they had done to the administrators of the Raj.

A century later similar fears arose when Soviet leaders sought to expand their sphere of influence into Central Asia, an effort that observers believed was connected to propaganda about the imminence of a world-wide proletarian revolution. Iran and Afghanistan once again became locations where international tensions became so fierce that NATO states and the

Soviet Bloc alike feared the outbreak of a new world war—demonstrating once again how a periphery can affect the centres. Since nobody except factions of Afghans and Persians profited from this situation, Russians and Americans tended to back away from what would be a very inconvenient conflict—the wrong war, in the wrong place, at the wrong time. While nations were tempted to thwart extremists from taking control of one of these unruly nations, as the British and Americans were accused of doing in Iran in 1953—as if Iranians and other peoples operated on the 'rent a mob' principle, or as children who could play no role in determining their own destiny—that seemed far safer than challenging a world power at a time or place that could lead to world war.

When Soviet leaders overthrew the weak pro-Communist government of Afghanistan in 1979, President Jimmy Carter and others saw this as an ideological and strategic challenge. Carter, who had overseen a significant reduction in American military resources, now began the build-up that was later associated with Ronald Reagan. Some political experts saw the Afghan invasion as a revived Russian search for a warm-water port; this paranoia ignored the likelihood that Pakistan and India that would resist such an imperialist venture, and few asked how the Soviets would use a warm water port. They had Cam Ranh Bay in Vietnam, a beautiful location, but useful only to show the triumph of Socialist forces over Capitalism. What would they use a similar base in Pakistan for?

Jimmy Carter also faced a challenge by the new Islamist government in Iran. While the American public was outraged by the occupation of the American embassy in Tehran, policy experts were more interested in driving the Red Army out of Afghanistan. As the Great Game became a more important narrative, few Westerners argued that a Soviet state in Afghanistan might be better than the tribal despotisms of the Afghan resistance; Carter, like Reagan after him, seemed to not understand that if one believed in universal education, women's rights, and secular values, one should not support a guerilla war conducted by ethnic groups which disliked and feared one another, some of whom were religious fanatics who hated the West and its values as much as they did the Soviet Union, and its efforts to promote atheism. In such a dry and mountainous region the Red Army was unlikely to be successful even if the West did not supply weapons and advice to the Afghan tribesmen.

Carter, besieged by economic problems at home, was slow to grasp why the rhetoric was so anti-American. After all, he had helped remove the shah. Nor were educated secular Iranians pleased. They had hoped that the revolution would bring democracy; instead, they got radical mullahs and revolutionary guards who regarded them as traitors to their faith and the nation. The mullahs who came to power presented a challenge that was to change the regional balance of power. Carter had got what he wanted, and he did not like what he saw. Nor did the many secular Iranians who had believed the revolution would bring Western-style democracy to their country.

The crisis lessened after Ronald Reagan became president in 1980—the Iranians, apparently believing Carter's election rhetoric that Reagan was trigger-happy, released the diplomatic hostages that enthusiastic students had taken. Reagan was thus able to give some attention to Afghanistan, but he did so only in the context of the Cold War—that is, as a revival of the Great Game.

As far as Ronald Reagan saw it, the Evil Empire had to go, and the Berlin Wall was its most prominent symbol; his generals were so fixated on the mass formation of Soviet tanks along the Iron Curtain that they could not think of any other type of confrontation than the Second World War with better equipment and Germany as an American ally. This made it easy to overlook problems in distant and relatively unknown lands. Weapons went to Central Asian peoples hostile to Communists and to Arabs and Israelis, but with little thought as to what came next.

It was even easier to ignore Afghanistan after the Red Army pulled out in early 1989, a quiet departure soon overshadowed by the collapse of the Soviet Union and Saddam Hussein's seizure of Kuwait. The victorious Afghans then fought a bitter civil war that by 1996 had been won by the Taliban, a fundamentalist group largely composed of Pashtuns from the southern mountains and Pakistan. As the Taliban imposed Sharia law over their defeated enemies, they developed their own exaggerated combination of ambition and arrogance.

They believed that distance made them secure from any great power and their mountains and deserts made them secure from attack. Giving refuge to al Qaeda seemed to be a religious duty that was also risk-free. After the al Qaeda attack on New York on 9 September 2001, they rejected American requests to turn over the terrorist leaders and close the training camps.

The Taliban leaders thought that mocking President George W. Bush was safe, because it was impossible for Americans to bring heavy equipment to bear against them; moreover they had anti-aircraft missiles supplied by the US or captured from the Soviets, and they enjoyed much support in the Muslim world. Jokes circulated, 'What can the Americans do? Sue us?'

The surprising American reaction combined air power, irregular forces and alliances with the anti-Taliban opposition. Al Qaeda was almost destroyed, and the al Qaeda leader, Osama bin Laden, barely escaped the final encirclement. The offensive demonstrated that Special Forces using innovative methods, backed by air power, were effective in fighting on the periphery of power. But that lesson was incompletely employed later and almost forgotten during the 2003 war in Iraq.

The generals did not quite get their way in that war either. The dash to Baghdad was more like an old-fashioned cavalry charge than the employment of overwhelming numbers and firepower that characterised 'the American way of war' most recently seen in 1991 to expel Saddam Hussein from Kuwait. Genghis Khan would have approved, but he would have followed up his victory by a massacre of all potential rebels.

Iraqis still remember the total destruction of Baghdad by the Mongols in 1258. That is why complaints that the Americans were worse than the Mongols resonated for Iraqis, but seemed so strange to the foreign occupiers—moreover, Iraq was one of the most secular Arab states, with many educated citizens, and most of the institutions of parliamentary government. Surely everyone would welcome replacing a viscous dictator with a liberal democracy?

George W. Bush's ambition to convert Afghanistan into a modern state went ever further than his plans for Iraq. The most he achieved, however, in these two costly wars was to turn over deceptively stable situations to his successor, Barack Obama. After the new president hurriedly withdrew from Iraq, the vacuum was filled first by incompetent, corrupt and vengeful Shiite politicians supported by the ancient enemy, Iran, then by al Qaeda coming back as the representative of Sunni interests, only to be eclipsed by a new force, the Caliphate, that expanded quickly and brutally across the borderlands of Syria and Iraq. The dark side of Islam—the willful ignorance of the village and clan—drew recruits from all the backward areas of the Islamic world and unassimilated young Muslims from Europe and America who yearned for a more authentic and meaningful life. We've seen it before.

The future of Afghanistan is unclear. Obama called that the 'necessary war', but he pushed to end American involvement before the end of his term of office. The entire Middle East and much of Central Asia is a mess at the time of writing, but that does not make those regions any less good examples of how the periphery can affect the centre.

Religion is important for focusing the discontent of Muslims, but one has to ask why the same faith that had once managed to live with Sufi cults, Alawites, Druses, Christians and even scattered Jewish communities now became intolerant and violent.

Was this the work of Wahhabi imams supported by Saudi princes? Or a means of bringing tribal peoples together against a common foreign enemy?

One can disagree with any or all of the statements above and still believe that the essential conflict was not the Great Game, but primitive societies in rebellion against all modern states. Tribal societies are by nature hostile to the urbanised centres and to anyone who threatens their ancestral habits and ways of life. Such societies are by nature warlike—easily provoked to violence, resolute in their resistance, and not prone to forgetting or forgiving insults.

The few Westerners who today enter troubled regions for tourism, mountain climbing, to serve as teachers or doctors, or simply to escape the materialism of the modern world often find the experience less rewarding than expected. Still, the lure of exotic travel and the romanticism of meeting ancient, unchanging 'primitive' peoples is very strong; those who choose to be charmed by long-barrelled muzzle-loaders usually do not notice that the natives now carry these only on ceremonial occasions; when tribesmen go to war now, they carry AK-47s.

Intelligence

No war against tribes can be fought successfully without knowing who the enemy is and what they want. If the intruding power is not strong enough and ruthless enough to massacre entire peoples—as the Mongols were wont to do—it had to know who were likely to be friends and who were determined enemies. The eyeball test rarely worked. Natives all looked as much alike to the foreigners as the outsiders did to the natives. Often it was possible to recruit tribal enemies, sometimes rival leaders volunteered, and sometimes criminals could be hired, but getting an informant into the inner circles of resistance was difficult and getting information out was almost impossible. The boy who was the central figure in Kipling's *Kim* (1901) was a successful agent in the Great Game because he seemed so innocent and he was well-trained; moreover, as the orphan of a Protestant Irish soldier, Kim had a good reason to be loyal to the British, not to the Indians or Tibetans whose culture and philosophies he found so attractive; certainly he had no reason to think well of the Russians, whose plans he helped thwart. *Kim* is, in short, essential reading for anyone wanting to understand how to gather information in any land similar to colonial India.

It was the same in America during the War for Independence. One frustrated royal officer complained that George Washington had not outfought the British commanders, but had out-spied them. CIA trainers, in fact, lecture on the techniques used by Washington's spies in New York, so similar were their practices to the tradecraft of today.

Generals Always Fight the Last War

This truism can be understood in various ways: 1) Generals always remember the war they knew as young officers. 2) It is less expensive to continue to use existing equipment than to buy new, untested weapons. 3) Generals must prepare for the most likely war even when they suspect that is not the one they will actually have to fight. This is especially true for a young officer prepared for pitched combat between large armies, finding himself in charge of a platoon in some obscure skirmish on an unfamiliar frontier. 4) Politicians, especially those who look at *The New Yorker* cartoons of be-medalled generals gloating about opportunities to kill someone, assume that all generals are war-mongers, and that the best way to keep the peace is to guarantee that the generals do not have new toys to play with.

The only ones who are absolutely certain how a future war will be fought are the aggressors. Defenders are uncertain what the aggressors will do, and where and when, and so must have a variety of strategies to deal with possible scenarios.

Generals who are certain what an aggressor might do could be suffering from too many blows on the head, but most likely they developed their conformist habits of thought in a peacetime army; that is, junior officers who avoid giving their superiors sleepless nights are most likely to be promoted. Only after a lost war are superiors likely to listen to new ideas. There is also the Black Swan scenario—that is, major changes come about by surprise because nobody could foresee them. Since nobody knows what the Black Swan will be, nobody knows how to prepare for its appearance. Therefore, it is business as usual until the crisis comes.

Generals rarely like wars on the periphery. When they have to fight one, say, as the Americans did in Vietnam, they follow a strategy likely to lead to failure, much as the British did in the American War for Independence. The Americans never lost a major battle in Vietnam, and the British only lost a few in America, but those victories were almost irrelevant. In such conflicts it is essential to secure as much of the population as possible, eliminate hostile local leaders and win over new ones. The British in their long war, 1775-1783, with only enough men to occupy a few key cities, could not protect loyalists elsewhere; this made the loyalists less willing to risk their 'lives, fortune, and sacred honour' than the patriots were.

American public opinion about Vietnam changed as casualties mounted into the tens of thousands and there seemed to be no 'light at the end of the tunnel'. British generals, though better supported (perhaps because there was no television), had to avoid losing men who could not be replaced; they did not give up on the war until the coalition of hostile European states became so dangerous that peace with the detested Americans was unavoidable.

The political conflict in America reflected a periphery rebelling against the centre, but the military conflict was one of European-style armies facing each other. The British wanted a resolution that would permit a permanent reconciliation. George Washington opposed fighting a guerrilla war because he feared this would lead to the British laying waste to the land; instead, he insisted that the future of the nation depended on the Continental Army, and that the customary laws of war be observed, together with the traditional military forms and practices.

The end of the war was not pretty, especially not the flight of loyalists to Britain or British colonies, but an orderly country emerged from the conflict.

There are points at which the American War of Independence is similar to the Vietnamese War. Both were simultaneously a combination of civil war and a national effort to drive away a foreign army. The Communists had a strong army in North Vietnam, but it was restrained by Soviet and Chinese fears that the conflict would lead to World War III. Americans, similarly cautious, concentrated on the guerrilla army, the Viet Cong, in the South. American and allied forces employing conventional arms, however, seemed only to encourage more Vietnamese to join the Viet Cong. It appeared that the Americans were facing a long jungle frontier war with an enemy that was both motivated and able to fight effectively.

The stalemate was broken when the Americans began employing small unit tactics that emphasised winning over villagers—and most importantly, the highland tribes that hated all Vietnamese, especially the newcomers infiltrating from the North who took over their lands and villages; meanwhile they trained and armed a large South Vietnamese army. The strategy seemed to be turning the war around when the Viet Cong launched the Tet Offensive in January 1968. The Viet Cong essentially eliminated itself as a military force, but the psychological effect was profound—many Americans were persuaded that the war was lost. Fighting, of course, continued until the combination of President Richard Nixon's opening to

China, his more intensive bombing campaign in North Vietnam and the closing of Haiphong harbor led to a negotiated end to the fighting in 1972.

It hardly mattered by then what happened in the guerilla campaign. The American army had won that war, but it had not been permitted to move against the enemy in the North. Trained to attack, American soldiers and marines wore out when standing on the defensive. Nixon's one great effort to wipe out North Vietnamese bases in Cambodia produced anti-war protests at home and enabled the Khmer Rouge to make themselves stronger in the Communist-held areas.

The end of the war, which still remains a controversial subject, came only after Nixon's fall in the Watergate scandal and the international forces had all gone home. Until then every North Vietnamese offensive had been turned back by the combination of South Vietnamese regular army units and American air power. After the Democrats in the US Congress cut off supplies, money, and air support to South Vietnam and Cambodia, the demoralised South Vietnamese army collapsed when North Vietnamese armoured divisions rolled across the border.

That story, and its tragic aftermath, repeated itself in Cambodia and the infamous 'Killing Fields' where everyone who could speak French, wore glasses, or seemed in any way Westernised, was hacked to death or shot.

What becomes clearer with the passage of time is how every military expert and politician was wrong about these wars at one time or another. Similarly, the strategy and tactics of the War on Terror—as George W. Bush characterised efforts to end the many irregular conflicts around the world and to neutralise threats from Iran and North Korea—were based on assumptions that may have been incorrect. That is the thesis of Ahmed in *the Thistle and the Drone*—that modern jihadists are motivated less by religion than by the cultural practices of their tribal society that emphasise strict morality, loyalty, revenge, and concepts of masculine courage and duty.

Such concepts are not unique to primitive societies. The North Vietnamese and Viet Cong shared them, too. They also echo in General Douglas MacArthur's 1964 speech at the United States Military Academy when he was given the Thayer Award: 'Duty, honour, country: Those three hallowed words reverently dictate what you ought to be, what you can be, what you will be. They are your rallying point to build courage when courage seems to fail, to regain faith when there seems to be little cause for faith, to create hope when hope becomes forlorn.'

This sets the stage for a ritual combat between similar, or only slightly different military ethos. Under the right circumstances Crazy Horse and

Custer—heroes of wars on the American Great Plains—can admire one another's courage. Or Indian and Briton, as Kipling put it:

'Oh, East is East, and West is West, and never the twain shall meet,
Till Earth and Sky stand presently at God's great Judgment Seat;
But there is neither East nor West, Border, nor Bread, nor Birth,
When two strong men stand face to face, though they come from the
ends of the earth.'

Respect aside, the confrontation of their military forces can be bloody; and the result of the long conflict of unequal forces will end according to which side is willing to persevere the longest, or if the stronger side can offer suitable terms for ending the war or finding a means to track the elusive tribal enemy to his last redoubt and destroy him.

The successful strategy employed by the Americans and South Vietnamese against the Viet Cong was similar to that of the Marine Corps described earlier, one it had developed over many decades in peripheral wars. Later it worked effectively in Afghanistan and Iraq. But in all cases there was a strong mobile force available to rescue small units when attacked by overwhelming numbers.

The generals of the Vietnam to Afghanistan era were not always wrong, but at times the 'perfumed princes' seemed almost as out of touch with reality as their elected leaders. Competence at the middle levels of command and of the troops made up for many deficiencies, but ignorance of the requirements of warfare on the periphery led to inappropriate responses; even the Powell Doctrine , which would have made any involvement in a peripheral combat difficult, would have abandoned the world to its most ruthless extremists.

This short sketch of recent wars may not persuade everyone, but perhaps it will stimulate thought. Most likely, it will be remembered, as cautionary tales usually are, only when it is too late to matter.

However, if we give up all hope, defeat is certain.

The Periphery always fights for itself

It is easy to forget that the regions we often think of as peripheral have an existence separate and distinct from our technologically more advanced societies. Those who consider the virtues of the 'more civilised world' superior do so partly because they are appalled by the poverty, ignorance and incompetence of those they want to help. The motto WAWA (West

Africa Wins Again) and the proverb that No Good Deed Goes Unpunished come from hard experience. This is true whether the more civilised peoples happen to be secular, Christian, Muslim, Hindu, or Communist. It was also true in the centuries described in this book, when more civilised peoples saw in the weaknesses of peripheral peoples opportunities to do good both for them and for themselves, or simply to exploit momentary opportunities, leaving the devil to pick up the pieces.

This has often resulted in fierce armed resistance, followed by bloody cycles of repression and uprisings which lead local factions to imagine how they could exploit the situation for themselves. Moreover, some Westerners sympathise so totally with whatever group seems to be oppressed that they can see no good in their own nations. This is nothing new. Well over a century ago Gilbert and Sullivan mocked these people in *The Mikado*, having the Lord High Executioner present 'a little list' of society's people who never would be missed: 'Then the idiot who praises, with enthusiastic tone, All centuries but this, and every country but his own.' For these ideologues there is no foreign crime that cannot be understood and forgiven, no distant custom that is not superior to whatever the West has to offer, and they deride Western democracy as a sham or no better than the tribal councils of the once proud and independent peoples who now suffer under either the jackboots of some Western military or its puppet or under the insulting patronage of Western do-gooders.

There is no winning this debate. Who knows but that the critics might be, in part or in whole, right. But we should note that when 'backward' people get cell phones, it takes them no time to learn how to use them, even how to set off an IED with one. Moreover, the world is evolving so rapidly that whatever wisdom can be shared here, or by the critics of Western democracies, will be at least partially out-of-date very quickly.

That is why historians prefer the predictable world of the past. We may not like what we see there, but we are not morally responsible for what happened, and we are not able to influence what came later. Some historians may want to change the interpretation of the events, but that is part of the great academic debate that every historian must either enjoy or endure.

The fact remains that each periphery has a history beyond that part seen in the conflict with the more civilised centre or centres. We can do no more than allude to those histories, some of which are found in post-colonial scholarship so biased that only a satirist can do it justice. That is part of our current reality, and if the past is any basis for making a prediction, the weaker (or less useful) interpretations will eventually disappear. No author is read forever or even for very long. If a book is in tune with the times when written, it will not be so in a generation; if not in tune, it won't be read at all.

What survives are ideas that penetrate so subtly into commonplace thought that their authors are forgotten.

The Long-Term View

The centres of world civilisation have remained amazingly stable over the centuries—China, India, Egypt, Turkey, Italy—with more recent expansion to western Europe, Russia and the Americas. One can quibble about this and that, but those are areas which even our most geographically challenged youth today recognise.

It is the periphery that still remains obscure. One jungle, one desert is considered pretty much like all the others. It's like Gaston's retort to Gigi that life is a bore:

'It's the same dull world wherever you go
Whatever place you are at
The earth is round
But everything on it is flat.'[4]

Well, Gigi did not think so, and neither do the kind of people who will read about life and war on the frontier. The frontier peoples won't just go away. Today, just as in the past, the problems they present bedevil politicians and military leaders who have 'more important' plans that they are loath to put off. As Neville Chamberlain put it in September 1938 upon returning from having signed the Munich Agreement: 'How horrible, fantastic, incredible it is that we should be digging trenches and trying on gas-masks here because of a quarrel in a far away country between people of whom we know nothing.' He was speaking of Germans and Czechs! It may be an urban legend that a British newspaper once had a headline 'Fog in Channel. Continent Cut Off', but Chamberlain's statement accurately reflected his insular attitude.

Yet Kabul and Khartoum won't go away. And the Third World has moved to the First World. Timbuktu is in the news again, but more than ten times as many Muslims live in London than there. Algerians in Paris remained out of the sight of tourists until 2015.

Distant regions that were important were once referred to as spheres of influence. Today the Russian 'Near Abroad' (ближнее зарубежье) is more accurate and less offensive. In any case, this may be a matter of semantics. Everyone knows that there cannot be a centre without a periphery, and while a country bumpkin's jaw will drop at the sight of Paris by night or London by day, the sophisticates of those cities are more likely to sneer at the visitor's village than admire it.

The costs of intervening in either 'the Great Game' or the petty quarrels of the periphery are real. In *Arithmetic on the Frontier*, Kipling commented about the brains packed with knowledge from Oxford and Cambridge that were smashed by some uneducated Afghan: 'Two thousand pounds of education Drops to a ten-rupee jezail.' And to what point?

> 'When you're wounded and left on Afghanistan's plains,
> And the women come out to cut up what remains,
> Jest roll to your rifle and blow out your brains
> An' go to your Gawd like a soldier.'

Yet there is a cost to not intervening, as Kipling also said: 'War is an ill thing, as I surely know. But 'twould be an ill world for weaponless dreamers if evil men were not now and then slain.'

Kipling is often dismissed as an imperialist, but most often by those who have not read *Recessional*. Or who missed this passage:

> 'At the end of the fight
> Lies a tombstone white
> With the name of the late deceased;
> And the epitaph drear,
> A fool lies here,
> Who tried to hustle the East'

How far away is the periphery today? By air it can be a short distance indeed. Or only a few minutes by tube.

---

1. Anyone visiting the American state of West Virginia will note that however much people there disagree about politics, religion, and sports, they all believe in the 2nd Amendment to the US Constitution that guarantees the right to bear arms.
2. Uncultured is a much stronger word in Russian than in English because good manners and a good education are so much more highly valued.
3. A number of bankrupt British lords saved themselves by marrying American heiresses, including Winston Churchill's father. What is often ignored in this stereotype is that the women were educated and self-confident, attractive mates in every sense.
4. Lyrics from the 1958 musical based on the charming 1944 story by Colette.

Chapter 12

Lessons For The Future
Islam And Islamic Terrorism

In early 2015 a new threat to world stability emerged: ISIL. Also known as the Islamic Caliphate, Islamic State or the Islamic State of Iraq and the Levant, ISIL overran large parts of Iraq and Syria, whilst Muslim extremists in North Africa declared their allegiance. This breakaway offshoot of al Qaeda gloried in horrific crimes, videotaping its beheadings and burnings for a world audience. As young people from many nations hurried to join, its propaganda boasted of its intention to unite Islam, introduce Sharia law, then face the Apocalypse. As one spokesman put it, 'We will conquer your Rome, break your crosses, and enslave your women.'[1]

Normally, rapidly rising movements cannot hold cities and towns—without an air force, powerful allies, or sources of weapons and ammunition, they fade away. However, there are exceptions. Fidel Castro comes to mind.

The West and moderate leaders from the Middle East responded slowly. Not wanting to commit ground troops to the war they thought was over, they had limited options. Also, they believed that Iran was a greater threat, but Iran was effectively an ally against ISIL, as well as working with the Russians to support the Alawite dictator in Syria they detested. But what paralysed Western leaders most was the fear that intervention would be seen as a war on Islam.

Experts are debating as to whether there is any overlap between Islam and Islamic terrorism, each side often reducing the Islamic world to a stereotype favourable to its views of what should be done.

This distorts the complexity of the situation. The majority of Muslims are Sunnis (Arabs, Turks, Pakistanis, Indians, and Indonesians), who come in the full spectrum of devoutness. And there are sects which reflect accommodations with local conditions and ancient religious practices. In recent decades—thanks partly to Saudi financial support for Madrasas (religious schools)—the Wahhabi fundamentalist view of Islam has become more prominent. That is, young people who memorise the Koran are more likely to believe that Sharia law should replace constitutions and democracy than to accept western cultural practices as moral and good.

Any moderate Sunni who debates theology with fundamentalists is at a disadvantage because some passages in the Koran denounce Jews, heretics, and traitors, while the subtleties of law and tradition are difficult to explain.[2] Christianity once debated whether gentile converts had to follow Judaic dietary laws, but St. Paul broke Christians free of the Old Testament. Later, Christians managed to get around Christ's specific orders against the use of violence, but Muslim scholars struggle to explain that the greater jihad means a struggle for personal improvement, and only the lesser jihad means holy war. The Arab public, in contrast, sees its model as Saladin (d. 1193) taking Jerusalem from the crusaders. Thus Islamic heroes trump holy men—the text is the text, and there is little encouragement for scholars to interpret it as Westerners do the Old and New Testaments, much less allow the rest of the faithful to do so.

The Shiites in Iran and the surrounding region are a different problem. Their plan seems to be to drive ISIL out of Iraq and restore Syria to the Alawites, then—unless the recent understanding with President Obama works out as hoped—build atomic bombs and destroy Israel (the Near Enemy), after which they turn on Europe and the United States (the Far Enemy). This scenario, like that of ISIL, will bring on the Apocalypse. This may be largely propaganda, but the Iranian Revolutionary Guard regularly chants 'Death to America' and condemns 'the Great Satan'. American conservatives believe that wily Muslim leaders have outwitted the gullible liberal president once again, so that the world is now more dangerous, not less so. President Obama, however, believes that ancient rivalries, like outdated nationalisms and old-fashioned theologies, should give way to dealing with the threat that climate change presents to the planet.

Atomic weapons may have kept the Cold War cold, reduced Pakistan-India conflicts to an armed truce, and guaranteed Israel from another surprise attack, but the threat of mutual annihilation may not work with either Islamic extremists or Western voters.

The Saudis take the Iranian threats sufficiently seriously to talk with friendly nuclear powers about purchasing atomic weapons. Meanwhile, Americans—who long exerted the dominant influence in the region—are debating whether the crisis reflects President George W. Bush's foolish overthrow of Saddam Hussein, or President Barack Obama's premature withdrawal from Iraq, or President Obama's support of the Arab Spring that removed dictators who had suppressed radical Islamists for decades.

Israel, of course, believes that its very existence is threatened. Lebanon fears domination by whichever side wins in Syria. Turkey is in an ambiguous position, its government having abandoned the secular policies of Kemal Ataturk (1881-1938) without having completely crushed the modernists. In any case, Turks do not want to once again rule Arabs and fight Persians; however, if Iran gets an atomic bomb, they will feel threatened, too.

Such is a short term view of a problem that might change quickly in ways that we cannot foresee.

What We Don't Know

Donald Rumsfeld, George W. Bush's Secretary of Defense, made a comment that deserves to be remembered: 'Reports that say that something hasn't happened are always interesting to me, because as we know, there are known knowns; there are things we know we know. We also know there are known unknowns; that is to say we know there are some things we do not know. But there are also unknown unknowns—the ones we don't know we don't know. And if one looks throughout the history of our country and other free countries, it is the latter category that tend to be the difficult ones.'

This reflection was seconded by Nassim Nicholas Taleb's theory of the Black Swan. Biologists had never seen a black swan before the discovery of Australia; hence, they believed that all swans were white. Taleb's point was that history (and every other human activity) is punctuated by unlikely, and hence unexpected, events.

That is certainly what we have seen recently in the debate over the extent and importance of climate change. This was once called global warming, but when a black swan appeared in the form of temperature readings not following the computer models, it was renamed climate change. Then, in 2013 Geoffrey Parker—a noted military historian—published *Global Crisis*, describing how the Little Ice Age of the late 1600s brought starvation, a breakdown of commerce, and political crises to the great states of Eurasia. He ended with an exhortation to act immediately on the threat of climate change. President Obama endorsed this long view, saying that the real problem of the Middle East is climate change.

It would be awkward to think that after all our studies of politics, religion, and technology, that we discover that they are less relevant than our modern reliance on coal and oil. On the other hand, perhaps these studies show how our ancestors responded to changes they could not see.

What Military History Can Teach Us

In 2007 Victor Davis Hanson wrote an essay entitled 'Why Study War?' As he saw it, war is more than battle—it consists of the circumstances, the people, the pressures, and the decisions that first led to war, then to the ways it would be fought, and finally to the means of ending the conflict. This is in line with Clausewitz, for whom war was a continuation of politics. But war is different than politics in that once states begin to fight, they find it difficult to stop—after a short period people forget why they got into the war in the first place; then they can justify their sacrifices only by victory, which requires more sacrifices, until the war becomes an end in itself.

Hanson says that military history can provide examples of how crises played out in the past, but that no two events are identical. Instead, there are generalisations. For example, the greatest modern aggressors succeeded partly because they were daring, and partly because their potential victims were reluctant to do what was necessary to stop them. This is why the Romans warned, *si vis pacem, para bellum*. Hanson, of course, is aware that a perpetual arms race is not desirable, but neither is unilateral disarmament. Political matters are best handled by diplomacy, but, awkwardly, the always quotable Theodore Roosevelt (American president 1901-09) probably got it right when he said that in diplomacy—as in dealing with thugs in dark alleys—it was best to 'speak softly and carry a big stick'.

Military history can tell us about the advantages and disadvantages of such an attitude, then explain why personalities and political genius (or idiocy) drive the decisions that can affect all of us. It can also remind us of the sacrifices that past generations made to assure us that we can read about their deeds, their valour and their suffering; and to remind us that there is no such thing as 'a war to end all wars'—as Woodrow Wilson put it in 1917.

John Keegan (1934-2012) introduced similar reflections into *The Face of Battle*. Most importantly, he disposed of the tidy reconstructions of how battles are fought. In place of order and logic he gave us confusion, hesitation, incomplete information, and unpredictability. The politician, he suggested, acts as much out of ignorance and emotion as does the infantryman trying to make sense of the violence around him. This explains partly why politicians mistake wishes for knowledge and instinct for experience. Keegan's view is that no one should be confident about what will happen once the dogs of war are let slip.

Keegan also took sure aim at a target parodied by Gilbert and Sullivan in their 1879 comic operetta, *the Pirates of Penzance*—the modern major general:

'For my military knowledge, though I'm plucky and adventury,
Has only been brought down to the beginning of the century;
But still, in matters vegetable, animal, and mineral,
I am the very model of a modern Major-General.'

In Keegan's view any historian who tries to ignore military history is short-changing readers. History may not be all wars and politics, but history without them imposes very strange limitations on what we can learn about ourselves.

Historians Cannot Escape Cultural Trends

The difficulty in finding the right balance of fact, theory, and interesting narrative is nowhere truer than in the phenomenon of multiculturalism. In the beginning this school seemed to imply that every culture had laudable aspects; later it meant that all cultures were equal. However, a glance through any great city's telephone book will show that among the abundance of culinary traditions that make dining adventurous and enjoyable there will be more French, Italian and Chinese restaurants, together with fast food from America, India and Turkey than those featuring the cuisine of frontier societies. This suggests that not all cultures are equally valuable in all ways.

Not every great mind has agreed on what makes any culture significant. Americans Mark Twain (1835-1910) and H.L. Mencken (1880-1956) argued forcefully that there was no worthwhile American culture. A modern version of this is that only Western hegemony makes McDonald's hamburgers popular, not the dependable quality, speed, and service, much less the clean bathrooms. One might suspect that complaints about this shift in cultural values is only frustration with having lost a world that most people could not afford to live in.

This has a close connection to a widely held belief—best expressed by the late Edward Said—that Western culture is biased, overbearing and destructive. While Said's most thoughtful followers have moved on to more sophisticated analyses, many scholars will still criticise anyone who suggests that some blame for current crises in the Middle East, Africa or Asia lies with the political leaders there; they condemn such views as Eurocentric, a codeword for racist.

A Conundrum

Ahmed tells us that every tribal situation can be understood to reflect the pull of the three sources of power: first, the tribal leaders; second, the mullahs; lastly, the formal government. Depending on the circumstances, one of these will be dominant. Usually this is the tribal chief, who is often the head of the most important clan. When his authority is challenged, it is usually by the government representative (who often does not understand the subtleties of customary law); only when a legal matter between two tribes cannot be worked out between them is the government's authority considered legitimate. Should one chief not accept his judgement, the matter could be sent to a meeting of tribal heads—the Jirga. This is a slow process, but it is better than war.

Each new leader in a tribe must prove himself to his independent-minded followers. If he is successful—especially as a warrior leading warriors—his men will follow him anywhere. If he fails, he is abandoned, usually for a brother or cousin, but almost always someone with a genealogical claim to be head of the tribe.

On rare occasions a religious leader will challenge the tribal head. Usually this fails. Few mullahs or imams have family connections, proven competence in political matters, and military experience. Chaos follows. Thus, in 2007 when al Qaeda in Iraq made itself temporarily superior in the Sunni districts of Saddam Hussein's shattered land, those jihadists almost immediately made their new subjects furious by the hurried imposition of Sharia law—a gross violation of tribal and religious traditions. This made possible the American response of combining a surge of new troops and arming tribal leaders that temporarily swept the religious radicals out of their strongholds.

Four years later, when President Barack Obama pulled American troops out of Iraq, he failed to guarantee that the tribal chiefs would share in the governance of their peoples. Instead, the Shiite central government moved so strongly to restrict their influence that al Qaeda soon reappeared, then the more radical ISIL. No responsible historian can guarantee how this will end. In fact, it has been suggested that historians have a poor record even in predicting the past. Each generation rewrites its history, and not always for the better.

Historians can see many analogous situations to Ahmed's formula—in medieval Europe there were powerful local families, the Church, and the distant ruler. Time and again these vied for supremacy, with each power struggle eventually resolved by a slight rearrangement of *ante bellum* situation or a face-saving compromise that changed little. Few readers can follow the intricate negotiations and skirmishes of those events without becoming bored. These matters were important only to the participants—in short, something like domestic politics in any modern country.

Tip O'Neill (1912-94), the liberal Massachusetts politician who was speaker of the American House of Representatives for a critical decade, famously said, 'All politics is local'. This attitude made it possible for him to sit down with fellow Irishman, President Ronald Reagan, tell jokes and share a drink, then work out ways to resolve their political differences. Because the multitude of local political interests make it difficult for a centralised bureaucracy to please everyone, only well-informed, flexible politicians can put together compromises that get them through the immediate future.

This could give us some insight into situations which could lead either to war or to peace. First, there has to be some willingness to compromise, then the leading personalities must find compromises that most people can accept. This is easiest in long-established states with a tradition of respecting one's opponents and being willing to talk with them. That is not the case in all new countries (or even all old countries, all the time). Governing is an art, not a science.

The puzzle for today's politicians is how to figure out how all the moveable parts work, especially in unfamiliar regions. To an outsider any Muslim political process seems immobile—long talks, some beverages (tea or coffee where alcohol is forbidden), more hyperbole than Westerners are used to hearing outside a sports bar—and suddenly something seems to change. How did this happen?

According to Ahmed, the War on Terror empowered the mullahs at the expense of tribal chiefs and the government, then the various Talibans turned on the mullahs as too moderate. Mobilising thousands of young men trained in the Madrassas, they went after everyone who threatened both their old practices and their new theology. Out went mystic Sufi philosophers, secularists, crusaders and pagans. Everyone was an enemy.

This was new and yet it was familiar. At its heart was the same tribal resistance that in Afghanistan had frustrated Alexander the Great, various great warlords of the past, British generals, and now elected native Afghans. If the past repeats itself, some unelected warlord will come to power.

It's Not All Tribalism

Human beings are complex, both as individuals and in groups. How can we explain the age-old enmity of Arab Sunnis and Shiites, and why both hate

Turks and Kurds, who in turn do not like one another? We know how these conflicts began, but the hatred persisting through the years may be best explained as inertia—there are few reasons for it other than tradition. Sunni Arabs dislike Sunni Turks and Turks disdain Arabs.

Awkwardly for those who prefer consistency in history, these groups have often found ways to co-exist, and to permit other religious communities to exist among them—even to flourish. Islam was once famed for its toleration (its limitations seemed generous by comparison to medieval Christendom); Buddhism was celebrated for passivism and Hinduism for its willingness to incorporate diverse religions into its pantheon. However, Christians and Jews chaffed at being second-class citizens, while Muslims denounced toleration of paganism (Hinduism) as heresy.

Historical memory is often filtered through religious prejudices and cultural differences. Persian versus Turk, and Iranian versus Arab reflect ancient conflicts and grievances that are not unlike what historians deal with in explaining the European past.

Popular historical memory is difficult to change or even modify. Today in the Islamic world only one version of the life of Mohammed is permitted—and no pictures. Early Islamic life was not so restricted, but that was then.

Islamic fundamentalism is something similar to that which Christians practised long ago. But the Christian tradition was always inquisitive, and once Renaissance scholars began looking at texts and traditions with a modern eye, everything eventually changed. Today few Christians or Jews pay any attention to the bloody passages of their sacred scripts, but the equivalent verses of the Koran are calls for battle. Christians have clerical hierarchies, Shiites do, too. But the Sunni tradition is more complex, leading to various imams issuing *fatwas* against perceived enemies of their interpretation of Islam.

Even more to the point, the problem is not confined to the Islamic world. Africa, Asia and South America have insurgencies and terrorist groups with no connection to Islam. They are willing to get weapons and training wherever they can, much as they once relied on the Soviet Union and the CIA. But the real problem is discontent, which can range from lack of employment and poverty to a feeling of inferiority and resentment.

Why History?

Voltaire said more than 200 years ago, 'Indeed, history is nothing more than a tableau of crimes and misfortunes'. Perhaps we can someday prove him wrong. But in the meantime we must start conversations about what we should do about ourselves, our society and the world.

We live in a world where the youth thinks of itself as *alienated*. Adults understand that life is unfair, but youth believes everything can be changed. Moreover, dissatisfaction with modern, industrial society is not limited to 'primitive' peoples. Educated young Westerners are seeking an *authentic* life. They look for it in Eastern religions, drugs, alcohol, sustainable living, environmentalism, and sex; some give up on education and the work ethic; some see dropping out of society and protesting its institutions as viable expressions of their discontent. 'Primitive' peoples, in contrast, see the disordered lives of Western youth as proof of their own moral superiority, and, in turn, disordered Westerners admire them for the purity of this vision whether or not that corresponds to reality.

Much of what was almost universally accepted as proper is now challenged. Everyone once expected to be treated with dignity; now they believe that only full acceptance as equals is acceptable—or being left alone to follow their ancient practices, perhaps reforming them to get rid of foreign ideas and influences.

Getting from 'here' to 'there' has never been easy. What the gunpowder empires demonstrated is that modernisation was not about acquiring weapons, but about changing traditional thinking. Proud and lazy aristocrats who refused to lead, then resisted putting weapons and authority into the hands of talented men from the lower classes, were doomed; also, cultures that lacked a military tradition found it hard to meet challenges by enemies that were proud of their prowess. The future may lie with educated men and women who understand how to create and manage great enterprises and complicated bureaucracies, but there are many who have been passed over by the juggernaut of historical change. They form a restless underclass at home and jealous masses abroad that yet have to be brought into the system.

The first people in any new nation to accept modernisation are the military. When officers observe the corruption and incompetence of the government, the vanity, arrogance and popularity of demagogues, and the ignorance of clerics, they begin to question whether change can be made quickly enough; using their monopoly of firepower and discipline, they seize power; then they learn how hard governing is. Military coups are less of a problem in states with a tradition of stability, competence and democracy, but even there large sections of the populace can be disaffected. Protesters for every cause imaginable are now easily mobilised by cell-phones; race and ethnicity become more important than nationality, and religion is either all-important or irrelevant. Modern economies are complex, vulnerable to sudden dislocations, and everyone depends on computer networks. We could be forgiven for thinking that we live in a dangerous age.

We do. But we are not the first generation to do so. Hopefully, knowing that our ancestors somehow made it—though we can sometimes hardly see how they did it—will give us the strength to make it ourselves.

In short, we must be emotionally and mentally ready to deal with small wars. Only those who believe that the world follows orders from superpowers can believe that dissatisfied peoples and thugs will not use force to get what they want, or that those who have legitimate complaints will be patient forever. Rights conflict with rights, understandable fears and hopes are mirrored in opposing hopes and fears, and there are a few who are mentally deranged.

In Ecclesiastics 1, the prophet says 'What has been will be again, what has been done will be done again; There is nothing new under the sun.' That seems to be true. But how would we know if we do not know what the past was like? Perhaps all wisdom is in vain, but Martin Luther reputedly said that even if the world should end tomorrow, he would still plant a tree. Why should we succumb to a philosophy of hopelessness?

---

1. Graeme Wood, 'What ISSI Really Wants." *The Atlantic* (March 2015).

2. Polygamy was explicitly permitted in the Koran, but under conditions that Islamic scholars said make it impossible. Hence, in many Muslim-majority states a man can have only one wife.

Bibliography

Ahmed, Akbar *The Thistle and the Drone. How America's War on Terror Became a Global War on Tribal Islam.* Washington: Brookings Institution Press, 2013.

Arnold, Udo. ed. *Von Akkon bis Wien. Studien zur Deutschordensgeschichte von 13. bis zum 20. Jahrhundert.* Marburg: Elwert, 1978.

Ashley, Maurice. *The Glorious Revolution of 1688.* New York: Charles Scribner's Sons, 1967.

Axworthy, Michael. *The Sword of Persia: Nader Shah, from Tribal Warrior to Conquering Tyrant.* New York: Taurus, 2006.

Ballard, George Alexander. *Rulers of the Indian Ocean.* London, 1927.

Barker, Thomas. *Double Eagle and Crescent: Vienna's Second Turkish Siege and Its Historical Setting.* Albany: State University of New York Press, 1967.

Barrow, Cecil, and Hunter, Mark (eds.), *De Quincey's Revolt of the Tartars and The English Mail-Coach.* London: George Bell & Sons, 1896.

Barzun, Jacques. *From Dawn to Decadence, 500 Years of Western Cultural Life, 1500 to the Present.* New York: HarperCollins, 2000.

Baxter, Stephen. *William III and the Defense of European Liberty, 1650-1702.* New York: Harcourt, Brace & World, 1966.

Bishop, Morris. *The Life and Adventurers of La Rochefoucauld.* Ithaca, New York: Cornell, 1951.

Black, Jeremy, ed. *The Origins of War in Early Modern Europe.* Edinburgh: John Donald, 1987.

Bolger, Daniel. *Why We Lost.* New York: Houghton Mifflin Harcourt, 2014.

Bonney, Richard. *The European Dynastic States, 1494-1660.* Oxford, 1991.

Boot, Max. *The Savage Wars of Peace. Small Wars and the Rise of American Power.* New York: Basic Books, 2002.

Boot, Max. *War Made New. Technology, Warfare, and the Course of History, 1500 to Today.* New York: Gotham, 2006.

Bovill, Edward William. *The Golden Trade of the Moors.* London: Oxford, 1968.

Brauer, Jurgen, and van Tuyll, Hubert. *Castles, Battles & Bombs. How Economics Explains Military History.* London and Chicago: University of Chicago Press, 2008.

Buchanan, Brenda, ed. *Gunpowder, Explosives and the State.* London: Ashgate, 2006.

213

Chambers, David Sanderson. *Popes, Cardinals and War. The Military Church in Renaissance and Early Modern Europe*. New York: Taurus, 2008.

Chase, Kenneth. *Firearms. A Global History*. Cambridge: Cambridge University Press, 2003.

Citino, Robert. *The German Way of War from the Thirty Years War to the Third Reich*. Lawrence: University of Kansas, 2005.

Clark, Christopher. *Iron Kingdom: the rise and downfall of Prussia, 1600-1947*. Cambridge: Belknap, 2005.

Collins, James. *The State in Early Modern France*. New York: Cambridge University Press, 1995.

Cracraft, James, ed. *Peter the Great Transforms Russia*. Lexington, Mass.: D. C. Heath, 1991.

Crefeld, Martin van. *Supplying War, Logistics from Wallenstein to Patton*. Cambridge: Cambridge University Press, 1977.

Curtis, Edward. *Organization of the British Army in the American Revolution*. EP Publishing, 1972, reprint of the 1928 Yale edition.

Dalrymple, William. *Return of a King: the Battle for Afghanistan, 1839-42*. New York: Knopf, 2013.

Davies, John. *A History of Wales*. London: Penguin, 1993.

Darwin, John. *Unfinished empire: the global expansion of Britain*. New York: Bloomsbury Press, 2013.

Davidson, Basil. *Black Mother. The Years of the African Slave Trade*. Boston: Little, Brown and company, 1961.

Davies, Brian. *Warfare, state and society on the Black Sea Steppe, 1500-1700*. London: Routledge, 2007.

Davies, Norman. *God's Playground, a History of Poland*. New York: Columbia, 1982.

Douglas, Hugh. *Jacobite Spy Wars, Moles, Rogues and Treachery*. Bodmin: Sutton, 1999.

Duffy, Christopher. *The Fortress in the Age of Vauban and Frederick the Great, 1660-1789*. London, 1985.

Fairweather, Jack. *The Good War: Why We Couldn't Win the War or the Peace in Afghanistan*. New York: Basic Books, 2014.

Faroqhi, Suraiya. *The Ottoman Empire and the World Around It*. London: Tauris, 2004.

Ferguson, Niall. *Empire. The Rise and Demise of the British World Order and the Lessons for Global Power*. New York: Basic Books, 2002.

Ferguson, Niall. *Civilisation: The West and the Rest*. New York: Penguin, 2011.

Ferguson, Niall. *The War of the World: History's Age of Hatred*. London: Allen Lane, 2006.

Finkel, Caroline. *Osman's Dream, the Story of the Ottoman Empire 1300-1923*. New York: Basic Books, 2005.

Fisher, Godfrey. *Barbary Legend. War, Trade and Piracy in North Africa 1415-1830*. Oxford: Clarendon Press, 1957.

Flores, Jorge, and Vassallo e Silva, eds. *Goa and the Great Mughal*. London: Scala, 2007.

Foster, Robert Fitzroy. *Modern Ireland, 1600-1972*. London: Penguin, 1988.

Fortescue, John William. *A History of the British Army*. Vol 1: *to the Close of the Seven*

Years War. London: Macmillan, 1910.

Gezari, Vanessa. *The Tender Soldier. A True Story of War and Sacrifice*. New York: Simon and Schuster, 2013.

Gilbert, John. *A Jacobite Narrative of the War in Ireland, 1688-1691*. New York: Barnes and Noble, 1971.

Gipson, Lawrence Henry. *The British Empire before the American Revolution*. Caldwell, Indiana: Caxton, 1936-70.

Glubb, John. *Soldiers of Fortune. The Story of the Mamelukes*. New York: Dorset, 1973.

Goffman, Daniel. *The Ottoman Empire and Early Modern Europe*. New York: Cambridge University Press, 2002.

Gray, Richard, ed. *The Cambridge History of Africa*. Vol. 4, *from c. 1600 to c. 1790*. Cambridge University Press: Cambridge, 1977.

Guchinova, Elza-Bair. *The Kalmyks*. Trans. David C. Lewis. New York: Routledge, 2006.

Hellie, Richard. *Enserfment and Military Change in Muscovy*. Chicago: University of Chicago Press, 1971.

Hodgson, Marshall. *The Venture of Islam: Conscience and History in a World Civilisation;* Vol. 3: in *The Gunpowder Empires and Modern Times*. Chicago: University of Chicago, 1974.

Hughes, Lindsey. *Peter the Great: A Biography*. New Haven: Yale, 2002.

Ingrao, Charles. *The Habsburg Monarchy, 1618-1815*. 2d ed. New York: Cambridge University Press, 2000.

Jasienica, Pawel. *The Commonwealth of both nations*. 3 vols. Miami: American Institute of Polish Culture, 1987-92.

Kagan, Frederick, and Higham, Robin, eds. *The Military History of Tsarist Russia*. Basingstoke: Macmillan Palgrave, 2002.

Kaplan, Jeffrey. *Terrorist Groups and the New Tribalism: Terrorism's Fifth Wave*. London: Routledge, 1212.

Keegan, John. *Fields of Battle. The Wars for North America*. New York: Knopf, 1996.

Kennedy, Paul. *The Rise and Fall of the Great Powers*. New York: Vintage Books, 1989.

Kenny, Kevin, ed. *Ireland and the British Empire*. Oxford, 2004.

Khodarkovsky, Michael. *Russia's Steppe Frontier. The Making of a Colonial Empire, 1500-1800*. Bloomington: Indiana, 2002.

Kilmeade, Brian, and Yaeger, John. *George Washington's Secret Six. The Spy Ring that Saved the American Revolution*. New York: Sentinel, 2013.

Kinross, John. *The Ottoman Centuries. The Rise and Fall of the Turkish Empire*. New York: Morrow Quill, 1977.

Kipling, Rudyard. *The Naulahka. A Story of East and West. New York:* Doubleday and McClure Company, 1899.

Kirby, David. *Northern Europe in the Early Modern Period. The Baltic World 1492-1772*. London: Longman, 1990.

Kurlansky, Mark. *A Basque History of the World*. New York: Penguin Putnam, 1999.

Kwass, Michael. *Contraband: Louis Mandrin and the Making of a Global Underground*. Cambridge, Massachusetts: Harvard, 2014.

Lamphear, John, ed. *African Military History*. London: Ashgate, 2007.

Laqueur, Walter. *No End To War, Terrorism in the twenty-first century*. London: Continuum, 2003.

Laroui, Abdallah. *The History of the Maghrib. An Interpretive Essay*. Princeton, New Jersey: Princeton, 1977.

Leach, Douglas. *Arms for Empire. A Military History of the British Colonies in North America, 1607-1763*. New York: Macmillan, 1973.

LeDonne, John. *The Grand Strategy of the Russian Empire, 1650-1831*. Oxford: Oxford University Press, 2004.

Lewis, Bernard. *What Went Wrong? The Clash Between Islam and Modernity in the Middle East.* New York: Oxford University Press, 2002.

Lynn, John. *Battle. A History of Combat and Culture from Ancient Greece to Modern America*. Cambridge: Westview, 2003.

Lynn, John. *The French Wars 1667-1714. The Sun King at War*. Oxford, Osprey, 2002.

Lynn, John. *The Wars of Louis XIV*. New York: Longman, 1999.

Lynn, John. *Women, Armies and Warfare in Early Modern Europe*. Cambridge: Cambridge University Press, 2008.

Macdonald, James. *A Free Nation Deep in Debt: the Financial Roots of Democracy.*. Princeton and Oxford, 2006.

McKay, Derek. *Prince Eugene of Savoy*. London: Thames and Hudson, 1978.

Maland, David. *Europe at War, 1600-1650*. Totowa, NJ: Rowman and Littlefield, 1980.

Martin, Mike. *An Intimate War: An Oral History of the Helmand Conflict 1978-2012*. London: Hurst, 2014

Massie, Robert. *Peter the Great, His Life and His World.* New York: Knopf, 1980.

McNeill, William. *Europe's Steppe Frontier*. Chicago: University of Chicago Press, 1964.

McNeill, William. *The Pursuit of Power: Technology, Armed Force, and the Society Since A.D. 1000*. Chicago: University of Chicago Press, 1984.

McNeill, William. *The Rise of the West, a history of the human community*. Chicago: University of Chicago Press, 1963.

Meserve, Margaret. *Empires of Islam in Renaissance Historical Thought*. Cambridge, Massachusetts: Harvard, 2008.

Mill, James. *The History of British India*. New York: Chelsea, 1968.

Miller, James. *Swords for Hire. The Scottish Mercenary*. Edinburgh: Birlinn, 2007.

Morgan, Edmund. *American Heroes: Profiles of Men and Women Who Shaped Early America*. New York: Norton, 2009.

Mitford, Nancy. *The Sun King*. New York: Harper & Row, 1966.

Murphey, Rhoads, *Ottoman Warfare, 1500-1700*. New Brunswick: Rutgers, 1999.

Nicoll, Fergus. *Gladstone, Gordon and the Sudan Wars. The Battle over Imperial Intervention in the Victorian Age*. London: Pen and Sword, 2013.

Oliver, Roland, ed. *The Cambridge History of Africa*. Vol. 3, *from c. 1050 to c. 1600*. Cambridge University Press: Cambridge, 1977.

Parker, Geoffrey. *The Military Revolution, Military Innovation and the rise of the West, 1500-1800*. Cambridge: Cambridge University Press, 1996.

Parker, Geoffrey. *Global Crisis: War, Climate Change and Catastrophe in the Seventeenth Century*. New Haven: Yale, 2013.

Parvev, Ivan. *Habsburgs and Ottomans Between Vienna and Belgrade (1683-1739)*.

New York: Columbia, 1995.

Perdue, Peter. *China Marches West: the Qing Conquest of Central Eurasia.* Cambridge, Massachusetts: Harvard University Press, 2005.

Salzman, Phillip. *Culture and Conflict in the Middle East.* Amherst, New York: Humanities, 2007.

Scholefield, Alan. *The Dark Kingdoms. The Impact of White Civilisation on Three Great African Monarchies.* London: Heinemann, 1975.

Schevill, Ferdinand. *A History of the Balkan Peninsula.* New York: Harcourt, 1922.

Scottti, Anthony. *Brutal Virtue. The Myth and Reality of Banastre Tarleton.* Westminster, Maryland: Heritage, 2007.

Showalter, Dennis. *The Wars of Frederick the Great.* London, 1996.

Simms, Brendan. *Three Victories and a Defeat. The Rise and Fall of the First British Empire.* New York: Basic Books, 2007.

Simms, J.G. *Jacobite Ireland: 1685-1691.* London: Routledge and Kegan Paul, 1969.

Stone, Daniel. *The Polish-Lithuanian State, 1386-1795.* Seattle and London: University of London, 2001. Vol. IV of *A History of East Central Europe.*

Stoye, John. *The Siege of Vienna.* New York: Holt, Rinehart and Winston, 1965.

Stradling, R. A. *The Spanish Monarchy and Irish Mercenaries: the Wild Geese in Spain 1618-68.* Dublin: Blackrock, 1994.

Streusand, Douglas E. *Islamic Gunpowder Empires: Ottoman, Safavids, and Mughals.* Boulder, CO., Perseus 2010.

Sutton, John. *The King's Honour & the King's Cardinal. The War of the Polish Succession.* Lexington: University of Kentucky Press, 1980.

Tanner, Marcus. *Ireland's Holy Wars: The Struggle for a Nation's Soul, 1500-2000.* New Haven: Yale, 2001.

Thomson, Janice. *Mercenaries, Pirates and Sovereigns, State-building and Extra-territorial Violence in Early Modern Europe.* Princeton: Princeton, 1994.

Tilly, Charles. *Coercion, Capital, and European States, A.D. 990-1990.* Cambridge, Massachusetts: Blackwell, 1994.

Tombs, Robert and Isabella. *That Sweet Enemy. The French and the British from the Sun King to the Present.* New York: Knopf, 2007.

Thubron, Colin. *Shadow of the Silk Road.* London: Chatto & Windus, 2006.

Urban, William. *Dithmarschen, a medieval peasant republic.* Lewiston, New York: Edwin Mellen, 1991,

Urban, William. *Medieval Mercenaries: the Business of War.* London: Greenhill, 2006.

Urban, William. *Bayonets for Hire: the Business of War, 1550-1763.* London: Greenhill, 2007.

Urban, William. *Matchlocks to Flintlocks. Mercenaries in Europe and Beyond, 1500-1700.* London: Frontline, 2011.

Urban, William. *Bayonets and Scimitars. Arms, Armies and Mercenaries, 1700-1789.* London: Frontline, 2013.

Waterson, James. *The Knights of Islam. The Wars of the Mamluks.* London: Greenhill, 2007.

Webb, Stephen S. *Lord Churchill's Coup: The Anglo-American Empire and the Glorious Revolution Reconsidered.* New York: Knopf, 1995.

Webb, Stephen S. *Marlborough's America.* New Haven: Yale, 2011.

Wolf, John. *Louis XIV.* New York: Norton, 1968.

Index